CIO and Corporate Strategic Management:
Changing Role of CIO to CEO

Petter Gottschalk
Norwegian School of Management BI, Norway

IDEA GROUP PUBLISHING
Hershey • London • Melbourne • Singapore

Acquisition Editor:	Michelle Potter
Senior Managing Editor:	Jennifer Neidig
Managing Editor:	Sara Reed
Development Editor:	Kristin Roth
Copy Editor:	Amanda O'Brien
Typesetter:	Sharon Berger
Cover Design:	Lisa Tosheff
Printed at:	Integrated Book Technology

Published in the United States of America by
    Idea Group Publishing (an imprint of Idea Group Inc.)
    701 E. Chocolate Avenue
    Hershey PA 17033
    Tel: 717-533-8845
    Fax: 717-533-8661
    E-mail: cust@idea-group.com
    Web site: http://www.idea-group.com

and in the United Kingdom by
    Idea Group Publishing (an imprint of Idea Group Inc.)
    3 Henrietta Street
    Covent Garden
    London WC2E 8LU
    Tel: 44 20 7240 0856
    Fax: 44 20 7379 3313
    Web site: http://www.eurospan.co.uk

Library of Congress Cataloging-in-Publication Data

CIO and corporate strategic management : changing role of CIO to CEO / Petter Gottschalk, editor.
    p. cm.
  Summary: "This book holds key information in improving a CIO's role, which would then advance his/her chances of moving into a CEO role. It provides analysis within theoretical frameworks and consulting recom-mendations, starting with the demand side of CEO successions, specifically highlighting approaches in IT foundations, e-business development and IT sourcing decisions"--Provided by publisher.
  ISBN 1-59904-423-4 (hardcover) -- ISBN 1-59904-424-2 (softcover) -- ISBN 1-59904-425-0 (ebook)
  1. Executive ability. 2. Chief information officers. 3. Chief executive officers--Selection and appointment. 4. Executive succession. 5. Strategic management. I. Gottschalk, Petter, 1950-
  HD38.2.C56 2006
  658.4--dc22
                            2006019161

British Cataloguing in Publication Data
A Cataloguing in Publication record for this book is available from the British Library.

CIO and Corporate Strategic Management:
Changing Role of CIO to CEO

Table of Contents

Foreword

Petter Gottschalk's book takes a wide-ranging look at CIO roles and skills, and, in particular, explores the strategic and leadership competencies that support a progression to becoming a CEO.

How realistic is it for a CIO to become a CEO, particularly as it has been found that many IT managers are not interested in becoming the CEO? It is true that historically not many have made this transition. What are the biggest pros and cons for a CIO who wants to take the top job? Arguably, the biggest advantage is the cross-functional expertise that IT gains, together with a focus on logical, forward thinking and planning. This allows a "big picture" view that Dr. Gottschalk highlights with his expansive review of technology-enabling business models. Of course, in the extreme, strengths also can become a weakness. Strong logic may not be the best tool to deal with the "shades of grey" needed for stakeholder management and uncertain futures.

In practice, many IT managers have not yet evolved the skills and behaviors to become a CIO. According to surveys by Henley Management College and the British Computer Society, the most important factors in building a successful career in IT are leadership and communication skills (ranked by 69% of respondents as the most important), followed by management skills (22%) and professional skills (16%).

Henley Management College, where Dr. Gottschalk also obtained his doctorate, is well-known for its research on leadership. Building on some of these findings and research with CIOs, we have found a three-level path requiring an evolutionary blend of five skills. The entry level to IT requires "technical" skills. Progression to IT manager needs both professional and management skills. At the CIO level, it is the business and interpersonal skills that become most important. These latter skills are the ones that offer the potential to become a CEO.

However, in our research, IT directors raised serious concerns about a non-technical skills gap among their staff. Fifty-three percent indicated that there was a shortage of people with the right level of personal skills, such as communication, people management, and leadership; 51% said there was a lack of business and management skills. Just 2% said that their organisation lacked IT managers with the right technical skills. This requirement for well-rounded IT professionals means that respondents are as likely to look outside of the organisation for new recruits with the right skills as they are to promote internally.

In my own career as a CIO, one of the biggest initiatives I had was working with the European CEO to develop and implement a new business model for key accounts. It needed strategic insights both in business processes and emerging technologies, but probably the biggest challenge was dealing with multiple stakeholder relationships internally and externally across diverse cultures.

So how can organisations develop their future CIOs and CEOs? This book provides relevant theory and practical advice for the future CIO or for the CIO who aspires to be a CEO. Its consolidation of theory from a range of different fields makes it a valuable reference book for IT management courses. At the same time, the practical insights into strategy and leadership make it a useful primer for managers. Dr. Gottschalk's experience both as a CIO and CEO, supplemented by his extensive publishing record, are clearly evident in this recommended book.

Dr. Sharm Manwani
Henley Management College
June 2006

Dr. Sharm Manwani, PhD, is a senior faculty member at Henley Management College, a leading UK business school, where he researches and lectures in information management. Prior to this role, he held leadership positions with multinational companies, most recently as VP and CIO, IT & Business Processes at Electrolux. Dr. Manwani consults with leading companies on strategy, IT leadership, and program management. His commitment to professional activities includes being a fellow of the BCS and judging computing awards. He has an MBA and doctorate from Henley and is currently researching IT management capability. Dr. Manwani co-authored the CIO Elective for the Henley MBA, launched in August 2005.

Preface

How can the CIO become the next CEO in the organization? This book holds key information in improving a CIO's role, which would then improve his or her chances of moving up into a CEO role. Thus, readers may find this book to be a good tool for those interested in moving up the corporate ladder.

However, this book does not have information involving the "how" and the "who," nuts-and-bolts details that CIOs need to have to perform well in a competitive environment. Rather, this book is written in an academic style where research literature from various sources are presented to illustrate issues that are relevant for an aspiring CIO who wants to be CEO some day.

The CIO position emerged in the 1970s as a result of increased importance placed on IT. In the early 1980s, the CIO was often portrayed as the corporate savior who was to align the worlds of business and technology. In the 1990s, it was postulated that the CIO would become the next CEO, as information became a firm's critical resource.

Many predictions about CIO roles went wrong, and many CIOs have failed. The traditional discrepancy between technology management and business management in role perception still exists. More importantly, new challenges have emerged that have to be solved to make the CIO a success. This is the topic of this book.

So many organizations fail in their applications of modern information technology, and so many chief information officers fail in organizations. The objective of this book is to learn from the past to develop a revised understanding of successful CIO leadership for the future. The mission is to reduce the gap and bridge it between technology and business management through IT strategy and IT governance.

Value configuration, strategic thinking, management roles, and technology management are some of the scholarly values of this book. It makes a significant contribution to the discipline by presenting and discussing the role of the person in charge of information technology in business and public organizations.

This book holds key information in improving a CIO's role, which will then improve their chances of moving up into a CEO role. Thus, readers may find this book to be a good tool for those interested in moving up the corporate ladder.

The CIO position depends on IT maturity, IT management maturity, value configuration, and so forth. For example, a less mature organization might need a CIO who is able to organize the infrastructure and architecture, while a more mature organization might need a CIO who is able to apply modern information technology in emerging business models. Therefore, this book applies the contingent approach to the role of the CIO. The contingent approach is dependent on the situation at a specific point in time as well as organizational evolution. What seems smart to do in one organization might be unwise in another organization because they are not in the same situation. According to the contingent approach, changing roles from CIO to CEO depends on the situation.

The CIO is already thinking like a CEO when developing strategy. As we shall see in the Y model for strategic IT planning, the CIO applies the same techniques to analyze the current and desired business situation as does the CEO.

CEO succession is perhaps one of the most crucial events in the life of any firm because of the substantive and symbolic importance of the CEO position. CEO succession has been commonly viewed as an important mechanism for organizational learning and adaptation. A change in CEO can fundamentally alter the knowledge, skills, and interaction processes at the top of a company, and these alterations can in turn significantly influence post-succession firm performance.

A distinction can be made between two types of CEO succession — inside and outside. Some have emphasized the role of outside successions in organizational learning and adaptation. Others argue that research evidence indicates that outside, new CEOs rarely succeed in their efforts to improve firm performance. It is plausible that although outside successions bring in new competencies and skills, they are disruptive to firms from a process standpoint, and thus the enhanced cognitive repertoire may not get translated into improved firm performance. Further, the simple distinction between inside and outside succession does not recognize crucial differences between relay and non-relay inside successions, which may have different implications for organizational learning and adaptation.

The CIO belongs to the set of internal candidates for a firm's CEO position, which includes senior executives. Such executives have opportunities to participate in major strategic decisions. Their titles (typically, they have the title of executive or senior vice president) reflect strategically important positions in their organization's hierarchies with significant responsibility for overall organizational performance.

In addition to the pool of candidates in the intra-firm market, there is a pool of candidates in the intra-industry market. Potentially, a pool of industry candidates for succession to a particular CEO position is quite large, depending on the number of firms within the focal firm's industry and the number of senior executives within these firms.

Both the CIO and the CEO are practicing leadership. One of the defining characteristics of leadership is the ability to develop and implement appropriate responses to a variety of problem situations. Leaders must solve an array of problems including resource allocation, interdepartmental coordination, interpersonal conflict, and subordinate morale, to name a few.

This book discusses many important management topics such as strategy, governance, planning, and leadership. It covers a wide range of MIS topics and management research: from leadership and strategy to theory of firms, IT outsourcing, IT governance, and knowledge management.

This book is mainly written for academics and students, as it is full of theories, models, hypotheses, and a lot of common sense. At the same time, this book avoids prescriptions that some practitioners find useful. Prescriptions are dangerous and often misleading, as they are dependent on the situation. Therefore, this book applies the contingent approach to management, where different situations require different management skills and different approaches for the CIO to become the next CEO.

Although this book is not a how-to guide for aspiring CIOs who want to be CEOs, it highlights issues from research studies that should enable practicing CIOs to reflect on similarities and differences between the two positions as well as paths from one position to the other. Therefore, this book is also written for practicing CIOs.

This book should fit many MIS courses, where the leadership focus is present. For example, this book would fit a "strategic IT issues" course, as it links information technology to strategic management. Such a course would be more appropriate at the graduate, rather than the undergraduate level, in universities and colleges.

This is a textbook that will be useful to all business schools where MIS courses are taught. Probably, the book will be most useful to graduate students. In addition, practicing CIOs and persons recruiting CIOs will find this book most helpful.

I did the move from CIO to CEO myself once. I was CIO at ABB Norway, managing an IT staff of 80. Higher level ABB management thought I did a good job, and I was still up-and-coming at the age of 37. I was offered the job of CEO at ABB Datacables, one of many ABB companies, with two cable-manufacturing plants and with a staff of 400 people. I accepted the job and ran into quite a surprising situation. Being a CEO was completely different from being a CIO. And, becoming a CEO and having a local CIO in the organization was quite confusing. Yes, I still believed in the potential of IT. But no, I did not spend much time dealing with IT issues together with the CIO. I spent much time dealing with the unions to prevent strikes, I visited many customers, and I traveled a lot for coordination purposes within the global ABB family. Strange, but it went well in the end. My CEO successor was not the CIO. That's my story.

Overview of Book Chapters

This book is concerned with the changing role of CIO to CEO. How can the CIO become the next CEO in the organization? To understand this question — and to answer it — we need to understand the CEO role and the CIO role. Therefore, Chapter I of this book presents the CEO role, while Chapter II presents the CIO role. The focus in Chapter I is CEO successions, as the CIO might be a potential successor CEO of an incumbent CEO. The focus in Chapter II is CIO work, as the CIO is waiting for an opportunity for promotion and, in the meantime, is trying to qualify him or herself.

The CIO is further explored in terms of leadership roles in Chapter III. Leadership roles can be defined for both CIOs and CEOs, enabling a comparison for the change from CIO to CEO. Generally, CEOs have been found to be more externally oriented than CIOs. CEOs have external relationships with stakeholders such as shareholders, banks, major customers, joint venture partners, and supply chain partners. CIOs also have external activities, such as vendor contacts and computer society meetings. In the internal management, the CIO is mainly focused on personnel leadership and resource allocations, which is similar to the internal management of the CEO.

In Chapter IV, a theoretical basis is provided for further discussions of strategy and management. The chapter focuses on resource-based theory of the firm as well as the value configuration of a value shop. A value configuration describes the firm in terms of its primary and secondary activities that create value for its customers. The traditional value configuration is a value chain that produces goods from inbound to outbound logistics. Alternative value configurations are value shop and value chain. The value shop creates value by solving client problems by means of primary activities such as problem finding and acquisition, solutions to the problem, and implementation of the best solution to client problem.

The contingent approach to moving the CIO to the CEO position implies that the CEO candidacy of a CIO is dependent on the situation. One important situational factor is the value configuration of the organization. The main purpose of information systems in the value chain is to make production more efficient. The CIO must focus on systems such as enterprise resource planning (ERP) to make a significant contribution to firm performance. The CIO becomes an expert at the operational level, including supply chain management. Unfortunately for the CIO, operational expertise will seldom be the critical qualification for the next CEO.

The main purpose of information systems in the value shop is to add value to the knowledge work. The CIO in the value shop is close to the knowledge work of professionals by providing support through knowledge management systems. In contrast to CIOs in the value chain, CIOs in the value shop are closer to the people in the organization. The CIO must relate to professionals and executives in their knowledge work. In contrast, CIOs in value chains relate to topics such as logistics, production, supply chains, and projects, which are less person-focused and more task-focused.

Resource-based theory is applied in Chapter V to identify strategic IT resources. Corporate strategic management, in general, and strategic planning, in particular, are presented in Chapter VI. The Y model for strategic planning is introduced to illustrate the commonalities of corporate strategy and IS/IT strategy. Not only is there mutual influence and interaction between corporate and IS/IT planning, the procedures and methods are similar as well.

When the CEO and the top management team develop corporate strategy, they apply methods such as SWOT analysis (strengths, weaknesses, opportunities, and threats), value configuration analysis, competitive forces analysis, marketing analysis, and product portfolio analysis. Similarly, the CIO applies the same kind of methods when developing IS/IT strategy.

At the level of strategic management, the positions of CEO and CIO have more similarities than at the level of operational management. In strategic management, competitive forces are just as important to the CEO as they are to the CIO when developing strategy. While the CEO may want to form alliances with customers to reduce customer power, the CIO may want to form supply chains with customers to improve the relative power of the firm even more.

Challenging tasks for the CIO are discussed, such as the CIO developing e-business in Chapter VII, the CIO sourcing IT services in Chapter VIII, and the CIO enabling IT governance in Chapter IX. IT governance comes after e-business and outsourcing, as the governance structure is dependent on business model as well as sourcing decisions for IT services.

To expand his or her power base, the CIO might take and include the position of the chief knowledge officer (CKO) as presented in Chapter X. The CKO is an important role for both operational and symbolic reasons. Operationally, CKOs perform a variety of key roles, including serving as the chief designer of the knowledge architecture, the top of the reporting relationship for knowledge professionals, the head technologist for knowledge technologies, and the primary procurement officer for external knowledge content. Symbolically, the presence of a CKO serves as an important indicator that a firm views knowledge and its management as critical to its success.

Finally, in Chapter XI, the demand side and the supply side are presented to discuss the CIO as a potential candidate to become the next CEO. From the demand side, there is a need for a new CEO. The question we raise is whether or not the CIO is a candidate for the job. Promoting the CIO to the post of CEO represents an inside succession. It can either be a relay or non-relay succession. If the CIO is selected and crowned as an heir apparent it is a relay succession. An incumbent CEO works with the CIO as an heir apparent and passes the baton of leadership to the heir.

Taking a supply-side perspective, the CIO must represent attractive executive capital for the firm. Examples of tasks CIOs should perform — or attempt to perform — to develop their executive capital and potential are presented throughout this book. Important general tasks include mobilizing strategic IT resources, applying IT resources to the value configuration, and participating in corporate strategic management. More specific tasks include developing e-business, sourcing IT services, supporting IT governance, and linking information management and knowledge management.

Chapters dealing with the chief executive officer and CEO successions, CIO leadership roles, and theories of the firm manifest the background information for this book. These are handled within the context of modern business competition and globalization.

From the CIO perspective, there is nothing more critical than strategic management of IT or developing e-businesses or enabling e-governance in the modern corporate setting. Each of these items is addressed in this book in a practical manner, yet still well grounded in the academics.

Petter Gottschalk
Norwegian School of Management BI
Oslo, Norway
June 2006

Chapter I

The Chief Executive Officer

Introduction

The chief executive officer (CEO) is the only executive at level 1 in the hierarchy of an organization (Carpenter & Wade, 2002). All other executives in the organization are at lower levels. At level 2, we find the most senior executives. Level 3 includes the next tier of executives. In our perspective of promoting the chief information officer (CIO) to be the next CEO, we first have to understand the role of the CEO. Therefore, the first chapter of this book is dedicated to the topic of CEO successions (Zhang & Rajagopalan, 2004).

Being a CEO involves handling exceptional circumstances and developing a high level of tacit knowledge and expertise; these characteristics and experiences contribute to the accumulation of firm-specific human capital. The time a CEO spends in the position represents a significant investment in firm-specific human capital for both the individual and the firm. The firm is investing its resources to compensate the CEO, and the CEO is investing his or her productive time. Both make these investments with the expectation of future return, so age is a major factor determining the level of firm-specific human capital investment (Buchholtz, Ribbens, & Houle, 2003).

Being a CEO means bearing full responsibility for a company's success or failure, but being unable to control most of what will determine it; having more authority than anyone else in the organization, but being unable to wield it without unhappy consequences. Porter, Lorsch, and Nohria (2004) make this sound like a very tough job. They argue that this comes as a surprise to CEOs who are new to the job.

Some of the surprises for new CEOs arise from time and knowledge limitations—there is so much to do in complex new areas, with imperfect information and never enough time. Others stem from unexpected and unfamiliar new roles and altered professional relationships. Still others crop up because of the paradox that the more power you have, the harder it is to use. While several of the challenges may appear familiar, Porter et al. (2004) discovered that nothing in a leader's background, even running a large business within his or her company, fully prepare them to be CEO.

CEOs have long been recognized as the principal architects of corporate strategy and major catalysts of organizational change, and the extent to which CEOs can effect change in corporate strategy is thought to be determined largely by the power they possess and how they decide to wield it (Bigley & Wiersema, 2002).

Bigley and Wiersema (2002) argued that CEOs' cognitive orientations should influence how they wield their power to affect corporate strategy. On the one hand, predictions about a CEO's use of power require an understanding of the CEO's cognitive orientation toward his or her firm's strategy, because power is simply the ability to bring about a preferred or intended effect. On the other hand, hypothesized associations between a CEO's cognitive orientation and corporate strategy presupposes that the CEO has sufficient power to bring about the preferred or intended effects.

CEOs' strategic beliefs are likely to be instantiated to a significant degree in their firms' current strategies. When a top executive seeking advice confirms and/or restores his or her confidence in the correctness of strategic beliefs, the CEO will be less likely to change firm strategy. McDonald and Westphal (2003) theorized that relatively poor firm performance can prompt CEOs to seek more advice from executives of other firms who are their friends or similar to them and less advice from acquaintances or dissimilar others and suggests how and why this pattern of advice seeking could reduce firms' propensity to change corporate strategy in response to poor performance.

McDonald and Westphal (2003) tested their hypotheses with a large sample. The results confirm their hypotheses and show that executives' social network ties can influence firms' responses to economic adversity, in particular by inhibiting strategic change in response to relatively poor firm performance. Additional findings indicate that CEOs' advice seeking in response to low performance may ultimately have negative consequences for subsequent performance, suggesting how CEOs' social network ties could play an indirect role in organizational decline and downward spirals in firm performance.

In *MIT Sloan Management Review,* Johnson (2002) phrased the question: Do CEOs matter? To answer this, he cites two critical dimensions that influence the magnitude of a CEO's impact on a company. First, resource availability, which is dependent upon an organization's level of debt (higher debt means less cash available to direct toward investments or acquisitions) and level of slack (that is, the number of extra people or amount of assets that the CEO can easily redeploy to take advantage of an opportunity). Second, opportunity availability, which is determined by independence, concentration, and growth. CEOs at the helms of companies with low debt levels and high slack levels — thus high resource availability — will exert more powerful impact on their organizations, and CEO impact increases as opportunities become scarcer.

CEO Successions

CEO succession is perhaps one of the most crucial events in the life of any firm because of the substantive and symbolic importance of the CEO position. CEO succession has been commonly viewed as an important mechanism for organizational learning and adaptation. A change in CEO can fundamentally alter the knowledge, skills, and interaction processes at the top of a company, and these alterations can in turn significantly influence post-succession firm performance. Zhang and Rajagopalan (2004) studied CEO successions, and the following description of this topic is based on their research.

A distinction can be made between two types of CEO succession — inside and outside. Some have emphasized the role of outside successions in organizational learning and adaptation. However, Zhang and Rajagopalan (2004) argue that research evidence consistently indicates that outside new CEOs rarely succeed in their efforts to improve firm performance. It is plausible that although outside successions bring in new competencies and skills, they are disruptive to firms from a process standpoint, and thus the enhanced cognitive repertoire may not get translated into improved firm performance. Further, the simple distinction between inside and outside succession does not recognize crucial differences between relay and non-relay inside successions, which may have different implications for organizational learning and adaptation.

In relay succession, a firm identifies an heir apparent to its CEO well in advance of the actual succession event and uses the interval between designation and promotion to groom the heir for the top job. A relay CEO succession has two phases: During the first phase, the firm decides whether or not to designate an heir; during the second (the grooming phase), the firm decides whether or not to promote the heir to the CEO position. Both phases offer significant opportunities for organizational learning and adaptation. In the first phase, learning and adaptation occur primarily at the firm level. The firm assesses the availability and desirability of various candidates for the CEO position and evaluates their qualifications in light of key internal and external contingencies in order to decide whether to designate one of them as the heir apparent.

The second phase can be characterized as a two-way learning and adaptation process that occurs at both the individual level of the heir apparent and at the firm level. At the individual level, the heir now has the opportunity to carry out some of the tasks of the CEO position and to thereby acquire and enhance position-specific knowledge and develop broader leadership skills consistent with the position. Meanwhile, at the firm level, because one candidate has been designated the heir, the firm can now conduct a more focused assessment of this particular candidate's capabilities (cognitive and interpersonal) and continuously update its evaluation of whether the candidate's capabilities fit the CEO position. It can then use this evaluation to subsequently decide whether or not to promote the heir apparent. In this sense, the grooming phase is also a probation period for an heir apparent.

Contrary to the traditional wisdom that outside CEOs are better equipped to turn around poor performance, research results by Zhang and Rajagopalan (2004) suggest that outside successions do not significantly differ from non-relay inside successions in terms of post-succession firm performance, even under conditions of poor pre-succession performance and/or high post-succession strategic instability. Outside successors are usually prized for their new skills, perspectives, and their willingness to initiate changes. Indeed, it has been well noted in the literature that, relative to inside CEOs, outside CEOs are more likely to initiate strategic changes. Most often, though, previous studies have focused upon the impact of outside CEOs on strategic change rather than on the performance consequences of strategic change. The finding that outside CEOs are more likely to initiate strategic change does not necessarily imply that such change improves post-succession firm performance. Indeed, because outside successors are more likely to lack firm-specific knowledge, it is harder for them to formulate and implement appropriate strategic change. In addition, outside CEO successions often disrupt firms, and outside successors find it more challenging to get support from other senior executives within firms. Therefore, it is not surprising that outside succession may not lead to better post-succession firm performance.

In comparing post-succession firm performance following different types of CEO succession, Zhang and Rajagopalan (2004) found the best performance following relay succession. Further, post-succession firm performance did not differ for non-relay inside succession and outside succession. These findings thus highlight the value of a potential new CEO's learning experience (in relay succession) before he or she assumes the CEO position.

In an earlier study, Zhang and Rajagopalan (2003) classified newly chosen CEOs' origin into three categories — intra-firm, intra-industry, and outside-industry — and examined their firm-level and industry-level antecedents. In their sample of CEO successions, intra-firm succession was positively associated with the presence of an heir apparent and the number of non-heir inside directors. Intra-industry succession was positively associated with strategic homogeneity among industry firms and a focal firm's strategic conformity to industry central tendencies.

Taking a supply-side perspective, prior studies have often used the overall size of a firm as a proxy for the size of the available pool of candidates. It has been argued that large firms tend to have intra-firm successions because they have larger internal labor markets and thus can find more internal candidates who appear to have the ability to solve critical organizational contingencies. Consistent with this argument, several studies have found that intra-firm succession is positively associated with firm size.

However, Zhang and Rajagopalan (2003) drew upon three theoretical perspectives — the executive human capital, agency theory, and power perspectives — to suggest that the actual pool of qualified candidates for the CEO position within the firm is likely to be much smaller than that suggested by the firm's overall size. First, the executive human capital argument indicates that the requirements of the CEO job are substantially different from those of other organizational positions (such as the CIO position). This is a position with considerable responsibility for overall firm performance, hence, only a small group of executives with experience at the highest levels of a firm are likely to possess the relevant managerial skills and expertise and to be considered serious candidates for this position. A new CEO is charged with challenging strategic mandates, and the learning process can be both time-consuming and stressful unless the candidate has significant prior senior experience within the firm.

Second, the power perspective suggests that in order to qualify for consideration, an internal candidate needs an established power base, especially in relation to the incumbent CEO and the board of directors. Holding a formal job title like president/chief operating officer (COO) and/or board membership often evidences such a power base. Some studies provide empirical evidence that power and politics can limit the potential of even very senior executives from ascending to the CEO position. Finally, from an agency theory perspective, a candidate is more likely to be considered seriously for the CEO position if the board of his or her firm has relevant information on the candidate's skills and competencies. Interactions with the board help to reduce the "adverse selection" problem that arises from information asymmetry between a board and a potential successor.

In sum, these theoretical perspectives can be integrated to define an intra-firm pool of qualified candidates for the position of a firm's CEO, the heir apparent of the firm is by far the most qualified and powerful contender. An heir apparent is the executive who holds the most senior formal position in a firm's hierarchy (below the CEO) and who has the opportunity to access the task of the CEO. Indeed, there is an implicit contract between an heir apparent and a board. Promoting an heir apparent to CEO represents a rule-bound behavior, and breaking this contract can signal instability and uncertainty in a succession process. Given the seriousness of this contract, a firm's board is likely to have obtained and evaluated information about the competencies of a candidate (the firm's heir apparent) prior to approving the appointment. This, in turn, means a significant reduction in the information asymmetry between the board and the heir apparent. Although these factors clearly increase the likelihood of an heir apparent being promoted, Zhang and Rajagopalan (2003) refer to a study where nearly one-third of the heirs apparent in the sample were not promoted. Power struggles and politics often determine an heir apparent tenure outcome, hence, being an heir apparent does not guarantee promotion. These arguments lead to the hypothesis formulated by Zhang and Rajagopalan (2003) that the presence of an heir apparent will be positively related to the likelihood of intra-firm succession.

The second set of internal candidates for a firm's CEO position includes senior executives (other than an incumbent CEO and an heir apparent) who are also members of the firm's board. Such executives have opportunities to participate in major strategic decisions as board members. Their titles (typically, they have the title of executive vice president or higher) reflect strategically important positions in their organization's hierarchies with significant responsibility for overall organizational performance. The board membership of these executives is both a reflection of their demonstrated competencies and a formal channel outside board members can use to gain knowledge about the skills and competencies of these candidates. From a power perspective, inside directors are the mostly likely and viable challengers for a CEO position, and they often play a significant role in the dismissal of an incumbent CEO or in the non-promotion of an heir apparent. These arguments lead to the next hypothesis formulated by Zhang and Rajagopalan (2003) that the number of non-heir inside directors will be positively related to the likelihood of intra-firm succession.

Taking a demand side perspective, it is likely that who is considered a desirable candidate (and hence within the qualified pool) is primarily contingent upon the extent to which a firm desires firm-specific skills. Zhang and Rajagopalan (2003) argue that one key demand antecedent that makes internal hiring desirable is prior strategic persistence, or the extent to which a firm's strategy remains stable over time. Strategic contingency theorists have argued that executives with firm-specific skills are considered more desirable when the firm values continuity in strategy and adherence to historically established practices and norms. If a firm's strategy remains stable over time, the critical skills for a successor CEO are familiarity with the firm and expertise in its strategy and operations as well as interpersonal relationships. The successor's divergent or untested ideas about "what might be," rather than "what is," become less valued. In such cases, the successor's prior experience within the firm becomes a valued managerial asset. In contrast, if the firm's strategy changes over time, prior firm-specific skills are likely to be less valuable and may even be inhibitors to change. These arguments lead to the third hypothesis formulated by Zhang and Rajagopalan (2003) that prior strategic persistence by a firm will be positively related to the likelihood of intra-firm succession.

In addition to the pool of candidates in the intra-firm market, there is a pool of candidates in the intra-industry market. Potentially, a pool of industry candidates for succession to a particular CEO position is quite large, depending on the number of firms within the focal firm's industry and the number of senior executives within these firms. Zhang and Rajagopalan (2003) drew upon institutional theory and executive human capital to argue that the actual pool of qualified candidates within an industry is likely to be restricted to senior executives from similarly sized or larger firms and from strategically homogeneous firms.

According to institutional theory, organizations seek to enhance or protect their legitimacy by adopting industry practices or norms. Recruiting a new CEO is a particularly visible event, hence, it provides a significant opportunity to communicate a firm's intention to conform to or deviate from industry practices. Studies grounded in institutional theory indicate that firms are more likely to imitate other industry firms that are similar in size to them, or larger. In addition to conferring increased legitimacy from an institutional standpoint, the hiring of a senior executive from a similarly sized or larger firm is also appropriate for other reasons. First, organizations of similar size are often similar in terms of structural complexity, often rely on similar environmental resources, and often face similar structural constraints. Second, senior executives in relatively large firms also have higher visibility than those in smaller firms, so they are more likely to attract the attention of firms seeking CEO successors and executive search firms. Finally, in addition to enhancing legitimacy from a symbolic standpoint, successors' ties to similarly sized and larger firms in an industry also have strategic value for focal firms because such ties expand the latter's intra-industry network. Thus, the potential pool of firms within its industry from which a focal firm is likely to hire its CEO is most likely restricted to those that are of a similar or larger size. Accordingly, the fourth hypothesis formulated by Zhang and Rajagopalan (2003) said that the number of similarly sized and larger firms in an industry would be positively related to the likelihood of intra-industry succession.

The pool of qualified intra-industry candidates can be further narrowed to senior executives in strategically homogeneous firms by drawing upon arguments from an executive human capital perspective. The extent to which an intra-industry candidate can transfer his or her skills to a firm is likely to depend on the extent of industry homogeneity. This is because executives in homogeneous industries better understand the production technologies employed within their industries as well as the product-markets within which the focal firm competes. Hence, although outsiders generally possess less firm-specific human capital than insiders, the magnitude of this difference — and therefore the relative costs of inside and outside succession — is likely to be lower in industries comprised of homogeneous firms than in more heterogeneous industries. In line with this argument, Zhang and Rajagopalan (2003) formulated a fifth hypothesis that strategic homogeneity among similarly sized and larger firms in an industry will be positively related to the likelihood of intra-industry succession.

Turning to the demand side, it would be expected that a successor CEO's industry origin could be influenced by the extent to which the hiring firm values industry-specific skills and experience. Zhang and Rajagopalan (2003) draw upon strategic contingency theory to argue that one key demand antecedent that makes intra-industry hiring desirable is firm strategic conformity, or the extent to which a firm's strategy adheres to the central tendencies of its industry. Firms that adhere to industry central tendencies are more likely to value industry-specific skills than firms that deviate from industry practices. In firms whose strategies conform to their industries' central tendencies, the critical skills for successors are familiarity with those industries' strategies and practices. In contrast, firms with novel and unique strategies that deviate from industry tendencies are more likely to desire successors who have the ability to explore and evaluate a range of competitive behaviors beyond those that most firms in their industries have already adopted. These arguments lead Zhang and Rajagopalan (2003) to their sixth and final hypothesis that firm strategic conformity to an industry's central tendencies will be positively related to the likelihood of intra-industry succession.

In their empirical study to test these hypotheses, Zhang and Rajagopalan (2003) classified the origin of a new CEO into three categories: intra-firm, intra-industry, and outside-industry. Intra-firm succession was defined as one in which an executive with firm tenure of at least two years had been promoted to the CEO position. Similarly, intra-industry succession was defined as one in which the successor CEO had firm tenure of less than two years but had industry tenure of at least two years in the same industry that the hiring firm was in. Outside-industry succession referred to a succession in which the successor CEO had industry tenure of less than two years in the same industry. Among the 220 successions, there were 132 intra-firm successions, 43 intra-industry successions, and 54 outside-industry successions. Hypotheses 1, 2, 5, and 6 were supported. Hypotheses 3 and 4 were not supported in this study.

Khurana (2001) discussed why boards often make poor choices when attempting to find the right CEO. He recommends succession decisions that follow six steps:

1. **Establish the goals and objectives of the search:** Examine the strategic and market challenges facing the company. Identify the leadership skills and attributes necessary to meet those challenges.

2. **Carefully select the search committee:** Ensure that the search committee has individuals who have a deep knowledge of the company and its challenges. Ensure that the search committee is diverse in its functional backgrounds or cognizant of its potential biases.

3. **Separate the roles and responsibilities of the search firm and the search committee:** Enlist the entire board in gathering detailed information about candidates through trusted contacts. Allow the executive-search consultant to mediate between the candidate and the company during sensitive compensation negotiations.

4. **Define the candidate pool broadly:** Encourage less obvious candidates to be considered seriously. Use the succession to break the cycle of selecting conservatively while hoping for change. Choose the candidate who can best meet the long-term objectives of the company, not the short-term reactions of Wall Street and the business media.

5. **Analyze the multiple factors affecting company performance:** Realize that the CEO is an important element of company performance, but not the only one. Recognize the trade-offs involved in selecting an insider candidate versus an outsider candidate.

6. **Choose candidates on the basis of the goals and objectives of the search:** Use the requirements of the position in guiding the selection rather than evaluate candidates against one another. Avoid political compromises.

Choosing the right CEO will remain a challenge. Khurana (2001) lists seven pitfalls that are derailing searches for the next CEO: (1) missing the chance for organizational introspection, (2) choosing the wrong search committee, (3) outsourcing critical steps, (4) defining the candidate pool too narrowly, (5) equating candidates with their past companies, (6) overestimating the value of insider or outsider status, and (7) accepting false assumptions.

Non-CEO Executives

In a later study, Zhang (2005) examined how the presence of a COO/president, who is separate from the CEO, affected strategic change and CEO dismissal. With longitudinal data on the tenures of 207 CEOs, results suggest that the presence of a separate COO/president increases the magnitude of strategic change under conditions of low firm performance but it decreases the magnitude of strategic change under conditions of high firm performance. In addition, the presence of a separate COO/president increases the likelihood of CEO dismissal under conditions of low firm performance, and this effect is stronger when the magnitude of strategic change is high; but it has no impact on the likelihood of CEO dismissal under conditions of high firm performance. These results suggest that the impact of the presence of a separate COO/president on strategic change and CEO dismissal varies across different organizational contexts.

There can be two separate roles of a COO/president: one representing an heir apparent in training for the CEO position, and the other representing a co-leader delegated with internal operating authority. From a co-leader perspective, it is argued that the decision to have a COO represents a major structural choice: It explicitly divides between two people a set of top-level roles that are typically fulfilled by one person; it draws a structural distinction between strategy formulation and implementation; it adds an organizational layer; and it adds a highly paid executive position to the organization's costs. From a succession (heir apparent) perspective, it is argued that many firms identified an heir apparent in the COO and/or president position in advance of the actual succession event and used this position to groom the next CEO. Findings of Zhang and Rajagopalan (2003) have suggested that the presence of a separate COO/president increases the likelihood that a new CEO will be selected from within the firm. These studies suggest that a CEO and a COO/president in general are partners, considering that as co-leaders, they work closely in their positions and from a succession perspective, it is likely that the CEO will pass the leadership baton to the COO/president when succession occurs.

On the other hand, however, the relationship of a CEO and a COO/president (as a co-leader or an heir apparent) can involve rivalry. From the perspective of power circulation, the number of inside directors on the board might increase the likelihood of CEO turnover under conditions of poor firm performance. From the perspective of power contestation, the proportions of non-CEO inside directors and non-CEO executive ownership might have significant influence on the likelihood of CEO dismissal (followed by inside succession). Therefore, other senior executives can be power contenders to the CEO. Thus, a COO/president, as a co-leader who is only one step from the top post, can be a power contender to the CEO.

Studies from a succession perspective have similar suggestions (Zhang, 2005). For example, a CEO may have complex feelings toward a COO/president. While selecting a COO/president as an heir apparent gives the CEO opportunities to continue his or her influence over the firm, naming an heir apparent also reminds the CEO of his or her own mortality. In addition, from the point of view of the COO/president as an heir apparent, he or she may become impatient under the shadow of the CEO and wants to be his or her "own man." The relationship between a CEO and a COO/president might have built-in, and therefore endemic, hazards that are exacerbated rivalry and corresponding defensiveness.

The results of Zhang's (2005) study contribute to building a contingency view on the CEO-COO/president relationship. The findings suggest that the role of a COO/president with regard to a CEO is context-specific. While a COO/president in general is a partner to a CEO, the COO/president may become a contender to the CEO under conditions of low firm performance. Thus, examining the role of a COO/president with regard to a CEO without taking into account the organizational contexts may underestimate the complexity of their relationship. These arguments and empirical evidence also contribute to the understanding of the power circulation and power contestation within political coalitions. By focusing on the two top posts (a CEO and a COO/president), the study suggested that the relationships between the key members of dominant political coalitions vary across different organizational contexts and that organizational continuity is enforced by their collaboration under conditions of high firm performance, and organizational adaptation is achieved by their rivalry under conditions of low firm performance.

The findings of Zhang's (2005) study also contribute to a better understanding of the inner workings of corporate elites in general. Many studies using an upper echelon perspective have treated corporate elites as a "team." Recent studies have emphasized conflict and competition within corporate elites. While these studies have extended our knowledge of collaboration and competition within corporate elites, we so far know little about the conditions under which the corporate elites are more likely to be collaborative as a "team" and the conditions under which they are more likely to be competitive. The results of this study suggested that corporate elites are more likely to be collaborative as a team under conditions of high firm performance because they can benefit from the high performance, and they have developed equilibrium in their interests and power. In contrast, under conditions of low firm performance, change is expected and the prior equilibrium is disappearing, so competition within corporate elites will rise until a new equilibrium is formed.

Further, the findings of Zhang's (2005) study contribute to our understanding of the monitoring within corporate elites. While most studies in the literature have focused on monitoring from higher to lower levels of management, this study is one of the few that have examined monitoring in the other direction — from lower to higher levels of management. The study found that the presence of a separate COO/president increases the magnitude of strategic change and the likelihood of CEO dismissal under conditions of low firm performance. Thus, the presence of a separate COO/president represents a healthy antidote to the trend toward "celebrity" CEOs. However, it should be noted that the monitoring from lower to higher levels of management occurs only under conditions of low firm performance. Such context specificity is not surprising given that higher levels of management (e.g., a CEO) are more powerful than lower levels of management (e.g., a COO/president) in most circumstances.

Carpenter and Wade (2002) developed a theory wherein the pay of non-CEO executives can be explained by micro-level opportunity structures — the intersection of functional position, CEO background, human capital, and firm strategic resource allocation decisions. The theory suggests a positive association between pay and a position made visible by resource allocation decisions, a functional background similar to that of the CEO, and a position that helps the firm manage strategic resource allocations.

In their empirical study, Carpenter and Wade (2002) found that executives received greater cash compensation when they occupied positions in which they were likely to be associated with strategic resource allocation choices made by their firm and when they had functional responsibilities similar to the background of the CEO.

It is often assumed that executives, primarily CEOs, are compensated for the criticality of the tasks that they must manage. Similarly, it is reasonable to expect that such relationships extend to some extent to the pay of other executives throughout a firm. However, although that perspective has typically emphasized the external and macro-level determinants of pay (that is, environment, firm size, and corporate strategy), Carpenter and Wade's (2002) study showed how the many faces of firm strategy (actions and resource allocation choices) may result in different internal resource dependencies, and thus have different pay implications for particular executives. Furthermore, the study showed that executives themselves vary in the position and human capital requisite to managing the contingencies arising from differences in leadership (like CEO background) and strategic resource allocations. Consequently, functional position, along with education and work experience, created certain micro-level opportunity structures that executives converted into higher pay.

Carpenter and Wade (2002) characterized strategy as the pattern resulting from a stream of resource allocation decisions. Such a pattern is comprised, for instance, of a firm's resource allocation choices in research and development, marketing, diversification, capital investments, and international markets. This view follows the strategic choice perspective wherein firms are under considerable constraints imposed by their environments but also having some latitude in their actions. Those actions, in turn, may generate fundamentally different ways of allocating resources, as revealed by differences in patterns across firms. In the context of their study, Carpenter and Wade (2002) argue that such fundamental differences between firms are likely to create compensation differences among executives within firms.

Conflict and Competition

Following a power perspective, Shen and Cannella (2002b) studied antecedents of CEO dismissal followed by inside succession. Their theory highlights interest conflicts and competition within top management. They proposed that CEO origin, CEO tenure, non-CEO inside directors, and senior executive ownership are important antecedents of CEO dismissal followed by inside succession. Evidence from a sample of 387 large U.S. corporations suggests that non-CEO senior executives frequently play an important role in CEO dismissal.

CEO origin refers to whether an incumbent CEO was an employee of the firm he or she leads at the time of appointment as CEO. Origin has important implications for power dynamics within top management groups. Building strong social networks and coalitions within a firm is an essential task for those who aspire to be the CEO. When they are promoted to a firm's CEO position, inside successors not only have the approval of outside directors, but also have support within the top management group — though perhaps not complete support, owing to internal competition. In contrast, when outside CEOs take office, they lack the internal social networks and coalitions of inside CEOs. Accentuating this problem is the fact that senior executives from a firm's prior regime often have a hostile attitude toward outside CEOs because of the changes these outsiders may initiate. In addition, because outside successors are often appointed in periods of poor performance and are expected to turn their firms around, they are under pressure to take quick action in restructuring top management groups. This intensifies interest conflicts between outside CEOs and senior executives. Thus, compared to inside succession, outside succession increases tension within a top management group and places the outside CEO at a higher risk of power contests with senior executives. The high expectations the board and other stakeholders have toward outside CEOs make them more vulnerable when challenges from senior executives emerge (Shen & Cannella, 2002b).

New CEOs confront significant challenges upon taking office. Promotion to the CEO position typically leads to significant changes in both an executive's responsibility and task environment. New CEOs must adjust to their new roles and quickly develop good working relationships with the other members of their top management groups, boards of directors, and powerful outside stakeholders. The learning process is stressful and time consuming. At the same time, new CEOs are charged with specific strategic mandates, a charge that further increases the difficulty of their tasks. Finally, and perhaps most crucial for new CEOs, is their need to establish their authority in a top position.

Authority is legitimate power and is of two types — authorized power and endorsed power. Authorized power is granted by those superior to the power holder, and endorsed power is granted by those subordinate to the power holder. To establish their authority, new CEOs must be accepted by both their boards of directors and by subordinate executives. Although the official appointment represents authorization by the board of directors, it does not necessarily confer endorsement from subordinates. Further, the authorization of a board is likely to be somewhat tentative and can be revoked quickly if directors develop significant concerns about a new CEO's leadership capacity. Indeed, because there is little proof of accountability in office, the leadership capacity of new CEOs is under close scrutiny by outside directors. Thus, until they can prove their competence and meet the expectations of both their boards and subordinate executives, the authority of new CEOs will be much weaker than that of established CEOs (Shen & Cannella, 2002b).

Inside directors are directors who are also executives of the firm on whose board they serve. Although the effectiveness of inside directors in governance has been widely questioned, theories emphasizing managerial interest conflicts and competition suggest that the presence of non-CEO inside directors has important implications for the power dynamics within top management. First, inside directors are the most likely and viable challengers of a CEO. A seat on the board gives an executive exposure to outside directors and enables them to build social networks and coalitions on the board. This development narrows the power gap between them and the CEO and lends them more confidence with which to challenge the CEO. Second, for senior executives to successfully challenge a CEO and to advance their careers, they must be able to voice their concerns about the CEO to the corporation's board. Finally, the presence of non-CEO inside directors limits a CEO's influence over a board and increases the chance for senior executives to successfully challenge the CEO. Inside directors have valuable firm-specific information about a firm's activities and market position (Shen & Cannella, 2002b).

Haveman, Russo, and Meyer (2001) studied how regulatory punctuations impact CEO succession. Executive succession can impart new knowledge and skills that make it possible to cope with the dramatic shifts in critical contingencies that follow regulatory punctuations. If current executives are not willing or able to pilot their organizations through the new competitive channels, organizations will search for new talent. Executive succession also has symbolic value, as it projects an aura of change in organizational direction. When uncertainty mounts, yesterday's leaders tend to be seen as having caused today's crisis, and their replacement symbolizes salvation and renewal.

Haveman et al. (2001) found that immediately following any regulatory punctuation, CEO succession rates will not rise; instead, CEO succession rates will rise gradually as time passes. However, as might be expected, the regulatory punctuation did not increase the likelihood of outside succession.

Institutional investors have begun to advocate specific changes in corporate governance that are thought to protect the interests of shareholders but that threaten the interests of top managers. Thus, this is another kind of conflict and competition. The focus of institutional investors is on pressuring boards of directors to exercise independent control over management on shareholders' behalf. They advocate changes in board structure that will increase board independence from management, such as separating the CEO and board-chair positions and creating independent nominating committees. Moreover, they pressure boards to dismiss CEOs of underperforming companies and repeal takeover defenses that were believed to protect managers from market discipline. The common, underlying rationale for institutional investors demanding these changes is rooted in the agency conception of corporate governance, which suggests that boards must exercise discipline and control over management, because executives, if left to their own devices, will tend to pursue policies that benefit themselves at the expense of shareholders (Westphal & Khanna, 2003).

Westphal and Khanna (2003) studied how social processes by which the corporate elite may have resisted pressure from stakeholders to adopt changes in corporate governance that limit managerial autonomy. Senior managers and directors of large established companies tend to possess a shared class-wide rationality or group consciousness as members of a unified business elite. Members of this inner circle of business leaders are normatively expected to protect the interests of corporations and the executives who run them. A central interest to be protected is the autonomy and final decision-making authority of top managers themselves. Boards are often a critical mechanism by which the solidarity of the corporate elite is maintained and the interests of corporate leaders are served. Boards provide a locus for socialization of directors who violate the priorities of corporate leaders, demonstrating that such sanctioning is effective in determining deviant behavior.

Westphal and Khanna's (2003) findings suggest that control in corporate governance can be viewed as a social phenomenon. In recent years, the corporate governance literature has drawn largely from economic perspectives such as agency theory, and in some cases micro-political perspectives, to explain the determinants of corporate control. These perspectives tend to assume that control lies with individuals or small groups, such as individual CEOs, boards, or owners, thus lending a somewhat atomistic, and perhaps oversimplified perspective to theory and research on corporate control.

In contrast, Westphal and Kanna's (2003) study suggests how control can be exercised by the corporate elite as a larger social group. From a theoretical perspective, directors exercise social control over other directors not because it serves their own personal interests (whether economic or political), but because those directors violated normative expectations for members of the corporate elite by failing to respect the autonomy of managers on another board.

According to Westphal and Bednar (2005), CEOs often fail to initiate strategic changes in response to poor firm performance. Strategic persistence in response to poor performance results, in part, from a range of cognitive biases or perceptual distortions in executive decision-making. For example, CEOs have been shown to over-attribute poor firm performance to uncontrollable or temporary conditions in the external environment and under-attribute performance problems to the current corporate strategy. Executives fall prey to such attribution biases for a variety of reasons. They may become socialized into belief systems that take for granted the value of the current strategy. To the extent that they helped to formulate the strategy or previously endorsed the strategy, implicitly or explicitly, executives may be reluctant to acknowledge to themselves, colleagues, or external constituents that the strategy is not working. Moreover, there is evidence that executives tend to respond to poor performance by restricting their search for new information, ignoring information that reflects negatively on the current strategy, or engaging in a biased pattern of advice seeking that affirms their strategic assumptions and bolsters their confidence in the current strategy.

Outside directors may have social ties to the CEO or professional ties to the firm that make them reluctant to challenge the CEO's view about the viability of the current corporate strategy. Empirical evidence from the corporate governance literature does not consistently support this explanation, however. Although there is some evidence that boards comprising outsiders who lack social ties to management are more effective in controlling agency costs from overly generous executive compensation contracts, there is less evidence that directors' independence affects the likelihood of strategic persistence in response to poor performance or environmental change. Outside directors who lack social ties to the CEO or professional ties to the firm are not necessarily more likely to challenge top managers on strategic issues (Westphal & Bednar, 2005).

Succession Planning

According to Freeman (2004), the literature on CEO succession planning is nearly unanimous in its advice: Begin early, look first inside the company for exceptional talent, see that candidates gain experience in all aspects of the business, help them develop the skills they will need in the top job. It all makes sense and sounds pretty straightforward.

Nevertheless, the list of companies with CEOs lasting no more than a few years after taking the reins continues to grow. Freeman (2004) draws a conclusion from what he calls this parade of chief executives marching out the door: Implicit in many, if not all, of these unceremonious departures is the absence of an effective CEO succession plan.

Charan (2005) argued there is a CEO succession crisis. He suggests that the most important thing companies can do to improve successions is to bolster their leadership development and focus on those very rare people in their ranks who might one day be CEO. Organizations must identify high-potential candidates early in their careers, and global companies must look in all the countries where they operate. As candidates enter the development pipeline, managers must constantly align their charges' education and on-the-job experience with the emerging landscape. And they must rigorously assess the candidates' performance at each developmental stage.

But leadership development is just part of the solution. Boards, too, can greatly improve the chances of finding a strong successor by acting vigilantly before and during the search. Senior executive development should be overseen by the board's compensation and organization committee, which needs to receive periodic reports on the entire pool of potential CEOs and regular updates on those bobbing near the top of it. And directors should personally get to know the company's rising stars. The goal of all these interactions and deliberations is for board members to reach

rule violation in CEO succession. Third, understanding the outcomes of heir apparent tenures could improve understanding of coalition behaviors in firms' upper echelons. Finally, identification of the antecedents of heir apparent promotion and exit has practical implications for more effective management of relay succession.

Cannella and Shen (2003) treated promotion and exit as two competing outcomes for heir apparents. At the same time, they also emphasized that heir apparent promotion and exit are not a simple either-or situation, thus, the factors investigated would have asymmetrical implications for their occurrence. Their empirical results support this treatment. For example, CEO power not only strongly decreases the likelihood of promotion, but also decreases the likelihood of heir exit when firm performance is low. Similarly, although outside director power has no direct effect on promotion, it significantly influences heir exit. Further, the effect of outside director power is importantly influenced by the performance context. This observation warns against simple symmetrical thinking about heir apparent promotion and exit: Factors that decrease the likelihood of promotion will increase the likelihood of exit, and vice versa.

Cannella and Shen (2003) found that relay succession is guided by rules and most often unfolds as planned. Powerful CEOs and outside directors can intervene in the process but often do not. Intervention is most likely in situations of extreme importance — either high or low. Although relay succession is generally regarded as a smooth power transition process, it may also be characterized by interest conflicts and power struggles. Powerful outside directors help ensure the promotion of heirs when performance is strong and work to oust them when performance is poor.

The relay succession process places incumbent CEOs in a difficult situation that leads them to have mixed feelings toward their designated successors. The strongly negative association between CEO power and promotion found in the study by Cannella and Shen (2003) suggests that powerful CEOs are reluctant to relinquish their power and thus may strive to postpone heir apparent promotion. However, at the same time, CEO power did not have a direct effect on exit, which suggests that incumbent CEOs do not appear to oust their heirs apparent unconditionally. This complexity is further indicated by the positive interactive effect of CEO power and industry-adjusted return on assets on heir apparent exit: CEO power increases the likelihood of heir apparent when industry-adjusted ROA is above average but decreases it when industry-adjusted ROA is below average. This evidence is consistent with the argument that challenges to an heir from outside directors are very close to challenges to the incumbent CEO and that powerful incumbents protect their heirs apparent when performance is low.

Cannella and Shen (2003) noted that incumbent CEO age has a very strong effect on heir apparent promotion and exit. Unsurprisingly, promotions in relay succession were quite likely to happen when the incumbents are in their 60s, given that most mandatory retirement ages lie within this range. This evidence seems related to the finding that most relay CEO successions unfold as planned. The incumbent CEO retires on schedule, in conformity with the implied rules of relay succession.

Succession planning can be viewed as a component of a "passing the baton" process (Davidson, Nemic, & Worrell, 2001). A successful CIO can be promoted to president; a successful president would be promoted to CEO and a successful CEO to chair, with a new president awaiting the passing of the baton. In this passing the baton process, both duality and plurality will occur. Duality is when one executive is holding both the CEO and chair positions, while plurality is when one executive is holding the three titles of president, CEO, and chair. However, agency costs arise in both situations.

The agency cost perspective on executive duality and plurality is that the costs of this organizational structure would be greater than any benefits conveyed by such a unified command structure. The costs stem from the board's responsibility for ensuring that managers behave with shareholders' best interests in mind. If the chair of the board is also the CEO, then it is tantamount to the fox guarding the chicken coop. The board would be providing self-evaluation. However, Davidson et al. (2001) found in their study that duality and plurality announcements do not hurt shareholder wealth as long as there is an heir apparent.

In another study focusing on shareholder wealth, Shen and Cannella (2003) examined investor reactions to a specific form of succession planning — relay succession. Theory predicts that both the initiation and the outcome of a relay CEO succession process will influence shareholder wealth. The results show that investors generally do not react to the initiation of the process as indicated by heir apparent appointment, but react negatively when the process ends in heir apparent exit from the firm and react positively when the process ends in heir apparent promotion to the CEO position. Shen and Cannella (2003) also found a strong positive investor reaction to outside CEO promotion and a negative investor reaction to non-heir inside CEO promotion. Further, firm performance exerted an important influence on the wealth effect of heir apparent promotion and exit.

The question of internal versus external successors does regularly emerge in the popular business press. In Norway, where business organizations typically have a small size, it is argued that small organizations will find it more difficult to identify potential internal successors. This problem occurs because small organizations have a very limited number of candidates and because small organizations have a tendency to be more homogeneous in thinking style, making it less attractive to replace a CEO with a similar CEO in times of change (*Dagens Næringsliv*, 2005).

According to the Norwegian financial newspaper *Dagens Næringsliv* (2005), larger business organizations plan for successions and choose internal candidates. Examples include Orkla, Norsk Hydro, Elkjøp, DnB Nor, Møller Group, and Norske Skog. Orkla has 35.000 employees and revenues of $6 billion in food and paper production. The last three CEOs were internally recruited, maybe because the company has been profitable all the time. Similarly, Norsk Hydro has recruited its CEO internally for several decades. Both companies have succession planning in terms of rotation programs and management training.

In Sweden, the furniture giant Ikea with 84,000 employees in 44 countries recruits top managers internally. CEO Jeanette Söderberg has made it all the way from the cash register to the top position and was named executive of the year in Sweden in 2005 (*Dagens Næringsliv,* 2005).

Three Types of CEO Successors

Organization and strategy scholars studying CEO succession often dichotomize CEO successors into insiders and outsiders: Insiders are executives promoted from within the firm, and outsiders come to new CEO positions from other organizations. The assumption in most research is that inside successors are appointed under conditions of good company performance and reflect intent to maintain strategic continuity, and outside successors are appointed under conditions of poor company performance and reflect intent to initiate strategic change. Firms do not typically appoint outside successors unless they face the pressure of initiating strategic change, coupled with an unavailability of competent inside successor candidates. However, the appointment of an inside successor does not necessarily reflect intent to maintain strategic continuity. This proposition by Shen and Cannella (2002b) is grounded in a power circulation theory of control, and it separates their study from mainstream succession research.

The power circulation theory of control suggests that incumbent CEOs face a risk of power contests initiated by other senior executives as well as by outsider directors. Senior executives who are typically ambitious individuals with strong needs for power and control surround CEOs. The power of a CEO is thus, from time to time, subject to challenge and contestation from these senior executives. The likelihood of CEO turnover is significantly increased when questions arise about an incumbent's capabilities and viable inside candidates exist.

According to Andrews (2001), CEO turnover is not a simple solution to a company's problems. She argues that we live in a society that is quick to praise or blame individuals without looking at the context in which they operate. Boards of directors and shareholders need to create conditions in which their CEOs can succeed.

Performance consequences of CEO turnover depend on the circumstances. Andrews (2001) divided turnover circumstances into four categories: the voluntary (or natural) departure of a CEO who is then succeeded by an insider; natural departure followed by an outsider; forced departure followed by an insider; and forced departure followed by an outsider. When a natural departure was followed by the promotion of an insider, no change of any statistical significance occurred in company performance. Neither did performance change when a CEO's forced departure was followed by an insider filling the position. Firing a CEO signals a mandate for change. But an insider, linked to the political and operational status quo, rarely has the skills or the maneuvering room to make the kinds of dramatic strategic changes — such as downsizing or taking on substantial debt — that affect performance. However, when an outside hire replaced a fired CEO, company performance rose by more than 4% during the three-year period following the change.

Research on successor selection has also shown that inside successors are often appointed in periods of poor performance, even in situations of forced CEO departure. Although this phenomenon has been proposed to reflect managerial entrenchment, Shen and Cannella (2002b) believe that it more likely reflects the outcome of power struggles within top management. According to power circulation theory, an inside succession following a CEO's dismissal reflects a successful internal power contest against the CEO, and the successor is a contending executive who has won the support and approval of the board of directors. In this situation, the inside successor, whom can be referred to as a contender, is more likely to be charged with a mandate to initiate strategic change, as is the case in an outside succession, rather than a mandate to maintain strategic continuity.

In contrast, if an inside successor is appointed following the predecessor's ordinary retirement rather than dismissal, the successor's mandate is more likely to be to maintain strategic continuity, as proposed in previous research. Because successors who follow a CEO's ordinary retirement are often expected to continue and follow their predecessors' strategies, they can be referred to as followers.

Thus, as noted, including outsider successors, there are three types of CEO successors: followers, contenders, and outsiders. These three types of CEO successors will have different impacts on post-succession firm operational performance. Shen and Cannella (2002b) view three sets of factors as the source of performance effects: firm-specific knowledge, change initiatives, and the risk of adverse selection. In their conceptualization, change initiatives have two parts — a board mandate for alterations of the firm's strategic profile, and the new leader's propensity for and ability to make such alterations. The risk of adverse selection arises because information asymmetry between the board and successor candidates makes it difficult for the board to accurately assess if the abilities of a potential successor match the needs of the firm. The board may select someone who is poorly suited to the job. The following description of three types of CEO successors is adopted from Shen and Cannella (2002b).

Follower successors are inside executives who are promoted to CEO positions following the ordinary retirement of their predecessors. As insiders, they possess firm-specific knowledge. Further, because of their frequent exposure to their firms' boards of directors and other senior executives, coupled with their history of performance inside the firm, the risk of adverse selection is relatively low. However, follower successors have significant limitations in their ability to initiate strategic change because they are often selected and groomed by the outgoing CEOs. Incumbent CEOs often believe that their successors should be similar to them, and many incumbents do select such successors when they retire. Because of their close connections and similarities to their predecessors, follower successors are heavily influenced and socialized by their outgoing CEOs and may share with them the same or similar strategic perspectives. They are also significantly constrained by their within-firm social networks. Further, CEO successors promoted after their predecessors' retirements typically have mandates to maintain strategic continuity rather than to initiate change.

Therefore, although follower successors' firm-specific knowledge and the relatively low risk of adverse selection they pose can help reduce the disruption of CEO succession, their close connection to their predecessors and social networks within the firm, coupled with a likely mandate for continuity rather than change, will impede their initiating significant strategic change and make it difficult for them to significantly influence firm operational performance.

Contender successors are inside executives who are promoted to CEO positions after the dismissals of their predecessors. Like follower successors, contender successors' work experiences give them firm-specific knowledge, and their exposure to directors and other senior executives reduces the risk of adverse selection. What distinguishes contender successors from follower successors is their having mandates for change from their boards of directors and the high likelihood that they will be able to initiate and implement important changes.

Unlike follower successors, who are usually selected and groomed by the outgoing CEOs, contender successors are promoted after successfully challenging their predecessors. Because power contestation and CEO dismissal often occur in periods of poor firm performance, contender successors will be charged to initiate strategic change and improve firm performance. CEO dismissal is a very disruptive event, and boards of directors are very cautious in making dismissal decisions. In order to gain support from directors, contenders for succession must convince them that the incumbent CEOs' competencies are not up to the demands of the job and that they (the contenders) have different strategic perspectives and can perform better. Further, contenders may not only have board support, but also support among senior executives for their power contests against the incumbent CEOs. An established power base and support within top management will greatly facilitate the process of taking charge. Lastly, contender successors do not have to be concerned about offending their predecessors in initiating changes because their predecessors have been dismissed and have terminated all association with the firms. Contender successors may also be constrained to a certain degree by their within-firm social networks, but demands from the boards for change initiatives will push contenders to overcome such constraints in their actions. The firm-specific knowledge, different strategic perspectives, and supportive directors and executives possessed by contender successors not only help them reduce harmful disruption associated with CEO dismissal, but also enable them to formulate and implement appropriate strategic changes in a timely manner.

Outsider successors are most often selected in periods of poor firm performance and when directors cannot locate a competent successor within their firm. Outsider successors are prized for their fresh perspectives and their ability to initiate strategic change. Also, the popular business press has advocated outsider succession when corporate transformation is required. However, past research has reported mixed investor reactions to outsider succession, and little is known about its long-term implications. Although the objective of outsider succession is improved firm performance, three factors work against this outcome. First, outsider successors lack firm-specific knowledge. Facing mandates to turn performance around, outsider successors are often pressured to take quick action. However, without a deep understanding of their new firms' internal operations and external environments, it is difficult for outsider successors to quickly formulate and implement appropriate strategic changes.

Second, it is more difficult for directors to fully and accurately evaluate the capabilities of outside candidates (compared with inside candidates) because directors usually do not have a deep familiarity with them. This evaluation difficulty leads to a higher risk of adverse selection in that a newly appointed outsider successor may not fit a firm's strategic demands. Finally, outsider successors often face the challenge of finding competent and supportive senior executives within their new firms. Senior executives have often been selected by outsiders' predecessors and have close social and professional connections with them. These executives are often hostile toward outside successors. Constrained by their experiences and by hostility, these executives may have strong commitments to their firms' past strategies and will resist any significant changes initiated by the outsider successors. Although the outsider successors have the support of their boards, the lack of competent and supportive executive teams when they take office puts them at a significant disadvantage.

The sample in Shen and Cannella's (2002b) research consisted of 228 successions, including 159 follower successions, 41 contender successions, and 28 outsider successions. Findings from their study suggest that operational performance impact differs for contender and outsider successions when both are facing tremendous pressure to initiate strategic change. Contender successions were more successful than outsider successions. This result is mainly a consequence of the outsider successors' lack of firm-specific knowledge and the tremendous disruption already present in outsider succession.

CEO Charisma and Celebrity

There is some degree of controversy concerning whether it is possible for top-level leaders to have a substantive effect on the overall performance of the organization they lead. On the one hand, some have heralded leadership on the part of CEOs as an important ingredient for the revitalization of organizations, and as critically important to the top management of large organizations and, in the political area, of nations. On the other hand, proponents of external control assert that CEO leadership is inconsequential to organizational performance. Much of their reasoning is based on the notion that leadership is a perceptual phenomenon that allows observers to develop simple causal explanations for complex organizational events and performance (Waldman & Yammarino, 1999).

CEO charisma represents a potentially key component of strategic leadership. Charisma is based on behavioral tendencies and personal characteristics of the leader, including the articulation of a clear vision derived from firmly held values or moral justifications, role modeling of those values, communication for high performance expectations, and confidence in followers' abilities to meet those expectations, references to the greater collective and its identity, symbolic behaviors, and the assumption of personal risks and sacrifices. CEO charisma involves a relationship between a CEO and one or more followers in close organizational proximity, combined with favorable attributions, primarily from followers at distant organizational echelons, which results in internalized commitment to the vision of the leader, exceptionally strong admiration and respect for the leader, and identification of followers with the leader, the vision, and the collective forged by the leader (Waldman & Yammarino, 1999).

Waldman and Yammarino (1999) presented a model of CEO charismatic leadership in organizations and showed how such leadership can, through levels of management and analysis, impact organizational performance. They suggest that charismatic leadership will result in heightened work efforts by organizational members, which in turn will improve organizational performance.

CEO celebrity arises when journalists broadcast the attribution that a firm's positive performance has been caused by its CEO's action. In this definition, celebrity has three core components. First, journalists broadcast such attributions through the print and electronic mass media. Second, the attribution involves the causes of a firm's actions that lead to its positive performance. Third, firm actions (and, by implication, performance) are attributed to the CEO's volition. That is, celebrity does not involve attributions to other factors such as luck, environmental conditions, or the actions of other individuals and teams in the firm. Thus, celebrity does not necessarily arise if performance is attributed to a CEO's action that is portrayed as lucky or dictated by the CEO's environment. Hayward, Rindova, and Pollock

(2004) present the following example of a journalist's propensity to attribute a firm's outcomes, including its performance, to the actions of its CEO:

> *Welch has delivered extraordinary growth, increasing the market value of GE from $12 billion in 1981 to about $200 billion today. No one, not Microsoft's William H. Gates III or Intel's Andrew S. Grove, not Walt Disney's Michael D. Eisner or Berkshire Hathaways Warren E. Buffet, not even the late Coca-Cola Chieftain Roberto C. Goizueta or the late Wal-Mart founder Sam Walton, has created more shareholder value than Jack Welch.*

There is a tendency of journalists to attribute a firm's actions and outcomes only to the CEO. Journalists celebrate a CEO whose firm takes strategic actions that are distinctive and consistent by attributing such actions and performance to the firm's CEO. In doing so, journalists over-attribute a firm's actions and outcomes to the disposition of its CEO rather than to broader situational factors.

A CEO who internalizes such celebrity also will tend to believe this over-attribution and become overconfident about the efficacy of his or her past actions and future abilities. Hubris arises when CEO overconfidence results in problematic firm decisions, including undue persistence with actions that produce celebrity. The more that others provide an individual with attributional accounts, the more likely it is that the individual will adopt the view expressed by others. The more a CEO interacts with others who also accept his or her celebrity, the more likely he or she will accept the celebrity attribution as true (Hayward et al., 2004).

As a result of recent corporate scandals, reformers and investors have increasingly called for companies to separate the chairman and CEO jobs. Of the 100 largest British companies, all but a handful separate the CEO and chair positions. The U.S. model combines the two positions. Lorsch and Zelleke (2005) found that no compelling arguments exist for splitting the chairman and CEO jobs.

Founder-CEO Succession

Chief executive officers are critical players in their organizations. From their position at the top of a company, CEOs are able to direct their companies in the active pursuit of opportunities and can control the company's strategy and structure. More specifically, CEOs make material strategic choices that can influence firm performance, and the quality and performance of an organization's top managers is often the single most important determinant of both the success and survival of the organization. The CEO of an organization is a critical factor in its direction and performance. As a result, changes in CEOs — CEO succession events — are critical junctures for organizations (Wasserman, 2003).

The very first succession event in a firm is often when the founder-CEO is replaced. The critical differences between later-stage succession and founder-CEO succession include the higher level of attachment between founder-CEOs and the firms they create, the much larger equity holdings of founder-CEOs (which give them much more control of the firm), the fact that many founder-CEOs remain in the firm (even though it is being run by their successors), and the fact that nearly all early-stage succession events involve outside successors (in contrast to later-stage succession research, which has focused on the insider-outsider distinction). These differences make it hard to extrapolate from later-stage succession findings to founder-CEO succession.

Therefore, in order to examine founder-CEO succession, Wasserman (2003) used field research and grounded theory building to study the factors that should affect founder-CEO succession in Internet start-ups. He found that there are two central inter-temporal events that may affect founder-CEO succession: the completion of product development and the raising of each round of financing from outside investors.

CEO Characteristics

Organizational research has a long history of examining the association of executive characteristics with organizational decisions and attributes. Next, some of the commonly examined attributes of CEOs are discussed based on Barker and Mueller (2002).

CEO tenure. Researchers examining CEO tenure find that CEOs tend to make fewer changes in strategy as their tenure increases. This lack of change might occur because with each increasing year of tenure CEOs become more strongly committed to implementing their own paradigm for how the organization should be run. Longer tenured CEOs may lose interest in implementing organizational changes as their outside interests increase and the novelty of CEO's job decreases. Longer tenured CEOs may lose touch with their organizations' environments and therefore may not make the changes and investment desires to keep the firm evolving over time.

CEO age. One of the most enduring findings about executive age is that older executives tend to be more conservative. Empirical studies have found that older top managers (as opposed to younger managers), follow lower-growth strategies. Several psychological reasons are commonly offered for this pattern of findings. Older executives may have less of the physical and mental stamina needed to implement organizational changes. Based on learning theory, older executives may have greater difficulty grasping new ideas and learning new behaviors.

CEO career experience. The influence of an executive's career path on his or her decision-making has been discussed a lot by management researchers. This discussion has been focused on whether executives exhibit biases in decision-making that reflect the perspectives of the business functions in which they were trained. Experience with the goals, rewards, and methods of a particular functional area causes managers to perceive and interpret information in ways that suit and reinforce their functional training.

CEO education. The education levels of top managers have been studied. It was found that more educated executives have greater cognitive complexity. It is generally assumed that such cognitive complexity provides greater ability to absorb new ideas and therefore increases the tendency toward accepting innovations. More innovative organizations tend to be led by CEOs who have higher levels of education. In addition to education level, there seem to be differences between educational fields of study. Focusing on business education and the MBA degree in particular, theorists and critics have argued that MBA programs attract conservative, risk-averse students and teach analytic skills geared toward avoiding big mistakes or losses. Given this description, MBA programs are perceived as doing little toward developing innovative or risk-taking skills in students. This same argument could easily be applied toward legal education, which seems to place little emphasis on innovation.

Barker and Mueller (2002) applied these CEO characteristics to explain variation in firm R&D spending. For example, they suggested that CEOs with business or legal academic training may be less inclined to pursue innovation through R&D spending.

Innovation has long been the primary basis of advantage. If the company has a unique, first-mover product or service, the company can get far ahead of the competition. John Tyson, CEO of Tyson Foods, expanded the company's line of protein products. Kenneth Freeman, chairman of the board of Quest Diagnostics, handed over the CEO title to a scientist who can drive the company toward invention and organic growth. Robert Greifeld, Nasdaq's CEO, stressed that the most dramatic top-line growth opportunities come from finding new ways to make, do, or sell. George Nolan, CEO of Siemens USA, found that acquisitions have been an extremely important source of top-line growth as long as those acquisitions have been integrated into a solid strategic platform. Finally, Kenneth Lewis, CEO of Bank of America, emphasized organic growth after years of acquisitions (Gulati, 2004).

The failure and subsequent departure of a CEO is a costly misadventure for any organization. According to Conger and Nadler (2004), the most immediate and devastating impact is often on the company's market capitalization. In a matter of weeks, a floundering CEO can destroy a market valuation that has taken a decade to build. In addition, ousted CEOs rarely leave with empty pockets.

Conger and Nadler (2004) think of CEOs as broadly oriented in favor of content or context. The distinction might reveal a common pattern in cases of early-tenure CEO failure. Content-oriented CEOs focus on the substance of the company's business. Their interests and capabilities relate to corporate strategy, the core technology of the business, financial structure and performance, and business portfolio changes. In contrast, context-oriented CEOs focus more intensely on the environment in which content decisions are made. They are concerned with values, purpose, the interactions of the executive team, the engagement of leadership across the enterprise, the culture of the organization, and the processes that influence and shape these factors.

Conger and Nadler (2004, p. 54) argue that this CEO characteristic — either content-oriented or context-oriented — might strongly influence the success or failure of a CEO succession:

> *Now consider what happened in several instances in which an outstanding context leader was replaced by a content leader. Henry Schacht at Lucent, Paul Allair at Xerox, and John Pepper at Procter & Gamble were particularly good at creating collegiality at the top, building an executive team, engaging the organization, emphasizing values, and forming connections with many people in their companies. They also chose as their heirs apparent individuals with strong content orientations, people with the intellect, strategic insight, and analytic capabilities to complement their own strengths very effectively.*

> *Once the incumbents departed, however, and the new CEOs suddenly had to create a new context on their own, trouble started. Their lack of interest in context or inability to create the right one was problematic. They were unable to build and manage the necessary network of relationships inside and outside the organization. As a consequence, they were unable to engage the top team, build the collective intuition of the leadership group, create an environment in which others felt free to express dissenting views, and so on.*

> *Faced with performance shortfalls and disappointments, these content-oriented CEOs typically engaged in a cycle of failure. They became more entrenched in their search for the right answer and their belief in the power of that answer. They tended to pay even less attention to context and grew more detached from the reality of the team and organization they were leading.*

Just as outgoing chief executives, their boards, and incoming leaders bear part of the responsibility for the early-tenure flameouts of new CEOs, so too can they all be part of the solution. Outgoing CEOs can start by bearing in mind that a truly successful legacy is one in which their successors flourish (Conger & Nadler, 2000).

CEO Compensation

Recent research has suggested that stock options and equity ownership have different motivational implications for executive risk taking. Certo, Daily, Cannella, and Dalton (2003) examined investors' reactions to the differing incentive properties of stock options and equity ownership in the context of firms undertaking initial public offerings (IPOs). They found that stock options and equity ownership interacted to influence the premiums that investors applied to IPO firms.

Executive stock options have the potential to significantly influence CEO ownership and firm ownership structure. McGuire and Matta (2003) examined the ownership and performance implications of the exercise of CEO stock options. They found that the exercise of stock options has no impact on the levels of CEO equity and no relationship with subsequent firm performance. The decision to exercise stock options appeared to reflect risk-balancing concerns rather than expectations for future performance.

The CEO can be viewed as a resource. The CEO as a resource might have superior or inferior management skills. Top managers of poorly performing firms should think about voluntarily exiting because they do not represent valuable resources. We will present the resource-based theory of the firm later in this book. However, it should already be mentioned that Priem and Butler (2001) are skeptical of the CEO as a resource concept. They argue that there is no basis for discriminating among superior or inferior CEOs, other than waiting for performance results.

CEO compensation can influence the job of the CIO. Hall and Liedtka (2005) found that incentives created by CEO stock options and overall compensation significantly influence decisions to outsource information technology that is run by the CIO. The study provides evidence of a relationship between managerial self-interest and IT outsourcing.

Average CEO compensation has been high and steadily increasing over the period in which large-scale IT outsourcing has come into prominence. During 1992 through 2000 in the United States, for instance, the average value of the various components of CEO compensation grew from a total of $1.7 million to $8.5 million in large firms (Hall & Liedtka, 2005). CEO compensation plans also tend to be quite elaborate, providing a variety of incentives such as annual bonuses, stock options, stock grants, and long-term incentive payouts.

Principal-agent theory explains the existence of large, elaborate CEO compensation contracts and underscores the potential for compensation to influence CEO decisions. The theory begins with the assumptions that CEOs (agents) are effort averse and seek to maximize personal utility rather than that of their firms' shareholders (principals). To prevent CEOs from shirking or acting wastefully (e.g., over-consuming perquisites), shareholders can use compensation incentives that motivate CEOs to work harder and more responsibly than they would otherwise by tying CEO wealth to firm performance or shareholder wealth.

Consistent with the theory, empirical research finds strong evidence that CEO stock options and overall compensation balance drive a variety of accounting and finance choices. Further, the average relationship between compensation and CEO performance appears positive.

Not all CEO activities motivated by incentive compensation are in a firm's best interest, however. Noting that CEOs have private information and that perfect monitoring of CEO decisions is prohibitively costly (if not impossible), the principal-agent literature also argues that firms must endure some residual risk that CEOs will act opportunistically. For instance, CEOs can make both real and accounting decisions that increase their personal welfare despite the fact that the decisions are not in their firms' best interests. Given the dramatic increase in CEO compensation, the potential rewards of opportunism have increased as well. Recent accounting scandals have made the general public aware of the potential negative, almost irresistible compensation incentives contributed to the poor business decisions and ethical lapses that led to the collapse of Enron, WorldCom, and Tyco (Hall & Liedtka, 2005).

Hall and Liedtka (2005) found in their empirical study that CEO compensation appears to play a significant role in large-scale IT outsourcing decisions. The significant, positive coefficient reflects theory that, all else equal, stock option grants increase CEO willingness to make significant changes to firm structure. An important function of stock options is indeed to reduce the likelihood that CEOs will avoid beneficial changes to their firms by increasing the convexity of the relationship between wealth and performance. Not all decisions motivated by options, however, are desirable from the shareholders' standpoint. Rather, high proportions of option-based compensation can create an incentive for CEOs to engage in low-value activities to destabilize the firm.

Performance Consequences of CEO Succession

The general observation has been made that it is not the event of CEO succession per se, but the succession context that affects post-succession firm performance. Successor origin, a key successor characteristic that refers to whether a new CEO comes from inside or outside the firm whose chief executive he or she becomes, has been proposed as important. Successor origin both reflects succession context and has significant implications for subsequent firm performance. However, as discussed, empirical studies also report inconsistent evidence regarding the performance impacts of insider and outsider succession.

Shen and Cannella (2002a) strove to capture succession context more completely by simultaneously examining three important components of succession contexts. First, they focused on key characteristics of CEO successors, but diverged from previous research in that they did not dichotomize CEO successors into insiders and outsiders. Adopting a power circulation theory of control, which takes intra-firm contention into account, implies that there are two distinct types of insiders successors: those appointed following their predecessors' dismissals and those appointed following their predecessors' ordinary retirement. These two types are labeled contenders and followers, respectively. Thus, including outsiders, three types of CEO successors were examined. These three types of successors — contenders, followers, and outsiders — differ importantly with respect to their ability to manage change, their firm-specific knowledge, and the risk of adverse selection (selection of an unsuitable successor) they pose. It is expected that they have different impacts on firm performance.

Next, Shen and Cannella (2002a) focused on post-succession executive turnover at the top management level. According to upper echelons theory, it is not a firm's CEO alone, but its entire management team, that shapes strategic decisions. Senior executive turnover influences top management team composition and may have a significant impact on strategic decision-making and firm performance.

Lastly, CEO succession frequency was studied at the organizational level by examining the influence of a departing CEO's tenure. Frequent CEO successions may disrupt organizational continuity and hurt firm performance. At the same time, long CEO tenure has been found to be directly linked to top management's commitment to status quo and decreases in the fit between firm strategy, structure, and environmental demands. Drawing on the organizational change literature, departing CEO tenure can importantly affect subsequent firm performance through its impact on organizational inertia and the disruption surrounding a succession event.

Shen and Cannella's (2002a) empirical study of 228 successions did not support a hypothesis regarding a positive main effect of a successor contender (an insider who struggled with the departing CEO). However, the study supports the argument that senior executive turnover following a contender succession has a positive impact on firm performance. Further, both contender and outsider successors are positively correlated with post-succession senior executive turnover, which has been used as an indicator of strategic change.

These findings support the proposition that contender successors importantly differ from follower successors, though both are insiders. One explanation for not finding a main effect of contender successors on firm performance is that contenders, though they differ from followers, are still constrained by their social networks within their firms. Unless they can restructure their top management teams, they will not be able to improve firm performance. An alternative explanation follows the power perspective: Some contender successions after CEO dismissal may reflect the outcome of power struggles within top management rather than an intention to initiate strategic change. Because the prestige and material benefits associated with the CEO title, some ambitious senior executives may challenge an incumbent CEO simply to advance their own careers (Shen & Cannella, 2002a).

CEO Backgrounds

Ocasio and Kim (1999) developed a conceptual model of the circulation of corporate control to study the instability in formal authority at the top of large organizations. According to their model, chief executive selection is both a political contest for the top executive position and an ideological struggle among members of the firm's political coalition over defining the corporate agenda and strategy. They applied their model to analyze the selection of functional backgrounds of 275 new CEOs in large U.S. manufacturing firms. The distribution of functional backgrounds among the 275 new CEOs was as follows:

- 24% of the new CEOs had production and technical backgrounds.
- 21% of the new CEOs had financial and legal backgrounds.
- 18% of the new CEOs had marketing and sales backgrounds.
- 37% of the new CEOs had operations and other backgrounds.

An interesting question is whether or not new CEOs have the backgrounds of their predecessors. Ocasio and Kim (1999) found that in 100 internal successions:

- 54% of new CEOs with production and technical backgrounds had predecessors with the same background, which also was the most frequent predecessor background.
- 20% of new CEOs with financial and legal backgrounds had predecessors with the same background, while the most frequent predecessor background was operations and others.

- 40% of new CEOs with marketing and sales backgrounds had predecessors with the same background, which also was the most frequent predecessor background.

- 36% of new CEOs with operations and other backgrounds had predecessors with the same background, which also was the most frequent predecessor background.

Overall, it was more common to have a different background rather than the same background for a new CEO. Ocasio and Kim (1999) concluded that instability, rather than stability in power, is the norm for functional backgrounds of new CEOs.

Ocasio and Kim (1999) did also study determinants of functional backgrounds of new CEOs. Potential determinants in their study were strategic contingencies and political dynamics. An important strategic contingency was the number of merger and divestiture activities. The study showed that firms with large numbers of merger and divesture activities are less likely to select production and marketing CEOs than either those from finance or operations and others. The political dynamic variables in the model showed how the history of the functional background of the two previous CEOs affects the functional background of new CEOs selected. The effects of the immediate predecessor in the model supported the entrenchment of power at the corporate level for production and technical CEOs and marketing and sales CEOs, but not for finance CEOs.

CEO for the Information Age

Earl and Feeny (2000) argue that by now the vast array of Web applications for supply-chain integration, customer relationship management, sales force automation, work group collaboration — and the sale of everything from equities to automobiles — should make it perfectly clear that information technology has evolved beyond the role of mere infrastructure in support of business strategy.

The implications for existing and aspiring CEOs are equally clear, according to Earl and Feeny (2000): Information technology is now a survival issue. Board and executive team agendas are increasingly peppered with, or even hijacked by, a growing range of IT issues. They may be explicitly IT, but more and more frequently, IT issues are now wrapped inside wider questions of business strategy.

Earl and Feeny (2000) identified several archetypes of CEOs, but argue that only the last one, the believer, is ready for the information age:

- **Hypocrite:** Espouses strategic importance of IT. Negates this belief through personal actions.

- **Waverer:** Reluctantly accepts strategic importance of IT. But not ready to get involved in IT matters.

- **Atheist:** Convinced IT is of little value. Publicly espouses this belief.

- **Zealot:** Convinced IT is strategically important. Believes he or she is an authority on IT practice.

- **Agnostic:** Concedes IT may be strategically important. Requires repeated convincing.

- **Monarch:** Access IT is strategically important. Appoints best CIO possible, then steps back.

- **Believer:** Believes IT enables strategic advantage. Demonstrates belief in own daily behavior.

CEOs who already demonstrate their fitness for the information age share a common and intuitive belief. They see IT as a first-order factor of strategy making. Belief in the business-critical role of IT drives what believer CEOs do and the organizational climate they create. It influences how they live and what they practice (Earl & Feeny, 2000).

References

Andrews, K. Z. (2001, Winter). The performance impact of new CEOs. *MIT Sloan Management Review, 14.*

Barker, V. L., & Mueller, G. C. (2002). CEO characteristics and firm R&D spending. *Management Science, 48*(6), 782-801.

Bigley, G. A., & Wiersema, M. F. (2002). New CEOs and corporate strategic refocusing: How experience as heir apparent influences the use of power. *Administrative Science Quarterly, 47,* 707-727.

Buchholtz, A. K., Ribbens, B. A., & Houle, I. T. (2003) The role of human capital in postacquisition CEO departure. *Academy of Management Journal, 46*(4), 506-514.

Carpenter, M. A., & Wade, J. B. (2002). Microlevel opportunity structures as determinants of non-CEO executive pay. *Academy of Management Journal, 45*(6), 1085-1103.

Certo, S. T., Daily, C. M., Cannella, A. A., & Dalton, D. R. (2003). Giving money to get money: How CEO stock options and CEO equity enhance IPO valuations. *Academy of Management Journal, 46*(5), 643-653.

Charan, R. (2005, February). Ending the CEO succession crisis. *Harvard Business Review*, 72-81.

Conger, J. A., & Nadler, D. A. (2004, Spring). When CEOs step up to fail. *MIT Sloan Management Review*, 50-94.

Dagens Næringsliv. (2005, October 25). Sjefer fra eget hus gir fortrinn (Executives from own house gives advantage). *Dagens N, æ, ringsliv* (financial newspaper in Norway), 34.

Davidson, W. N., Nemic, C., & Worrell, D. L. (2001). Succession planning vs. agency theory: A test of Harris and Helfat's interpretation of plurality announcement market returns. *Strategic Management Journal, 22*, 179-184.

Earl, M. J., & Feeny, D. F. (2000, Winter). How to be a CEO for the information age. *Sloan Management Review,* 11-23.

Freeman, K. W. (2004, November). The CEO's real legacy. *Harvard Business Review*, 51-58.

Gulati, R. (2004, July-August). How CEOs manage growth agendas. *Harvard Business Review*, 124-132.

Hall, J. A., & Liedtka, S. L. (2005). Financial performance, CEO compensation, and large-scale information technology outsourcing decisions. *Journal of Management Information Systems, 22*(1), 193-221.

Haveman, H. A., Russo, M. V., & Meyer, A. D. (2001). Organizational environments in flux: The impact of regulatory punctuations on organizational domains, CEO succession, and performance. *Organization Science, 12*(3), 253-273.

Hayward, M. L. A., Rindova, V. P., & Pollock, T. G. (2004). Believing one's own press: The causes and consequences of CEO celebrity. *Strategic Management Journal, 25,* 637-653.

Johnson, L. K. (2002, Winter). Do CEOs matter? *MIT Sloan Management Review*, 8-9.

Khurana, R. (2001, Fall). Finding the right CEO: Why boards often make poor choices. *MIT Sloan Management Review*, 91-95.

Lorsch, J. W., & Zelleke, A. (2005, Winter). Should the CEO be the chairman? *MIT Sloan Management Review*, 71-74.

McDonald, M. L., & Westphal, J. D. (2003). Getting by with the advice of their friends: CEOs' advice networks and firms' strategic responses to poor performance. *Administrative Science Quarterly, 48*, 1-32.

McGuire, J., & Matta, E. (2003). CEO stock options: The silent dimension of ownership. *Academy of Management Journal, 46*(3), 255-265.

Ocasio, W., & Kim, H. (1999). The circulation of corporate control: Selection of functional backgrounds of new CEOs in large U.S. manufacturing firms. 1981-1992. *Administrative Science Quarterly, 44,* 532-562.

Porter, M. E., Lorsch, J. W., & Nohria, N. (2004, October). Seven surprises for new CEOs. *Harvard Business Review,* 62-72.

Priem, R. L., & Butler, J. E. (2001). Is the resource-based view a useful perspective for strategic management research? *Academy of Management Review, 26*(1), 22-40.

Shen, W., & Cannella, A. A. (2002a). Revisiting the performance consequences of CEO succession: The impacts of successor type, postsuccession senior executive turnover, and departing CEO tenure. *Academy of Management Journal, 45*(4), 717-733.

Shen, W., & Cannella, A. A. (2002b). Power dynamics within top management and their impacts on CEO dismissal followed by inside succession. *Academy of Management Journal, 45*(6), 1195-1206.

Shen, W., & Cannella, A. A. (2003). Will succession planning increase shareholder wealth? Evidence from investor reactions to relay CEO successions. *Strategic Management Journal, 24*(2), 191-199.

Waldman, D. A., & Yammarino, F. J. (1999). CEO charismatic leadership: Levels-of-management and levels-of-analysis effects. *Academy of Management Review, 24*(2), 266-285.

Wasserman, N. (2003). Founder-CEO succession and the paradox of entrepreneurial success. *Organization Science, 14*(29), 149-172.

Westphal, J. D., & Bednar, M. K. (2005). Pluralistic ignorance in corporate boards and firms' strategic persistence in response to low firm performance. *Administrative Science Quarterly, 50,* 262-298.

Westphal, J. D., & Khanna, P. (2003). Keeping directors in line: Social distancing as a control mechanism in the corporate elite. *Administrative Science Quarterly, 48,* 361-398.

Zhang, Y. (2005). The presence of a separate COO/president and its impact on strategic change and CEO dismissal. *Strategic Management Journal,* forthcoming.

Zhang, Y., & Rajagopalan, N. (2003). Explaining new CEO origin: Firm versus industry antecedents. *Academy of Management Journal, 46*(3), 327-338.

Zhang, Y., & Rajagopalan, N. (2004). When the known devil is better than an unknown god: An empirical study of the antecedents and consequences of relay CEO successions. *Academy of Management Journal, 47*(4), 483-500.

Chapter II

The Chief Information Officer

Introduction

The chief information officer (CIO) can be defined as the highest ranking IT executive who typically exhibits managerial roles requiring effective communication with top management, a broad corporate perspective in managing information resources, influence on organizational strategy, and responsibility for the planning of IT. This definition is in line with research which applied the following criteria when selecting CIOs for empirical observation: (1) highest ranking information technology executive; (2) reports no more than two levels from the CEO (i.e., either reports to the CEO or reports to one of the CEOs direct reports); (3) areas of responsibility include information systems, computer operations, telecommunications and networks, office automation, end-user computing, help desks, computer software and applications; and (4) responsibility for strategic IS/IT planning.

According to Gartner (2005), only a few CEOs view CIOs as boardroom peers. Most CEOs view their CIOs as effective operational leaders. Yet only a few view them as full business leaders. There is an opportunity for CIOs to build their relationship with their CEO and other stakeholders — to increase their influence and to enhance the contribution of information systems and information technology.

The CIO Position

The CIO position emerged in the 1970s as a result of increased importance placed on IT. In the early 1980s, the CIO was often portrayed as the corporate savior who was to align the worlds of business and technology. CIOs were described as the new breed of information managers who were businessmen first, managers second, and technologists third (Grover, Jeong, Kettinger, & Lee, 1993). It was even postulated that in the 1990s, as information became a firm's critical resource, the CIO would become the logical choice for the chief executive officer (CEO) position.

Job advertisements for information systems positions from 1970 to 1990 were reviewed by Todd, McKeen, and Gallupe (1995). They investigated specific positions related to programmers, systems analysts, and information systems managers. It is the latter position that is of interest here. At the time of the research, it was considered that successful information systems managers should have a blend of technical knowledge and sound business-related skills. Further, in general, they should possess effective interpersonal skills. Over the 20-year period, Todd et al. (1995) determined that there had not been much change in the required skills indicated in job advertisements.

Benjamin, Dickinson, and Rockart (1985) suggested that the emergence of the CIO role represented the recognition of the importance of the role to be played within the organization. Kaarst-Brown (2005), however, suggests it is unfortunate that 20 years later, in 2005, the CIO is still held in lower regard than those senior managers of other more traditional business units. Kaarst-Brown (2005) suggests the reasons for this gap may be attributed to some of the items on the following list:

- Personality conflicts
- Lack of corporate technology vision
- Poorly aligned IT goals
- Lack of business knowledge
- Lack of IT awareness among the business executives
- Incorrect formal structure and reporting relationships

However, Kolbasuk (2005) reported that the perception of CIOs within organizations may be evolving. She suggests they may finally be getting the respect they deserve as they become members of the board of directors of large companies. This movement to the board level in the organization indicates the perception of the CIO role is evolving from a manager primarily focused on regulations, back office operations, and administrative duties to applying information technology at a strategic level to facilitate competitive advantage through an understanding of how business processes function and may be adapted to a changing corporate environment.

As a manager of people, the CIO faces the usual human resource roles of recruiting, staff training, and retention, and the financial roles of budget determination, forecasting, and authorization. As the provider of technological services to user departments, a significant amount of work in publicity, promotion, and internal relations with user management remains. As a manager of an often-virtual information organization, the CIO has to coordinate sources of information services spread throughout and beyond the boundaries of the firm. The CIO is thus more concerned with a wider group of issues than most managers.

While information systems executives share several similarities with the general manager, notable differences are apparent. The CIO is not only more concerned with a wider group of issues than most managers, but also, as the chief information systems strategist, has a set of responsibilities that must constantly evolve with the corporate information needs and with information technology itself. It has been suggested that the IT director's ability to add value is the biggest single factor in determining whether the organization views information technology as an asset or a liability.

According to Earl and Feeny (1994, p. 11), chief information officers have a difficult job:

> *Chief information officers have the difficult job of running a function that uses a lot of resources but that offers little measurable evidence of its value. To make the information systems department an asset to their companies — and to keep their jobs — CIOs should think of their work as adding value in certain key areas.*

Creation of the CIO role was driven in part by two organizational needs. First, accountability is increased when a single executive is responsible for the organization's processing needs. Second, creation of the CIO position facilitates the closing of the gap between organizational and IT strategies which has long been cited as a primary business concern.

Alignment of business and IT objectives is not only a matter of achieving competitive advantage, but is essential for the firms very survival. Though the importance of IT in creating competitive advantage has been widely noted, achieving these gains has proven elusive. Sustained competitive advantage requires not only the development of a single system, but the ability to consistently deploy IT faster, cheaper, and more strategically than one's competitors. IT departments play a critical role in realizing the potential of IT. The performance of IT functions, in turn, often centers on the quality of leadership, meaning, the CIO.

As early as 1984, some surveys suggested that one-third of U.S. corporations had a CIO function, if not in title. While exact percentages differ, ranging from 40 to 70%, Grover et al. (1993) found that the number of senior-level information systems executive positions created over the past 10 years had grown tremendously. Early research conducted on the CIO position examined 43 of 50 top ranked Fortune 500 service organizations in the United States, and noted that 23 (58%) of these organizations had the CIO position. In 1990, the 200 largest Fortune 500 industrial and service organizations were examined, and it was found that 77% of the industrials had a CIO position as compared with 64% of the service organizations. It is very likely that these numbers have increased in recent years.

Few studies have examined the reasons behind the creation of the CIO position in firms. Creation of the position effectively increases accountability by making a single executive responsible for corporate information processing needs. In a sample of Fortune 500 firms (i.e., appearing on the list for four consecutive years), 287 firms with CIOs were compared in 1995 to firms without CIOs on a number of variables hypothesized to predict creation of the position. It was observed that a number of characteristics of the corporate board, including the number of outside directors and equity ownership of the directors, predicted the existence of the CIO position. A firm's information intensity was also found to be positively related to the creation of the CIO position. Furthermore, the CIO position was more likely to exist when the CEO appreciated the strategic value and importance of IT.

The CIO title itself has become a source of confusion. The term CIO has been somewhat loosely defined and is often used interchangeably with various titles such as IT director, vice president of IS, director of information resources, director of information services, and director of MIS, to describe a senior executive responsible for establishing policy and controlling information resources. Sometimes, the CIO label denotes a function rather than a title. Studies relating to the CIO have focused on the evolution of the position and the similarities between the CIO and other senior-level executives.

The CIO label itself has been met with resistance, and some firms have replaced the title with alternative labels such as knowledge manager, chief knowledge officer (CKO), or chief technology officer (CTO). It has been found that the CKO has to discover and develop the CEO's implicit vision of how knowledge management would make a difference and how IT can support this difference.

There are differences between the tasks of a CTO, CIO, and CKO. While the CTO is focused on technology, the CIO focuses on information, and the CKO focuses on knowledge. When companies replace a CIO with a CKO, it should not only be a change of title. Rather, it should be a change of focus. Alternatively, as we shall see later in this book, the CIO might expand his or her power base by including the roles of the CTO and the CKO in the position of the CIO.

Applegate, McFarlan, and McKenney (1996) indicate that the CIO is becoming a member of the top management team and participates in organizational strategy development. Similarly, it has been stated that CIOs see themselves as corporate officers and general business managers. This suggests that CIOs must be politically savvy and that their high profile places them in contention for top-line management jobs. The results of these studies indicate that today's CIO is more a managerially oriented executive than a technical manager. Some provide a profile of the ideal CIO as an open communicator with a business perspective, capable of leading and motivating staff, and as an innovative corporate team player. Karimi, Somers, and Gupta (2001) found that successful CIOs characterized themselves in the following way:

- I see myself to be a corporate officer.
- In my organization, I am seen by others as a corporate officer.
- I am a general business manager, not an IT specialist.
- I am a candidate for top-line management positions.
- I have a high-profile image in the organization.
- I have political as well as rational perspectives of my firm.
- I spend most of my time outside the IT department focusing on the strategic and organizational aspects of IT.

Business strategist is likely to be among the most significant roles that CIOs will fulfill in the digital era, according to Sambamurthy, Straub, and Watson (2001). As a business strategist, the CIO must understand and visualize the economic, competitive, and industry forces impacting the business and the factors that sustain competitive advantage. Further, the CIO must be capable of plotting strategy with executive peers, including the chief executive officer (CEO), chief operating officer (COO), and other senior business executives (Sambamurthy et al., 2001, p. 285):

> Business strategist *is likely to be among the most significant roles that CIOs will fulfill in the digital era. As a business strategist, the CIO must understand and visualize the economic, competitive, and industry forces impacting the business and the factors that sustain competitive advantage. Further, the CIO must be capable of plotting strategy with executive peers, including the chief executive officer (CEO), chief operating officer (COO), and other senior business executives. Not only are CIOs drawn into the mainstream of business strategy, but also their compensation*

is being linked with the effectiveness of competitive Internet actions in many firms. With an understanding of current and emergent information technologies and an ability to foresee breakthrough strategic opportunities as well as disruptive threats, CIOs must play a lead role in educating their business peers about how IT can raise the competitive agility of the firm. Obviously, to be effective business strategists, the CIOs must be members of an executive leadership team and part of the dominant coalition that manages the firm.

Blair (2005) cautions, however, that while there is a movement toward more of an emphasis for the CIO to understand the business, the CIO must still be the information technology champion within the organization. The CIO needs to know both the business and the information technology. Thus, while the CIOs of the future will be involved in strategy, they must understand information technology and how it can be applied to positively impact the business.

With an understanding of current and emergent information technologies and an ability to foresee breakthrough strategic opportunities as well as disruptive threats, CIOs must play a lead role in educating their business peers about how IT can raise the competitive agility of the firm. To be effective business strategists, the CIOs must be members of an executive leadership team and part of the dominant coalition that manages the firm.

Reporting Levels

Although it was originally expected that the CIO would have high levels of influence within the firm, as the definition of job responsibilities would suggest, recent surveys indicate that this may not be the case. CIOs may not actually possess strategic influence with top management, and they may lack operational and tactical influence with users. Some specific problems include higher-than-average corporate dismissal rates compared with other top executives, diminished power with belt tightening and budget cuts, high expectations of new strategic systems that CIOs may not be able to deliver, lack of secure power bases due to the fact that CIOs are viewed as outsiders by top management, and the fact that few CIOs take part in strategic planning and many do not report to the CEO.

Over time, the number of CIOs reporting to CEOs seems to increase. In 1992, only 27% of surveyed CIOs in the United States reported to CEOs, while this number had increased to 43% five years later, as listed in Figure 2.1. In 2005, Gartner (2005) found that 40% of the surveyed CIOs reported to the CEO, 18% to the CFO, 21% to the COO, and 21% to other executives.

Figure 2.1. CIO reporting in the U.S. and Norway over time

Chief Information Officer (CIO) reporting to:	USA 1992	USA 1997	USA 2000	USA 2005	Norway 1997	Norway 1999	Norway 2000
Chief Executive Officer (CEO)	27%	43%	33%	40%	48%	44%	41%
Chief Financial Officer (CFO)	44%	32%	20%	18%	21%	23%	16%
Other top executive in the company	29%	25%	47%	42%	31%	33%	43%

In Norway, the numbers in Figure 2.1 seem to indicate a stable level above 40% or maybe an insignificant decline in the fraction of CIOs reporting to the CEO. An interesting development is indirect reports moving from CFOs to other top executives.

It has to be noted that the difference in size of the business community between the USA and Norway makes the comparison weak. Also, European companies tend to have a very different executive reporting structure compared to companies based in the United States.

In a U.S. survey in 2000 cited by Schubert (2004), 33% of the CIOs reported to the CEO, while 20% reported to the CFO. Forty-seven percent reported to another top executive in the company, as listed in Figure 2.1. It is interesting to note that among those U.S. CIOs not reporting to the CEO in 2000, most of them reported to the chief operating officer (COO).

In most countries surveyed by Gartner (2005), CIOs tended to report to an executive other than the CEO. Not so in Japan and South Korea, where more than two-thirds of IT executives had the CEO for a boss. Regardless of whom they reported to, CIOs in the U.S., Canada, South Korea, and Singapore said they spent the most time interacting with other business executives.

In a Gartner (2005) CIO 100 survey in the US, 40% of the respondents held the title of CIO, 7% were both CIO and executive vice presidents (EVP), 16% were both CIOs and senior vice presidents (SVP), 22% were chief technology officers (CTO), and 15% had other titles such as director.

The CIO's pivotal responsibility of aligning business and technology direction presents a number of problems. Moreover, rapid changes in business and information environments have resulted in corresponding changes at the IT function helm. This role has become increasingly complex, causing many firms to look outside the organization for the right qualifications. Characteristics such as professional background, educational background, and current length of tenure have been examined in previous research. CIO problems seem to indicate that, when compared with other senior executives, CIOs do not have the authority or ability to achieve the kind of changes that were promised when the position was initially proposed. A second and possibly related explanation is that CIOs are experiencing managerial role conflicts that prevent them from meeting those expectations as originally envisioned in the CIO position.

Hybrid Manager

Robson (1997) has suggested that CIOs have to be hybrid managers to be successful. Hybrid managers require business literacy and technical competency plus a third dimension. This third item is the organizational astuteness that allows a manager to make business-appropriate IS use and management decisions that enhance or set business directions as well as follow them. It is fairly well recognized that hybrid managers are problematic, perhaps requiring built-in talent and personal qualities, but can be encouraged or discouraged. For this reason, undergraduate study can generally produce only hybrid users, while postgraduate and post-experience study can support the development of hybrid managers.

Hybrid users are the people involved in user-controlled computing, they combine a degree of technical competence with business literacy required to fulfill their primary role (Robson, 1997, p. 367):

> This management description is not just another term to describe the users engaged in the user-controlled computing. A clear distinction exists between hybrid users and hybrid managers and this distinction is one of emphasis and purposes. Hybrid users are the people involved in user-controlled computing, they combine a degree of technical competence (perhaps defined by notions such as the end-user continuum) with, of course, the business literacy required to fulfill their primary role. Hybrid managers, as opposed to managers who are hybrid users, require this business literacy and technical competency plus a third dimension. This third item is the organisational astuteness that allows a manager to make business-appropriate IS use and management decisions that enhance or set business directions as well as follow them. It is fairly well recognised that hybrid users can be trained whereas the more sophisticated development of hybrid managers is problematic, perhaps requiring inbuilt

talent and personal qualities, but can be encouraged or discouraged. For this reason undergraduate study can generally produce only hybrid users whilst postgraduate and post-experience study can support the development of hybrid managers.

The notion of hybrid management is an essentially British one and a significant amount of work on the concept of hybrid management has been done. Earl provided the initial working definition of hybrid managers that has been subsequently adopted by other works. Hybrid managers are a high risk, high cost, people infrastructure that enables the organisational integration of IS and business. This integration ensures both business-consistent IS and IS-exploitative business and so hybrid managers straddle two, previously disparate, disciplines. No amount of communication, or translation bridges, between the two separate disciplines can achieve the same degree of integration. Whilst there is no theoretical reason why hybrid managers cannot be drawn from any discipline, experience seems to show that it proves easier to add IS 'technical' knowledge to a base of business awareness than to inculcate IS technicians with a broader, organisational vision. The primary benefits of hybrid managers are that they create 'islands' of true business/IS understanding; these islands then provide the catalyst that leads to an organisational hybridisation. Even from the earliest stages of hybridisation programmes, organisational gains in flexibility and effectiveness are reported.

Since developing hybrid managers (or any form of management development) is a costly and uncertain exercise it can be a problem notion in recessionary times. The long-term benefits, rather than short-term gains, of such a development programme can look easy to 'trim' out of recession-hit budgets. And yet, paradoxically, it is precisely this type of people infrastructure that supports the cross-boundary, radical re-works typically associated with business process redesign to enable significant future cost savings. The business redesign focus of the 1990s demands the hybrid manager who is, not narrowly specialist, but capable of seeing the broad picture and the opportunities present in this total view. Hybrid managers will be critical to the survival of the IS function into the next decade. The continuing devolution of many IS areas requires a hybrid manager to manage the 'new' IS and indeed even the act of assessing the relative merits of different paths to devolution, and judging what not to devolve requires the skills as defined to be of a hybrid manager.

According to Robson (1997), hybrid managers will be critical to the survival of the IT function in the future. The continuing devolution of many IS areas requires a hybrid manager to manage the new IS and indeed even the act of assessing the relative merits of different paths to devolution, and judging what not to devolve requires the skills as defined to be of a hybrid manager.

This is certainly true if the company is to succeed in knowledge management. Knowledge management requires not only business literacy and technical competency; it requires first and foremost an ability to combine the two. Sometimes information technology is (part of) the solution to knowledge management challenges, sometimes it is not. Only business literacy combined with technical competency can enable a CIO to make an optimal judgment.

Announcements of CIO Positions

What most differentiates those firms able and not able to build strong IT management skills? A very likely answer lies with the quality of IT leadership, as evidenced in the capabilities and character of the IT function's most senior executive, popularly referred to as the chief information officer (CIO). The CIO position has gained increased prominence over the past decade. Not only has the CIO role become increasingly common in all types of firms, CIOs are also beginning to contend for CEO openings, especially with technology- and information-based businesses searching for a chief executive possessing a strong combination of technology and business skills (Chatterjee, Richardson, and Zmud, 2001).

In the U.S., Chatterjee et al. (2001) conducted an investigation to study if newly created CIO positions have any impact. The study's findings provide strong support for the proposition that announcements of newly created CIO positions do indeed provoke positive reactions from the marketplace, but primarily for firms competing in industries with high levels of IT-driven transformation. Within such industries, IT is being applied in innovative ways for competitive purposes. For firms to engage in such strategic behaviors, they must first develop and then effectively exploit an appropriate set of IT capabilities. Strong executive leadership, as reflected in the CIO role, is likely to play a crucial enabling role in the effective deployment of these IT capabilities, and hence be highly valued by a firm's shareholders. Just how valuable is a newly created CIO role? One way to consider the magnitude of the stock market reaction is to compute the impact on each firm's market valuation of common equity.

Even with the trend in escalated executive salaries, the expected return from such an investment in IT capability appears quite reasonable (Chatterjee et al., 2001, p. 59):

This study's findings provide strong support for the proposition that announcements of newly created CIO positions do indeed provoke positive reactions from the marketplace, but primarily for firms competing in industries with high levels of IT-driven transformation. Within such industries, IT is being applied in innovative ways for competitive purposes. For firms to engage in such strategic behaviors, they must first develop and then effectively exploit an appropriate set of IT capabilities. Strong executive leadership, as reflected in the CIO role, is likely to play a crucial enabling role in the effective deployment of these IT capabilities, and hence be highly valued by a firm's shareholders.

Just how valuable is a newly created CIO role? One way to consider the magnitude of the stock market reaction is to compute the impact on each firm's market valuation of common equity. A conservative approach would calculate this effect through the median statistic (multiplying the median stock market reaction by the median market valuation of common equity); a less conservative approach would use the mean statistic (multiplying the mean stock market reaction by the mean market valuation of common equity). For our entire sample of firms, the net impact per firm of a newly created CIO position is in a range from $7.5 million (median approach) to $76 million (mean approach). If only the IT-driven transformation subgroup is considered, the net impact is in a range from $8 million (median approach) to $297 million (mean approach). Even with the trend in escalated executive salaries, the expected return from such an investment in IT capability appears quite reasonable!

CIO Wisdom

In the book *CIO Wisdom: Best Practices from Silicon Valley's Leading IT Experts*, Lane (2004) discusses the extended enterprise CIO, background of the CIO, and reporting relationships.

The extended enterprise CIO. One of the many transformations in our business institutions during the past decade has been the growing importance of the extended enterprise. As our businesses changed, so have the information systems that support them. The changing roles of those systems and of the executives that are responsible for them become a map for the broader transformations — in our commerce, in our culture, and in our socioeconomic relationships. By better understanding the changing role of the CIOs in these institutions, we can better understand the institutions themselves.

The extended enterprise CIO is a partner in a networked community designed to deliver systems and services with and between customers, vendors, and partners, a matrixed role in a network of associations for which some executives are suited and others are not. More and more, CIOs are the executives who are forging alliances and ensuring alignment with critical owners of business relationships, both within and outside the corporate boundary.

Background of the CIO. The role of the CIO has become as varied as the business models in place today. Expectations of the CIO role often includes the following:

- **The technology leader:** This role incorporates the various engineering and information technology functions within a common functional area.

- **The business leader:** This role takes ownership of some IT-based tools and systems to satisfy their business requirements, which require that they become more knowledgeable about these tools and systems.

- **The strategist and mentor:** This role operates in a high-tech environment.

- **The corporate influencer:** This role is directly shaped by the type of business environment he or she must support, and his or her influence is driven by the characteristics of the business, including their relative maturity levels.

- **Reporting relationships:** The CIO who reports to a CFO is typically part of the administrative side of the business and is always expected to focus on cost reduction as a key strategy for the IT organization. The CIO who reports to the CEO possesses a higher degree of freedom and responsibility than a comparable CIO who reports to the CFO.

- **CIO challenges:** The CIO role is inherently challenged because it is constantly beset by conflicts and problems. A CIO has to wear many hats: service provider, business enabler, business partner, strategic visionary, and company executive.

Roles and Responsibilities

According to Schubert (2004), the state of the information technology leadership profession is no different from any other profession in its earliest stages: It is evolving. From an organizational context, because all companies work at a unique level of IT management maturity, the responsibilities of the person at the top of the IT organization follow those same idiosyncratic centralization cycles and respond to influences that the prevailing business climate has from the standpoint of overall organizational maturity. Amidst all this flux, CIOs can count on one consistency from organization to organization at all levels of IT maturity: The horizontal reach of and expectations put on the CIO are significantly greater than they were 10 years ago. Whether the CIO reports to the chief executive officer (CEO), the CIO is expected to be more businessperson than technologist; he or she is expected to lead and manage directly, by means of influence, or through a combination of both. Within this same context of greater horizontal reach, the organization may or may not expect the CIO to perform as a key member of the senior executive team directly participating in the development of key company strategies, tactics, and initiatives. Depending on the company, the culture, and the CEO in particular, the CIO either holds a key executive position with all its obligate leadership responsibilities or works as the head manager of the company's IT utility.

In the context of the significant economic and technological growth periods and significant economic downturns, more enlightened senior executive teams look to the CIO in times of growth to help them maximize the opportunities for the company and its employees to benefit from that growth: to gain significant competitive advantage. Similarly, those same enlightened senior executive teams look to the CIO in times of downturn to help them make the most of what they have, find ways to leverage any advantage against the competition, provide the technology to get the greatest productivity from their workforce, and to find ways to get more for less throughout the company (Schubert, 2004).

Looking at the CIO in the context of organizational authority, it is interesting to look at the range of the CIO reporting responsibilities. In a survey cited in Schubert (2004), 26% of 500 of the Fortune 1000 had CIOs who reported to the CEO, chairperson, or president, with the remainder reporting to lower-level executives. In the same survey, 30% of the 100 CIOs in the top-ranked companies reported directly to the highest executive.

Focus and prioritization always challenge people who work in senior executive position, especially the CIO. By the very nature of the job, he or she has a strategic as well as a tactical role. Although the CIO's role is supposed to be primarily strategic, CIOs are forever associated with the IT group. Consequently, the CIO must be prepared to handle any number of tactical issues, and even projects, whether the position involves direct IT group management responsibilities. As such, the CIO is continually challenged to stay focused on achieving strategic objectives while prioritizing key personal work activities and IT organizational work activities to meet enabling commitments to peers and partners (Schubert, 2004).

Specifically, the CIO works in partnership with peers to ensure that the company's organizational strategies are translated into actionable plans that the IT team can execute. The CIO demonstrates an enabling partnership relationship by visibly aligning and prioritizing IT resources with commitments made to peers (Schubert, 2004).

A special challenge might emerge for the current CIO when the new CEO has IT background. Nortel Networks Corp. named former Motorola Inc. executive Mike Zafirovski president and CEO in 2005. Before he started his new job, Zafirovski announced at a press conference that he plans to build support systems for customers and have a sharper focus on corporate IT (*Computerworld,* 2005).

According to Gartner (2005), CIOs face increasing demands on their time and attention. Time robs CIOs of management capacity. CIOs can expand their management capacity by leveraging an "office of the CIO." CIOs have big jobs with diverse business, technical, and organizational responsibilities. The complex issues surrounding these responsibilities require coordination and thought to resolve properly. The result is often long days, and sometimes even longer nights for the CIO. CIOs need a way to get more management capacity without increasing overhead and bureaucracy. Making time involves extending the management capacity of the CIO and the IS leadership team. Leading CIOs create an office of the CIO in response to these challenges.

The office of the CIO provides an organizational structure for extending management capacity without building overhead and bureaucracy. An office of the CIO leverages management capacity and builds the next generation of leaders in the IS organization. The office of the CIO is an organizational structure for the CIO, IS, and the business. CIOs define the scope and roles of the office to fit their needs. CIOs use the office to strengthen IS. Roles within an office of the CIO reflect its enterprise-wide focus and specialized position. Gartner suggests four alternative office models:

1. A semiformal office of the CIO provides a flexible tool for responding to IT issues. TRW Automotive's semiformal office is integrated into the IS leadership.

2. A collaborative office of the CIO provides agility to address issues, and resources to follow them through.

3. A coordinating office of the CIO connects IS across business units. Tyco Fire & Security uses the office to help run IS like a business.

4. A directional office of the CIO extends the CIO's leadership reach. Landsbond der Christelijke Mutualiteiten uses the office to direct IS and business change.

The office of the CIO is an enhancement to existing management and governance structures. CIOs choose a model most relevant to business needs, thereby avoiding to create an administrative function that would be seen as management overhead or bureaucracy (Gartner, 2005).

Leadership Behavior

Gartner (2005) has studied the changing role of the CIO. The study showed that critical issues for IT leaders include:

- Driving infrastructure management at a time when industries are colliding and technology is becoming a commodity
- Innovating at a time when corporate intellect appears to be the only thing that can be differentiated
- Prioritizing at a time when market opportunities are temporary and fleeting
- Increasing the perception of information about transactions becomes more important than the transactions themselves

Leaders have to lead transforming while performing. Leaders are required to bridge the gap between moving toward a bright new future and ensuring required performance levels. The process requires CEO competencies in CIOs. Based on talents, skills, supporting processes, and desire to get the right things done right, the CIO will develop vision, plan and achieve current performance and future transformation. In doing so, the CIO will demonstrate a leadership behavior characterized by (Gartner, 2005):

- **Researching:** The ability to quickly gather information from a broad variety of sources, analyze it, and synthesize a method or model that solves a problem or various problems in a creative or innovative manner.
- **Interviewing:** The ability to formulate questions used in conversation to elicit facts or statements from another individual, and a willingness to listen to what the individual has to say.
- **Engineering:** The ability to apply principles of logic, science, and mathematics to the understanding of systems and processes to improve them.
- **Lecturing:** The ability to expound on an important subject delivered before audience members to inform/instruct them and convince or persuade them to further action.
- **Arbitrating:** The ability to reconcile the differences in components of networked resources or assets to achieve a common objective.
- **Coaching:** The ability and willingness to transfer knowledge about a subject to individuals, enabling them to succeed at a given task, and (if necessary) to identify their weaknesses and aid them in correcting those weaknesses.

- **Organizing:** The ability to put things together in an orderly, functioning, and structured whole.

Gartner (2005) argues that what is required in CIO leadership is intellect, passion, and courage. The convergence of technology and business trends will require business and technology intellect. Passion is needed to create a common and cohesive vision. Courage is needed to take personal and professional risk, to make quick decisions in light of ambiguity, to be true to core values and the necessary values of future organization, and to recognize this is not an altruistic endeavor.

It is sometimes argued that there are differences in leadership behavior between public sector CIOs and private sector CIOs. Private sector leadership is generally regarded as superior to that of the public sector, and efforts are often made to transfer private sector leadership strategies to the public sector (Dargie, 1998). However, it is not clear that the contexts are sufficiently similar. Political scientists view the political nature of public management as a unique social context where the citizens and elected officials, not the individual executive, are the principal actors. This puts the public sector CIO in the role of balancing between the series of tensions that are intrinsic to the duality of the public domain.

Existing studies predict more formalized contact and external contact for public sector managers. In a survey by Dargie (1998), it was found that public sector chief executives spent nearly three-quarters of their time in meetings, and most meetings are also planned. Contact is formalized. Chief executives meet groups rather than individuals. They do not work alone. Work is office-based, and the public CIO meets predominantly contacts from within his or her own organization. Chief executives in the public sector spend most time in review sessions, with less time on strategy. Review describes the majority of meetings in which the public chief executive is involved: issue-based, agendered, multi-purpose, lengthy, and internal (Dargie, 1998).

In a later study, Dargie (2000) draws on case studies of chief executives from the public, private, and voluntary sectors, which looked at what chief executives do and how their role relates to the context in which they work. The private sector chief executives did not work with groups nor were they involved in decision-making committees — they preferred to meet people on a one-to-one basis. The voluntary sector chief executives acted in a supportive role for trustees, members, and volunteers.

CIOs Influence Behavior

In their roles as senior managers, CIOs are often responsible for the initiation and implementation of information systems that are vital to the success, and even survival of the firm. In doing so, CIOs must exercise influence successfully in order to attain these objectives (Enns, Huff, & Golden, 2003b).

The potential for the CIO — the company's senior information systems executive — to play a critical role in the strategy and change process of firms is arguably greater today than ever before. CIOs spend much of their time attempting to convince other top managers to commit to strategic IS initiatives, share in a vision for IS, and allocate resources to IS projects.

CIO Lateral Influence Behaviors

In order to develop and bring to fruition strategic information systems projects, chief information officers must be able to effectively influence their peers. Enns, Huff, and Higgins' (2003a) study examined the relationship between CIO influence behaviors and the successfulness of influence outcomes, and their research is presented in the following.

Since no idea is intrinsically strategic or important, the give-and-take of senior managers about what matters largely determines which initiatives are implemented. Within the give-and-take context, a critical part of the CIO's strategic role is to provide thought leadership to other top executives, making them aware of the potential for information systems to support and enhance the strategy of the firm. One way CIOs do this is to effect proactive influence behaviors to convince other top managers to allocate attention and resources to strategic information systems projects.

Indeed, CIOs have an inherent responsibility to do so. A CIO's hesitance to exert influence may increase the risks that the agenda for IS will be shaped by other, less knowledgeable sources.

Effective organizations recognize that having line managers take ownership of critical IS projects increases the likelihood of appropriate IS deployment and organization success. If a CIO wants a strategic application proposal implemented, he or she requires the commitment of the top management team, without which the project would stand a lesser chance of success. Similarly, the practitioner literature suggests that effective CIOs must skillfully apply their powers of influence to encourage other functional heads to become partners with them and embrace ownership of these initiatives.

In the past, when most CIOs were not part of the top management team, they often needed to apply different forms of upward influence to convince top management to seriously consider strategic information systems projects, with varying degrees of success. More recently, as they have gained acceptance on their firms' top management teams, CIOs require skills at applying lateral influence, in order to convince their peers in other functional areas to commit to SIS initiatives. There is evidence that CIOs may be less effective than their executive counterparts in proactively exerting peer-level influence. For example, CIOs may attempt to use "hard" tactics such as edicts, which do not work as well as "softer" tactics like persuasion and participation.

In order to clarify the CIO-peer influence context, it is important to distinguish between influence and authority. Authority can be viewed as the legitimate exercise of decision-making that affects the behavior of individuals. Thus, subordinates agree without question to the decisions of a superior and are willing to set aside any judgments about the suitability of a superior's request or behave as if they agreed with the superior. Similarly, authority can be viewed as designated across hierarchical management positions.

It is also commonly recognized that a superior relies on advice or information from others, including subordinates. This advice or information comprises influence. Thus, a person exerts influence by offering information, providing advice, persuading, and the like. Importantly, in contrast with authority that flows downward, influence can be multidirectional. Thus, individuals have the capacity to influence superiors or colleagues. The dispersion of influence permits actors from all levels in the organization to make their expertise felt in specific decision areas. The distinction between authority and influence is important in situations where CIOs do not possess formal authority. Specifically, CIOs must rely primarily on influence to affect the thinking and behavior of their peers.

Good working relationships with peers are a necessary condition for the success of IT executives. The CIO requires integrity and interpersonal skills in order to develop these important relationships. These effective working relationships set the stage for CIOs to successfully approach peers in a "personal informal" style, to make causal contact with peers to discuss these initiatives and build support before a formal proposal is discussed. CIO influence behaviors comprise an important part of the CIO-peer communications that lead to the development of shared vision and SIS project success.

Coalition and consultation tactics have been effectively used to convince executives of the potential strategic impact of IS, to gain acceptance of other executives, to achieve a shared vision of IS's role in the organization, and to create a positive impression of the IS department. Rational persuasion has been used to identify new uses of IT, create a positive view of IS, and to convince top managers of the need for greater central IT coordination. Also, CIO tactics used to overcome resistance to IS implementation include bargaining with IS resources (i.e., exchange) and co-opting opposition (i.e., consultation).

Influence tactics can be studied in terms of an agent (i.e., initiator) trying to gain something from the target (i.e., recipient). Here are some examples of such influence behaviors:

- **Rational persuasion:** The agent uses logical arguments and factual evidence to persuade the target that a proposal or request is viable and likely to result in the attainment of task objectives.

- **Consultation:** The agent seeks target participation in planning a strategy, activity, or change for which target support and assistance are desired, or is willing to modify a proposal to deal with target concerns and suggestions.

- **Ingratiation:** The agent uses praise, flattery, friendly behavior, or helpful behavior to get the target in a good mood or to think favorably of him or her when asking for something.

- **Personal appeals:** The agent appeals to target feelings of loyalty and friendship toward him or her when asking for something.

- **Exchange:** The agent offers an exchange of favors, indicates willingness to reciprocate at a later time, or promises a share of the benefits if the target helps accomplish a task.

- **Coalition tactics:** The agent seeks the aid of others to persuade the target to do something, or uses the support of others as a reason for the target to also agree.

- **Pressure:** The agent uses demands, threats, frequent checking, or persistent reminders to influence the target to do what he or she wants.

Influence behaviors, and their effectiveness, vary depending on whether the target is a subordinate, peer, or superior. For instance, rational persuasion is often linked with effective upward influence, while pressure behaviors are more commonly associated with downward influence and are most effective under these conditions.

Influence leads to a number of possible outcomes. Influence outcome might include commitment, compliance, and resistance. Commitment is evident when the target displays strong enthusiasm and special effort beyond what is expected. Compliance occurs when the target completes the request but is apathetic and makes minimal effort. Resistance is displayed when the target avoids performing the requested actions by arguing, delaying, and so forth.

Socialization Theory

Enns et al. (2003b) framed their analysis of CIO influence behavior around socialization theory, and the following description is adopted from their work. Socialization, broadly speaking, is the process by which an individual learns and adopts the norms, value systems, and behavior patterns of a group. For example, new organizational members learn how to act in their different surroundings by observation of and interaction with long-term members. Socialization is also formally accomplished via orientation programs, for example. Of particular importance are behaviors and norms that are learned through early organizational experiences, such as a first job or university experience, since they lead to relatively stable patterns of behavior. Thus, socialization theorists contend that a newly promoted manager will continue to engage in behaviors that were acceptable and reinforced in the manager's prior work environment. This is consistent with the concepts of manifest and latent roles. Manifest roles focus on the way group norms produce prescribed similarities in the behavior of those in equivalent roles. Latent roles are relatively stable and are acquired via different degrees of commitment to professional skills, reference group orientations, and loyalty to the organization.

The concept of latent roles suggests that people playing different manifest roles may be performing similar latent roles and, conversely, that those performing the same manifest role may be playing different latent roles. The concept of latent role may then aid in accounting for some of the differences (in behavior or belief) among those in the same manifest role.

The concept of latent roles is important in understanding CIOs since latent roles may impact the behavior of CIOs who have greater technical backgrounds. Despite the fact that they function in the manifest role of the CIO, with expectations that they behave in prescribed ways, CIOs may continue to act out their latent role, and behave more like their technologist colleagues.

Socialization theory also suggests that the work and educational experience of individuals has a bearing on their use of influence behaviors. It has been argued that individuals with greater technical backgrounds, in contrast to those who have limited technical backgrounds, tend to have different experiences that affect their use of influence behaviors. Technically oriented people, according to advocates of this perspective, tend to deal with objects and things, are more task-focused, and are less relationship centered. In addition, the socialization of technically trained individuals differs from that of non-technically trained managers. For instance, technically oriented individuals are often focused on contributions to their profession, as opposed to their organizations.

A survey instrument was developed by Enns et al. (2003b) and targeted CIOs working in U.S. and Canadian companies. Surprisingly, survey results provided no support for stereotypical accounts of CIOs or socialization theory as applied to CIOs.

Work Experience

According to McCall (2004), the primary source of learning to lead, to the extent that leadership can be learned, is experience. He argues that the role played by training and other formal programs is relatively modest in comparison to other kinds of experiences. The implication of this belief is rather profound, because it suggests that experiences (mostly assignments) rather than programs should form the core of executive development.

Work experience of CIOs can be captured using three measures: quantitative, qualitative, and interaction (Dawson & Watson, 2005). Quantitative measures are time-based and amount measures. Time-based measures are the traditional measurement of the length of time spent work in a task, job, or organization and are operational in terms of tenure. Amount measures are the number of times that a task has been performed and reflect the opportunity to practice and perfect the task. However, quantitative measures provide little insight into the value of experience since learning from experience is not automatic. Some people come away with nothing, the wrong lessons, or only some of what they might have learned (McCall, 2004).

The second measure is qualitative. Work experiences are associated with learning when they challenge the individual, and challenge is mostly likely to occur when there is a lack of congruence between the individual's knowledge, skills, and abilities and the demands of the assignment. Two individuals with equal job, organizational, and position tenure can vary widely in the amount of challenges encountered in their work experience and resulting job performance. Qualitative measures capture this challenge and allow a more full analysis of its value of the work experience. They best represent the specific nature of work situations that contribute to the richness of the experience construct, such as the variety and breadth of tasks and responsibilities performed in a job, the types of challenges encountered in an assignment, or the complexity of the task. Qualitative measures may be best represented by the specific nature of work situations that contribute to the richness of the experience construct, such as the variety and breadth of tasks and responsibilities performed in the job, the types of challenges encountered in an assignment, or the complexity of a task (Tesluk & Jacobs, 1998). Qualitative measures might include: (1) unfamiliar responsibilities; (2) new direction; (3) inherited problems; (4) problems with employees; (5) high stakes; (6) scope and scale; (7) external pressure; (8) influence without authority; (9) work across cultures; (10) work group diversity (Dawson & Watson, 2005).

The third measure is the interaction between the qualitative and quantitative dimensions and includes the experience's density, placement within the career, and criticality of the work experience. Density is intended to capture the intensity of experiences (Tesluk & Jacobs, 1998). High-density experiences have a greater number of challenges within a short time period and are associated with the developmental punch of

Figure 2.2. Framework of work experience measures (adapted from Quinones et al., 1995)

	Amount	Time	Type
Organization	Number of organizations	Organizational tenure	Organization maturity
Position	Number of tasks	Job tenure	Job complexity
Task	Number of times performing a task	Time on task	Task difficulty

the experience. They are particularly important because they have a disproportional influence on learning and the individual's career trajectory. They are career-making assignments (Quinones, Ford, & Teachout, 1995).

According to Quinones et al. (1995), work experience refers to events that are experienced by an individual that relate to the performance of some job. They created a framework specifying two dimensions along which work experience measures can vary. The dimensions of measurement mode (amount, time, and type) and level of specificity (task, job, organizational) formed nine separate categories of measures of work experience, as illustrated in Figure 2.2.

When applying the framework in Figure 2.2 to CIO experience, it can be argued that the closer positions and tasks match positions and tasks of a top executive, the more relevant the CIO is as a candidate for the CEO position. For example, an indication of job complexity might be the kinds of people who are involved in the same issues as the CIO.

According to Dawson and Watson (2005), the goal of work experience is to build the knowledge necessary to be successful. This is often referred to as tacit knowledge (Hedlund et al., 2003). Tacit knowledge is a factor of practical intelligence and is expressed in everyday phrases such as common sense. Tacit knowledge results from understanding work experiences and represents an individual's ability to learn from everyday problems.

Figure 2.3. Work experience influences CIO effectiveness through tacit knowledge (adapted from Dawson and Watson, 2005)

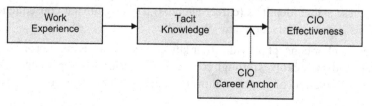

Dawson and Watson (2005) suggest a causal relationship between work experience and tacit knowledge, and between tacit knowledge and CIO effectiveness, as illustrated in Figure 2.3. It is assumed that quantitative measures of work experience, qualitative measures of work experience, as well as interaction measures of work experience will all be correlated with a CIO's tacit knowledge. Furthermore, a CIO's tacit business knowledge, tacit IS knowledge, tacit political knowledge, tacit power knowledge, and tacit operations knowledge will all be correlated with CIO effectiveness.Most CIO leadership studies use a role-based perspective. Dawson and Watson (2005) present six distinct CIO roles:

1. **IT educator:** concerned with ensuring that the human foundations for innovation are in place. In this role, the CIO is a champion for computer literacy.

2. **IT contract oversight:** concerned with ensuring that strategic partnerships with external vendors are optimized. In this role, the CIO negotiates and accomplishes contracts.

3. **IT support/utility provider:** focuses on classic IT support ensuring that the IT unit is operationally efficient and effective. In this role, the CIO ensures that the IT unit is responsive to customer needs.

4. **Integrator:** concerned with developing value-added integration among and between business units as well as with external partners. In this role, the CIO directs efforts to build an integrated delivery system.

5. **Informaticist/IT strategist:** concerned with developing sound data management and IT plans and processes. In this role, the CIO ensures that organizational data is secure and confidential.

6. **Business partner/strategist:** concerned with issues relating to the greater organization outside of the IT unit. In this role, the CIO helps to shape the organization's overall mission and vision.

CIO career anchor might have a moderating effect on the relationship between tacit knowledge and CIO effectiveness, as illustrated in Figure 2.3. Career anchor is a concept focusing on the pattern of self-perceived talents, motives, and values, which serve to guide, constrain, stabilize, and integrate a CIO's career. According to Feldman and Bolino (1996), the career anchor concept suggests that individuals develop "careers within careers" after their true abilities, needs, and values become crystallized through a variety of real-world work experiences. Moreover, once formed, these stable identities (career anchors) have significant consequences for individuals' career satisfaction and job stability.

The career anchor concept provides four key contributions. First, it proposes that a stable career identity evolves through concrete real-world work experiences. Second, it highlights the variety of careers within an occupation. Third, the differences within these career tracks can be as distinct as between those people in entirely different occupations. Finally, as an individual makes choices about jobs, the career anchor functions as a constraining force (Dawson & Watson, 2005).

The New CIO Leader

According to Broadbent and Kitzis (2005), CIOs are at a crossroads and must choose for themselves which path to follow: to become new CIO leaders or chief technology mechanics. Simply maintaining status is impossible, since focusing on managing request queues, keeping as large an IS organization as possible, being wowed by emerging technology, and operating IS divorced from business goals and specific business benefits is itself a choice to follow the path to enterprise irrelevance.

For those CIOs who aspire to more, to being integral parts of their enterprise leadership team, to having a valued and respected seat at the enterprise strategy table, there is an alternative. This alternative is built on the 10 areas of focus:

1.   Understand the fundamentals of your environment.
2.   Create your vision.
3.   Shape expectations for an IT-enabled enterprise.
4.   Inform expectations for an IT-enabled enterprise.
5.   Create clear and appropriate IT governance.
6.   Weave business and IT strategies together.
7.   Build a new IS organization.
8.   Develop a high-performing IS team.
9.   Manage enterprise and IT risks.
10. Communicate your performance.

The McKinsey consulting firm argues that the next-generation CIO must step up to the new responsibilities of an IT leader (Mark & Monnoyer, 2004). CIOs must delegate or shed some operational duties and spend more time helping business leaders identify and use technologies that will help companies innovate. Next-generation CIOs will (1) ensure that IT is efficient and then make the transition to effectiveness, (2) reengineer relationships with business leaders, and (3) invest in a business committee with technology oversight. A few leading companies have disbanded their technology committees — typically staffed by business managers and IT staff — and are asking senior-executive committees to take responsibility for IT-investment decisions.

According to Gartner (2005), the keys to being a successful CIO are the same around the world. Like CIOs in the United States, IT executives in Singapore, Sweden, and Germany cite good communication skills, ability to think strategically, and understanding business processes and operations as the skills that are most pivotal for success. Swedish CIOs add "being a good leader" to their list. Like CIOs in the U.S. and Germany, IT executives in Southeast Asia give strategic planning a high priority. But getting it done is less of a struggle for Southeast Asians. They rank finding time for strategic thinking and planning near the bottom in a list of 10 barriers to their effectiveness.

CIOs in Canada surveyed by Gartner (2005) spent the bulk of their time meeting with their company's executives and business partners. Their U.S. counterparts said they spend a good portion of their time with company executives and IT providers.

To be successful, most of the respondents (78%) in the survey by Gartner (2005) responded that aggressive leadership is most important. Also, good communication of goals throughout the organization (59%) and agility (59%) are important CIO skills.

Thompson (2005, p. 59), himself a CIO at the Shaw Group, noted the following characteristics of a successful CIO:

> *To be a successful CIO, you have to be a businessperson first, not an IT person. You have to sit amongst your peers at the executive committee level and stand toe to toe with them on business issues and talk the business, and walk your talk. That's the first characteristic that CIOs need to have — an understanding of the business and being able to make sure that you can communicate at the executive level.*

> *The second thing is you need to understand good talent, and be able to hire good people and to surround yourself with good talent... The third characteristic is to walk amongst the people. You can't expect your staff to do things you're not willing to do, to go that extra mile.*

Federal CIO

Responsibilities, reporting relationships, tenure, and challenges of federal chief information officers were discussed in a report to congressional requesters by GAO (2004). Here are some of the points in this report.

Agency CIOs come from a wide variety of professional and educational backgrounds, but they almost always have IT or IT-related work or educational experience. The median tenure of a federal CIO has been about 2 years. In contrast, both current CIOs and former agency IT executives most commonly cited 3 to 5 years as the time they needed to become effective. Among the reasons cited for a high turnover rate were the challenges that CIOs face, the political environment, and the pay differentials between the public and private sectors.

All CIOs had responsibility for information and technology management areas such as:

- Capital planning and investment management
- Enterprise architecture
- Information security
- IT/IRM strategic planning
- IT/IRM workforce planning

In addition to requiring that federal agency CIOs have many specific responsibilities, federal law also generally requires that these CIOs report directly to their agency heads. This requirement establishes an identifiable line of accountability and recognizes the importance of CIOs being full participants in the executive team in order to successfully carry out their responsibilities.

Agency Theory

The CIO is an agent for the organization in leading the IT function to the best value for the organization.

Agency theory has broadened the risk-sharing literature to include the agency problem that occurs when cooperating parties have different goals and division of labor. The cooperating parties are engaged in an agency relationship defined as a contract under which one or more persons (the principal(s)) engage another person (agent) to perform some service on their behalf which involves delegating some decision-making authority to the agent (Jensen & Meckling, 1976). Agency theory describes the relationship between the two parties using the metaphor of a contract. In an IT outsourcing relationship, this is a client-vendor relationship and an outsourcing contract.

According to Eisenhardt (1985), agency theory is concerned with resolving two problems that can occur in agency relationships. The first is the agency problem that arises when the desires or goals of the principal and agent conflict and it is difficult or expensive for the principal to verify what the agent is actually doing. The second is the problem of risk sharing that arises when the principal and agent have different risk preferences. These problems are well-known in IT outsourcing. An example might be that the client organization wants to reduce its IT costs, while the vendor organization wants to maximize profits. The agency problem arises when the two parties do not share productivity gains. The risk-sharing problem might be the result of different attitudes toward the use of new technologies. Because the unit of analysis is the contract governing the relationship between the two parties, the focus of the theory is on determining the most efficient contract governing the principal-agent relationship given assumptions about people (e.g., self-interest, bounded rationality, risk aversion), organizations (e.g., goal conflict of members), and information (e.g., information is a commodity which can be purchased). Thus, the question becomes: Is a behavior-oriented contract more efficient than an outcome-oriented contract? To a great extent, outsourcing contracts are tied up to service level agreements, where the outcome of the service is the focal point.

The agency theory is applicable when describing client-vendor relationships in IT outsourcing arrangements. Typically, the client organization (principal) transfers property rights to the vendor organization (agent). In the context of IT, assets transferred might be infrastructure, systems and documentation, and employees. For a certain amount of money, the vendor organization provides services to the client organization. This implies a change in legal relationships, and IT services are carried out using a more formal transaction process. The status of personal relationships also changes, from that of a manager and a subordinate, to that of a client-manager and a vendor. According to agency theory, control mechanisms also change, from that of behavioral control, to that of outcome-based control. If both parties to the relationship are trying to maximize their utility, there is good reason to believe that the vendor organization will not always act in the best interests of the client. Monitoring and bonding activities in reducing agency costs include auditing, formal control systems, budget restrictions, and the establishment of incentive compensation systems which serve to more closely identify the manager's interests with those of the outside equity holder.

The original impetus for the development of agency theory was large corporations' separation of control from ownership. Thus, its focus was never on organizational boundaries, as with transaction cost theory. Agency theory's primary interest is not the decision to source via the hierarchy or via the market. Although all contractual arrangements contain important elements of agency, agency theory is essentially concerned with the delegation of work by the principal to the agent via a contract, whether or not they are both within the same organization. However, agency and transaction cost theories share several concepts, such as opportunism, uncertainty, and bounded rationality, and there is a rough correspondence between transaction cost economics' hierarchies and markets and agency theory's behavior-based contracts and outcome-based contracts.

According to Hancox and Hackney (2000), the choice of contract type depends on the agency costs, which include the principal's effort in assessing the agent's performance and the agent's efforts in assuring the principal of his or her commitment. Agency theory holds that human beings act through self-interest and therefore, as contracting parties, they may have divergent goals. An important aspect of the theory is that both principal and agent wish to avoid risk when dealing with each other. The principal may prefer to place risk with the agent via an outcome-based contract, whereas the agent may prefer to avoid risk by having a behavior-based contract.

Outcome-based contracts are claimed to reduce agent opportunism because the rewards of both agent and principal depend on the same actions. Behavior-based contracts need the principal to have sufficient information to identify two possible dangers: First, whether there is adverse selection (the agent does not possess the skills he claims); second, moral hazard – the agent is shirking. Overall risk may be reduced by sourcing via the hierarchy, but agency costs also exist in hierarchies. Problems between agents and principals are greater in complex organizations with many managerial layers. Given that many public sector bodies are large and complicated both in the range of their activities and the structures adopted to manage and account for those activities, it may be that agency costs are inclined to be higher in the public sector. Non-market organizations may be especially susceptible to influence costs, where employees pursue their own agenda. This might imply that within a public sector organization if the employees of one department were motivated by self interest, then workers in other departments would be inconvenienced and resent the action, unless perhaps, they themselves were pursuing a similar or compatible agenda.

The technological and business complexity of IT means that there may be major problems for the principal in choosing a suitable agent and in monitoring the agent's work. Only the agent knows how hard he is working, and that can be especially important in multilateral contracting where one agent acts for several principals. This is often the case in IT outsourcing because of the market dominance of one large firm. Given the difficulties of behavior-based contracts suggested by agency theory, it is reasonable to assume that the overwhelming majority of clients would insist on outcome-based contracts when acquiring IT products and services. Such a strategy can only succeed if the client can confidently specify current and future requirements. But accurate predictions by the client may not always be in the vendor's interests, since vendor account managers often are rewarded according to contract profitability, which is principally achieved through charging the client extra for anything which is not in the contract.

Hancox and Hackney (2000) interviewed IT managers to find support for the agency theory in IT outsourcing. In their interviews, it was difficult to find examples of some of the ideas from agency theory, although a minority of the organizations had been disappointed with aspects of vendor performance and behavior.

Example of Agency Theory

Austin (2001) developed an agency model to study the effects of time pressure on quality in software development.

Agency situations arise whenever one person relies on another person to do work. The problem created is one of control, because the worker — the agent — can usually act in ways that are not observable to the person who wants the work done — the principal. Observation difficulties result from lack of time to comprehensively supervise (watching the agent every minute obviates the efficiency sought in hiring him), specialized skills possessed by the agent but not by the principal (which are often the principal's reason for employing the agent in the first place), or anything else that makes it difficult to attribute work or its consequences to a single agent. The central problem broached by this framework leads to the question: How can the agent, whose motives may not be aligned with those of the principal and who has the ability to act beyond the view of the principal, be influenced to behave in a way that is desirable to the principal?

Austin (2001) used an agency framework to model the behavior of software developers as they weigh concerns about product quality against concerns about missing individual task deadlines.

CIO Backgrounds

Enns et al. (2003b) studied the extent of technical background that CIOs have. Technical background can be conceptualized in a variety of ways, normally centering on the length and type of a CIO's education and work experience. In the study, CIO technical background was measured via four survey items about the technical component of the individual's work experience and formal education. Respondents in the survey rated their previous education, overall work history, and detailed work history on a scale (1 = non-technical, 7 = highly technical). The mean score of these ratings was used to produce an overall CIO technical score. Then, out of 69 responses, 42 CIOs were classified as technical, while 27 CIOs were classified as non-technical.

In another survey by CIO (2003) on work experience, survey respondents reported that they have been the CIO or have held an equivalent head of IT title for an average of four years and nine months. When asked how long they have been in their current job, the average length of time was four years.

In the same survey, 82% of the IT heads surveyed listed IT as a functional area that they worked in previously and that had an impact on their career path to CIO. Other areas most frequently listed included consulting (34%), administration (25%), engineering (20%), customer service (17%), and research and development (17%). Eighty-seven percent of the IT heads in the survey were male.

On average, CIOs earned in 2003 a total annual compensation, including base salary, bonus, and stock options, of $186,000. The highest paying industries for CIOs were insurance, where the average compensation was $223,000, followed by finance ($220,000) and computer-related business ($209,000). CIOs in manufacturing earned an average of $176,000 annually, while CIOs in education and government (federal, state, and local) earned the lowest compensation at $126,000 and $120,000, respectively (CIO, 2003).

The CEO-CIO Relationship

Building strong social networks and coalitions within a firm is an essential task for those who aspire to be the CEO. When they are promoted to a firm's CEO position, inside successors not only have the approval of outside directors but also the support within the top management group (Shen & Cannella, 2002b). For a CIO who aspires to become the next CEO, he or she needs to manage relationships, develop coalitions, and understand power dynamics in top management.

The quality of the CEO-CIO relationship influences the CIO's effectiveness and success as a business leader, and the value gained from information technology. CEOs are demanding and not always clear about their expectations. That can create a situation where their views are radically different from the CIO's perceptions, a situation fraught with risk for both. CEOs and CIOs often see the relationship between business and information differently. CIOs tend to view their role and contribution optimistically. CEOs, by contrast, are more critical (Gartner, 2005).

The difference between how the CEO views the CEO-CIO relationship and how the CIO views this relationship creates the potential for a dangerous disconnect, limiting the value generated by information technology and the power of the executive team. Understanding the CEO's expectations and view of the CIO helps create the right relationship based on personal style and enterprise need.

In the survey conducted by Gartner (2005), CIOs believed they are trusted and respected business leaders, and to a great extent they are right. But few CEOs share the same unqualified view. This is partly because CEOs have a broad span of control, with IT just one of many priorities. It is also because of CIOs' technology and operations focus, which does not always allow them to show traditional business leadership styles and behaviors.

In the survey by Gartner (2005), responding CEOs found that healthy relationships with other executives (CXOs) are very important for the CIO. Furthermore, the CIO must oversee that IT objectives are aligned with the CEO's objectives and overall business strategy. Survey results indicate that CIOs and CEOs are in agreement on the most important skills for the CIO's success. They stress strategic thinking and planning, as well as understanding business processes and operations.

CEOs hire CIOs to fit with enterprise needs and the changing context. CIOs must understand the type of relationship they are in and the actions required to reach the right relationship type. Four relationship types describe how CIOs relate to CEOs: at-risk, transactional, partnering, and trusted-ally. These relationships are not set in stone. Sudden events — a change of CEO or a strategic IT initiative — can change the balance. And, if both CEO and CIO are open to the possibility, they can change the relationship.

The first step for the CIO is to understand where his or her relationship is now, through self-assessment and dialog with the CEO. Then, the CIO uses that information to decide the next step, and move one step at a time, cementing credibility and the enterprise's appetite for change at each level.

According to Gartner (2005), CIO success stems from a four-step cycle — leading, shaping demand, setting expectations, and delivering. The CIO is recommended to build an action plan based on this cycle, tailored to personal relationship type. The plan might have tangible, time-bounded goals. Embedded in the plan might be six powerful and proven practices: get coaching and mentoring; make time for relationship building; take on non-IT responsibilities; build the strength of deputies; educate personally; and educate shareholders. This will increase the chances of achieving the right CEO-CIO relationship.

Gartner (2005) has the following note to CEOs:

The age of the operational CIO is almost over

Your relationship with your CIO matters. The CIO can be a powerful and positive member of your executive team. A recent study by Burson and Marsteller shows that 5% of Fortune Global 500 companies have CIO skills on their board. And these companies' stocks have outperformed the industry index by 6.4% per year since the CIO-skilled member was elected.

You set the tone of the relationship with your CIO. Successful CEOs are getting more from IT by building their CIO relationship. Getting CIO input into enterprise strategy has proved much more powerful than getting the CIO to execute a fixed strategy.

This trend is increasing, not decreasing, as enterprises become more reliant on IT to implement efficient processes and to drive sources of competitive advantage.

For an enterprise to be effective in using IT to drive innovation and growth, a good working relationship between the CEO and CIO is crucial. But there is still a lot of misunderstanding and suspicion amongst CEOs of CIOs and IT. To succeed, CIOs need to understand the CEO's perspective on them and on IT's role in the enterprise.

References

Applegate, L. M., McFarlan, F. W., & McKenney, J. L. (1996). *Corporate information systems management* (4th ed.). USA: Irwin.

Austin, R. D. (2001). The effects of time pressure on quality in software development: An agency model. *Information Systems Research, 12*(2), 195-207.

Benjamin, R. I., Dickinson, C., & Rockart, J. F. (1985). Changing role of the corporate information systems officer. *MIS Quarterly, 9*(3), 177-197.

Blair, R. (2005). The future of CIOs. *Health Management Technology, 26*(2), 58-59.

Broadbent, M., & Kitzis, E. (2005). *The new CIO leader: Setting the agenda and delivering results.* Cambridge, MA: Harvard Business School Press.

Chatterjee, D., Richardson, V. J., & Zmud, R. W. (2001). Examining the shareholder wealth effects of announcements of newly created CIO positions. *MIS Quarterly, 25*(1), 43-70.

CIO (2003). The state of the CIO 2003. *CIO Research Reports.* Retrieved from www.cio.com

Computerworld (2005). Premier 100 IT Leaders 2005 (January). Nortel Hires CEO (October). *Computerworld.* Retrieved from www.computerworld.com

Dargie, C. (1998). The role of public sector chief executives. *Public Administration, 76*, 161-177.

Dargie, C. (2000, July-September). Observing chief executives: Analysing behaviour to explore cross-sectoral differences. *Public Money & Management*, 39-44.

Dawson, G., & Watson, R. (2005). *An empirical analysis of the career paths of effective CIOs.* Working paper, University of Georgia.

Earl, M. J., & Feeny, D. F. (1994). Is your CIO adding value? *Sloan Management Review, 35*(3), 11-20.

Eisenhardt, K. M. (1985). Control: Organizational and economic approaches. *Management Science, 31*(2), 134-149.

Enns, H. G., Huff, S. L., & Golden, B. R. (2003b). CIO influence behaviors: The impact of technical background. *Information & Management, 40,* 467-485.

Enns, H. G., Huff, S. L., & Higgins, C. A. (2003a). CIO lateral influence behaviors: Gaining peers' commitment to strategic information Systems. *MIS Quarterly, 27*(1), 155-176.

Feldman, D. C., & Bolino, M. C. (1996). Careers within careers: Reconceptualizing the nature of career anchors and their consequences. *Human Resource Management Review, 6*(2), 89-112.

GAO. (2004). *Federal chief information officers: Responsibilities, reporting relationships, tenure, and challenges.* Report to Congressional Requesters, United States Government Accountability Office, GAO-04-823.

Gartner (2005). The changing role of the CIO. The state of the CIO around the world. CIO 100 2005: The bold 100. State of the CIO 2004: The CEO view. *Gartner Group Insight.* Retrieved from www.gartner.com

Grover, V., Jeong, S. R., Kettinger, W. J., & Lee, C. C. (1993). The chief information officer: A study of managerial roles. *Journal of Management Information Systems, 10*(2), 107-130.

Hancox, M., & Hackney, R. (2000). IT outsourcing: Frameworks for conceptualizing practice and perception. *Information Systems Journal, 10*(3), 217-237.

Hedlund, J., Forsythe, G. B., Horvath, J. A., Williams, W. M., Snook, S., & Sternberg, R. J. (2003). Identifying and assessing tacit knowledge: Understanding the practical intelligence of military leaders. *The Leadership Quality, 14,* 117-140.

Jensen, M. C., & Meckling, W. H. (1976). Theory of the firm: Managerial behavior, agency costs and ownership structures. *Journal of Financial Economics, 3*(4), 305-360.

Kaarst-Brown, M. (2005). Understanding an organization's view of the CIO: The role of assumptions about IT. *MIS Quarterly Executive, 4*(2), 287-301.

Karimi, J., Somers, T. M., & Gupta, Y. P. (2001). Impact of information technology management practices on customer service. *Journal of Management Information Systems, 17*(4), 125-158.

Kolbasuk, M. CIOs get respect. *Insurance and Technology, 30*(9), 18.

Lane, D. (2004). *CIO wisdom: Best practices from Silicon Valley's leading IT experts.* Upper Saddle River, NJ: Prentice-Hall.

Mark, D., & Monnoyer, E. (2004, July). Next-generation CIOs. *McKinsey on IT,* 7 pages.

McCall, M. W. (2004). Leadership development through experience. *Academy of Management Executive, 18*(3), 127-130.

Quinones, M. A., Ford, J. K., & Teachout, M. S. (1995). The relationship between work experience and job performance: A conceptual and meta-analytic review. *Personnel Psychology, 48,* 887-910.

Robson, W. (1997). *Strategic management & information systems* (2nd ed.). UK: Prentice Hall.

Sambamurthy, V., Straub, D. W., & Watson, R. T. (2001). Managing IT in the digital era. In G. W. Dickson & G. DeSanctis (Eds.), *Information technology and the future enterprise: New models for managers* (pp. 282-305). USA: Prentice Hall.

Schubert, K. D. (2004). *CIO survival guide: The roles and responsibilities of the chief information officer.* Hoboken, NJ: John Wiley & Sons.

Shen, W., & Cannella, A. A. (2002b). Power dynamics within top management and their impacts on CEO dismissal followed by inside succession. *Academy of Management Journal, 45*(6), 1195-1206.

Tesluk, P. E., & Jacobs, R. R. (1998). Toward an integrated model of work experience. *Personnel Psychology, 51,* 321-355.

Thompson, P. (2005). *Where business & IT meet.* In CIO Leadership Strategies. Aspatore Books. Retrieved from www.aspatore.com

Todd, P. A., McKeen, J. D., & Gallupe, R. B. (1995). The evolution of IS job skills: A content analysis of IS job advertisements from 1970 to 1990. *MIS Quarterly, 19*(1), 1-27.

Chapter III

CIO
Leadership Roles

Introduction

One approach to understanding the CIO position is to study managerial roles. In this chapter, 10 roles by Mintzberg, six roles by Grover et al. derived from Mintzberg, and six CSC roles are presented to shed light on the various leadership roles for CIOs.

Mintzberg's Roles

Mintzberg (1994) notes a number of different and sometimes conflicting views of the manager's role. He finds that it is a curiosity of the management literature that its best-known writers all seem to emphasize one particular part of the manager's job to the exclusion of the others. Together, perhaps, they cover all the parts, but even that does not describe the whole job of managing. Based on an observational study of chief executives, Mintzberg (1994) concluded that a manager's work could be described in terms of 10 job roles. As managers take on these roles, they perform management functions. These 10 roles consist of three interpersonal roles (figurehead, leader, and liaison), three informational roles (monitor, disseminator, and spokesman), and four decisional roles (entrepreneur, disturbance handler, resource allocator, and negotiator):

- **Figurehead:** performs some duties of a ceremonial nature. Examples include greeting visitors, responding to journalists' questions, and visiting customers and allies.

- **Personnel:** leader is responsible for motivation of subordinates and for staffing and training. Examples include most activities involving subordinates, such as settling disagreements between subordinates.

- **Liaison:** establishes a web of external relationships. Examples include attending conferences and giving presentations.

- **Monitor:** seeks and receives information to understand and learn from the environment. Examples include reading journals and listening to external experts.

- **Disseminator:** transmits information to other organizational members. Examples include forwarding reports and memos, making phone calls to present information, and holding informational meetings.

- **Spokesman:** involves the communication of information and ideas. Examples include speaking to the board of directors and top management and talking to users.

- **Entrepreneur:** acts as initiator and designer of much of the controlled change in the organization. Examples include user ideas converted to systems proposals and management objectives transformed to infrastructure actions.

- **Disturbance handler:** is responsible for solving conflicts in the organization.

- **Resource allocator:** is responsible for allocation of human, financial, material, and other resources. Examples include working on budgets, developing project proposals, and monitoring information technology projects.

- **Negotiator:** is responsible for representing the organization in negotiations. Examples include negotiations with unions concerning wages and with vendors concerning procurements.

According to Mintzberg (1994), these 10 roles are common in all managerial jobs regardless of the functional or hierarchical level. However, differences do exist in the importance and effort dedicated to each managerial role based on job content, different skill levels, and expertise. Mintzberg (1994) states that managers are in fact specialists, required to perform a particular set of specialized managerial roles that are dependent upon the functional area and hierarchical level in which they work.

Grover's Roles

Grover, Jeong, Kettinger, and Lee (1993) used the Mintzberg framework to study CIO roles. They selected six of the 10 roles which they found relevant for CIOs: personnel leader, liaison, monitor, spokesman, entrepreneur, and resource allocator. The four other roles (figurehead, disseminator, disturbance handler, and negotiator) were not operationalized because Grover et al. (1993) found that the activities constituting these roles were correlated with the activities of the other six roles and because they found that the activities that comprised those four roles were consistently important only for certain functions and levels of management. The six selected roles were related to information technology management by rephrasing them:

- As the **personnel leader**, the IS manager is responsible for supervising, hiring, training, and motivating a cadre of specialized personnel. Literature has emphasized the impact of this role on IS personnel. This role is mainly internal to the IS organization.

- The **spokesman** role incorporates activities that require the IS manager to extend organizational contacts outside the department to other areas of the organization. Frequently, he or she must cross traditional departmental boundaries and become involved in affairs of production, distribution, marketing, and finance. This role is mainly external in relation to the intra-organizational environment.

- As the **monitor**, the IS manager must scan the external environment to keep up with technical changes and competition. In acting as the firm's technical innovator, the IS manager uses many sources including vendor contacts, professional relationships, and a network of personal contacts. This role is mainly external in relation to the inter-organizational environment.

- As the **liaison**, the IS manager must communicate with the external environment including exchanging information with IS suppliers, customers, buyers, market analysts, and the media. This role is mainly external in relation to the inter-organizational environment.

- As the **entrepreneur**, the IS manager identifies business needs and develops solutions that change business situations. A major responsibility of the IS manager is to ensure that rapidly evolving technical opportunities are understood, planned, implemented, and strategically exploited in the organization.

- As the **resource allocator**, the IS manager must decide how to allocate human, financial, and information resources. The litany of past discussion on charge-back systems (users have to pay for IT services) and the importance of "fairness" in IS resource allocation decisions speak to the importance of this role. This role is mainly internal to the IS organization.

Figure 3.1. CIO roles on different arenas

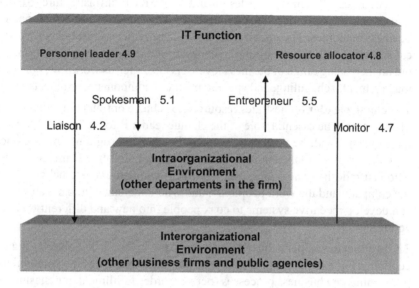

Three Leadership Arenas

The selected six CIO roles are illustrated in Figure 3.1,. The roles of personnel leader and resource allocator are both internal to IT functions. The entrepreneur absorbs ideas from the intra-organizational environment, while the spokesman influences the intra-organizational environment. The liaison informs the external environment, while the monitor absorbs ideas from the external environment.

A survey was conducted in Norway to investigate CIO roles (Gottschalk, 2005). CIOs were asked questions about the importance of the different roles. Survey results indicate some variation in the importance of roles. Responding CIOs found the role of entrepreneur most important and the role of liaison least important. This is indicated with numbers in Figure 3.1, where the scale went from 1 (not important) to 6 (very important).

CSC Roles

Computer Science Corporation (CSC, 1996) has suggested an alternative set of leadership roles to Mintzberg (1994). These six leadership roles are specifically tailored to information technology executives:

- The **chief architect** designs future possibilities for the business. The primary work of the chief architect is to design and evolve the IT infrastructure so that it will expand the range of future possibilities for the business, not define specific business outcomes. The infrastructure should provide not just today's technical services, such as networking, databases, and desktop operating systems, but an increasing range of business level services, such as workflow, portfolio management, scheduling, and specific business components or objects.

- The **change leader** orchestrates resources to achieve optimal implementation of the future. The essential role of the change leader is to orchestrate all those resources that will be needed to execute the change program. This includes providing new IT tools, but it also involves putting in place teams of people who can redesign roles, jobs, and workflow, who can change beliefs about the company and the work people do, and who understand human nature and can develop incentive systems to coax people into new and different ways of acting.

- The **product developer** helps define the company's place in the emerging digital economy. For example, a product developer might recognize the potential for performing key business processes (perhaps order fulfillment, purchasing, or delivering customer support) over electronic linkages such as the Internet. The product developer must "sell" the idea to a business partner, and together they can set up and evaluate business experiments, which are initially operated out of IS. Whether the new methods are adopted or not, the company will learn from the experiments and thus move closer to commercial success in emerging digital markets.

- The **technology provocateur** embeds IT into the business strategy. The technology provocateur works with senior business executives to bring IT and realities of the IT marketplace to bear on the formation of strategy for the business. The technology provocateur is a senior business executive who understands both the business and IT at a deep enough level to integrate the two perspectives in discussions about the future course of the business. Technology provocateurs have a wealth of experience in IS disciplines, so they understand at a fundamental level the capabilities of IT and how IT impacts the business.

- The **coach** teaches people to acquire the skills they will need for the future. Coaches have two basic responsibilities: teaching people how to learn, so that they can become self-sufficient; and providing team leaders with staff able to do the IT-related work of the business. A mechanism that assists both is the center of excellence — a small group of people with a particular competence or skill, with a coach responsible for their growth and development. Coaches are solid practitioners of the competence that they will be coaching, but need not be the best at it in the company.

- The **chief operating strategist** invents the future with senior management. The chief operating strategist is the top IS executive who is focused on the future agenda of the IS organization. The strategist has parallel responsibilities related to helping the business design the future, and then delivering it. The most important, and least understood, parts of the role have to do with the interpretation of new technologies and the IT marketplace, and the bringing of this understanding into the development of the digital business strategy for the organization.

These roles were applied in a survey in Norway (Gottschalk, 2005). CIOs were asked to rate the importance of each leadership role. The roles were rated on a scale from 1 (not important) to 6 (very important). The role of change leader received the highest score of 4.6, while the role of product developer received the lowest score of 3.3.

The Harvard Business Review invited leading scholars to answer the question: Are CIOs obsolete? They all responded with a no answer. Rockart found that all good CIOs today are business executives first, and technologists second (Maruca, 2000). Earl paid attention to recruiting new CIOs. His scenario suggests an acid test for selecting the new CIO. Does he or she have the potential to become CEO? If we could develop and appoint such executives, not only will we have CIOs fit for today's challenges, we may be lining up our future CEOs (Earl, 2000).

IT Project Management

Information technology (IT) functions of all sizes and in all industries face many new challenges in today's rapidly changing environment. Multiple and flexible ways of working require organizational structures to be flexible as well. Projects are a flexible and efficient way of working, whether the goal is to design, install, reengineer, or reorganize technology initiatives. However, IT projects are often driven by aggressive deadlines and periods of frequent change (Murch, 2000). Projects are temporary organizational structures and unique, goal-oriented work systems where technical, procedural, organizational, and human elements are integrated. To get the job done, resources must be identified and allocated, and activities must be properly organized and structured in accordance with business and technical requirements.

This section presents research investigating the emphasis placed on different managerial roles by IT project managers. Six managerial roles were applied in this research: personnel leader, resource allocator, spokesman, entrepreneur, liaison, and monitor. Two surveys were conducted in Norway to investigate these management roles. In the first survey, which focused on project management roles in internal IT projects, the respondents emphasized the personnel leader role significantly more than other managerial roles. In the second survey, which focused on project management roles in IT outsourcing projects, the respondents emphasized the spokesman role. With changing business environments, the locus of value creation is no longer within the boundaries of a single firm, but instead occurs at the nexus of relationships between parties. With the growing importance of pooling knowledge resources, knowledge management will have to transcend organizational boundaries in exchanges such as IT outsourcing relationships. Therefore, we would expect to find differences in our two surveys. The empirical results provide evidence that project managers in internal IT projects are more internally oriented than project managers in outsourcing projects. Future research should also take into account culture and structure dimensions as well as the specific industry of the IT project. This research concludes that project managers of both internal IT projects and outsourcing projects should be more externally oriented to meet future challenges. The contingent approach to leadership roles is applied in this research section.

The project management approach to solving IT problems and opportunities involves stakeholders such as CEOs, clients, IT managers, project managers, end users, and consultants (Ko, Kirsch, & King, 2005). Each role and responsibility of these stakeholders must be clearly defined in making the most of the potential of information technology. Information technology projects come in many different shapes and sizes. In this section we are studying two types: internal IT projects and IT outsourcing projects.

Internal IT projects are performed within the IT department. Both the project manager and the staff are members of the department (Gottschalk, 2006). The results of this type of project are typically used within the IT department or the user organization. Examples of internal IT projects include feasibility studies, development projects, design projects, implementation projects, upgrade projects, migration projects, and support services projects.

IT Outsourcing Projects

IT outsourcing is typically organized as a project. The project is concerned with turning over all or parts of an IT activity to an outside vendor. The user organization (client) transfers property decision rights over information technology functions to an external (vendor) organization (Koh, Ang, & Straub, 2004). The project is a process whereby an organization decided to contract-out or sell the firm's IT assets, people, and/or activities to a third party supplier, who in exchange provides and manages these assets and services (Kern & Willcocks, 2002).

This section investigates project management roles in internal IT projects versus IT outsourcing projects. We are studying how project managers in these two groups of projects perceive their leadership roles, and discuss the implications of the differences between them. The following research question is addressed: *What leadership roles are emphasized in internal IT projects versus IT outsourcing projects?* This IT management research is important because the contingent approach to leadership roles implies that the significance of each role is dependent on the situation. This section discusses a very important and interesting aspect of leadership roles and types with IT projects.

Many IT projects are internal projects carried out in the IT department. The project manager is often the IT executive or another member of the department. The challenges that face the project manager in carrying out such a project requests both project management knowledge and practice (e.g., planning and scheduling systems). A dominant focus in such projects has been on internal activities within the project and the base organization. Very often, little or no attention is given to the project environment and other stakeholders. Most of the project-planning models currently available tend to consider the project as though it was developed in a vacuum. The project manager is responsible for planning, organizing, coordinating, and controlling tasks to ensure successful project completion. In order to do this, the project manager has to allocate human, financial, and information resources to the project.

According to Mintzberg's (1994) role typology, we expect the internal roles — personnel leader and resource allocator — to be more emphasized in internal IT projects than in outsourcing projects, since outsourcing projects have an external emphasis (Lee, Miranda, & Kim, 2004; Willcocks, Hindle, Feeny, & Lacity, 2004). From the previous discussion, we find it reasonable to propose the following hypotheses:

H1: Internal roles are more important in internal IT projects than in outsourcing projects.

H1a: The personnel leader role is more important in internal IT projects than in outsourcing projects.

H1b: The resource allocator role is more important in internal IT projects than in outsourcing projects.

Project managers responsible for outsourcing projects in client organizations will have to focus on managing client characteristics, while project managers responsible for outsourcing projects from the vendor side will have to focus on both vendor-client relationships and the vendor's value proposition (Levina & Ross, 2003). Hence, we argue that the job of the project managers in outsourcing projects is oriented toward external roles.

According to this line of reasoning, we should expect that the most external roles (monitor and liaison) are more emphasized and important among project managers in outsourcing projects than among project managers in internal IT projects. From the discussion, we propose the following hypotheses:

H2: External roles are more important in outsourcing projects than in internal IT projects.

H2a: The liaison role is more important in outsourcing projects than in internal IT projects.

H2b: The monitor role is more important in outsourcing projects than in internal IT projects.

The last two management roles defined by Mintzberg (1994) — spokesman and entrepreneur — are somewhat difficult to classify in our research context, since they are external to the IT department/IT project and internal to the organization.

However, according to Grover et al. (1993) we should to some degree expect that the role of spokesman (with internal orientation to the organization and other departments) to be more emphasized by project managers in internal IT projects than project managers in outsourcing projects. The role of spokesman is a management role that incorporates activities that require the project manager to extend organizational interactions outside the department to other areas of the organization and top executives as well. Frequently, the spokesman must communicate across traditional departmental boundaries and become involved in matters concerning production, distribution, marketing, and finance. The spokesman role requires that the project manager acts as an information disseminator and politician (Inkpen & Tsang, 2005), ensuring that IT projects are properly connected to the top level of the firm and to key decision-makers in other departments. Hence, we propose the following hypothesis:

H3: The spokesman role is more important in internal IT projects than in outsourcing projects.

According to Frame (1995), the clients' and users' needs are the driving force behind projects. If articulating needs is done insufficiently, the project will be built on a poor foundation and major problems will arise when implementing the changes. As an entrepreneur, it is the project manager's role in outsourcing projects to identify the users' needs and develop a fully acceptable solution. This project management role is further emphasized by Edum-Fotwe and McCaffer (2000), who state that the project manager is required to provide innovative solutions, as well as the business processes involved in the achievement of the project's outcome.

Client consultation, communication, listening, feedback activity, and client acceptance are critical project success factors (Bahli & Rivard, 2005). We will therefore expect that the role of entrepreneur is more emphasized by project managers in outsourcing projects than project managers in internal IT projects. Hence, the fourth hypothesis is as follows:

H4: The entrepreneur role is more important in outsourcing projects than in internal IT projects.

The Grover et al. (1993) instrument, which operationalized the managerial roles identified by Mintzberg (1994) and adapted them to the IT context, was used as a basis to investigate the roles in internal IT projects and outsourcing projects. The rationale for choosing this instrument was based upon the high validity and reliability they and others have obtained within each of the managerial roles.

The present study consists of two surveys conducted in Norway in 2002/2004 to investigate the leadership roles. The survey instrument contains six five-point Likert scales, and the respondent is asked to rate the importance of each item as it relates to the management role.

The first questionnaire focused on the internal IT project and was mailed to 673 companies selected from the listing of members of the Norwegian Computing Society. It was assumed that these firms would tend to have internal IT projects and project managers with job attributes consistent with our management role classification. Based on the availability of correct addresses, 591 questionnaires reached their destinations. Questionnaires with incomplete responses were deleted. After two mailings, a total sample of 80 was returned, representing a response rate of 14%.

The second questionnaire focused on outsourcing projects. It was distributed at an internal seminar for project managers in IT outsourcing projects. Eighty-four responses were received.

In both surveys, the objective of the study was explained and respondents were assured of the confidentiality of their answers. We have no indications of non-response bias. There is little reason to suspect that non-responding project managers perceived their firm or project differently than those project managers who did respond, since the respondents included all sectors within the industry and the public sector.

Leadership Roles Research

Figures 3.2 to 3.9 contain the results of statistical analysis (both descriptive statistics and ANOVA) of the comparisons between internal IT projects and outsourcing projects (Gottschalk & Karlsen, 2005).

Figure 3.2 shows descriptive statistics regarding management roles in internal IT projects, where the response scale ranged from 1 to 5 (1 = not important and 5 = very important). Means and t-tests (to assess statistical significance of the difference between two independent sample means) were used to examine the data from the survey. *(Please note that these are interesting findings from an academic perspective, but they are less relevant for a practitioner CIO trying to understand how to become a CEO. If you are not interested, you can skip the rest of this chapter.)*

As can be seen from Figure 3.2, project managers in internal IT projects emphasize the internal roles — personnel leader and resource allocator — as the most important management roles. The management roles of monitor and liaison, which have a focus outside the project and base organization, are the least important roles. Using a t-test procedure, we found that there are 13 significant differences between the management roles. Most interesting is the fact that the personnel leader role is significantly more important than all the other management roles. From Figure 3.2 we can observe that the internal management role of personnel leader is considered to be significantly more important than the two external roles — monitor (t = 9.12, p = 0.00) and liaison (t = 8.22, p = 0.00). Statistical analysis also indicates that the resource allocator role is significantly more important than the monitor role (t = 6.33, p = 0.00) and the liaison role (t = 5.63, p = 0.00).

Figure 3.3 shows the descriptive statistics for project managers in IT outsourcing projects. As we can see, project managers in outsourcing projects chose the spokes-

Figure 3.2. Statistics for internal IT projects

Leadership	Mean	t-values				
		2	3	4	5	6
1 Personnel leader	4.33	2.65*	2.56*	4.38**	8.22**	9.12**
2 Resource allocator	4.04		0.30	2.20*	5.63**	6.33**
3 Spokesman	4.00			2.04*	4.88**	5.79**
4 Entrepreneur	3.70				2.30*	4.45**
5 Liaison	3.34					-1.54
6 Monitor	3.11					

*Note: The statistical significance of the t-values is ** for p<.01 and * for p<.05.*

Figure 3.3. Statistics for IT outsourcing projects

Leadership role	Mean	t-values				
		2	3	4	5	6
1 Personnel leader	3.29	-1.76	-4.03**	-2.23*	0.37	0.06
2 Resource allocator	3.59		-2.41*	-0.97	1.81	1.66
3 Spokesman	4.04			1.61	4.70**	4.59**
4 Entrepreneur	3.77				2.83**	3.03**
5 Liaison	3.28					0.35
6 Monitor	3.23					

*Note: The statistical significance of the t-values is ** for p<.01 and * for p<.05.*

man role as a top priority role. A t-test between the six different leadership roles gives seven significant t-values. The results indicate that the spokesman role is significantly more important than the other roles. Surprisingly, the liaison and monitor roles, which focus on contacts and personal relationships with people outside the project and scanning of the external environment, are given lowest priority.

The statistical technique used for testing the research hypotheses was the univariate analysis of variance (ANOVA). The principal consideration in the use of the two-group ANOVA is the sample size in each of the groups. In this study, one group had 80 responses, while the other group had 84 responses. Testing of the assumptions for using ANOVA was conducted and the criteria were met.

Hypothesis 1 examines whether project managers in internal IT projects are more internally oriented than project managers in outsourcing projects. This hypothesis had two sub-hypotheses (H1a and H1b).

In Figure 3.4, statistical results of the test of hypothesis H1a are shown. The analysis of variance (ANOVA) gives sufficient statistical evidence to conclude that project managers in internal IT projects emphasize the leader role significantly more than

Figure 3.4. Analysis of variance: personnel leader role

Source	DF	SS	MS	F	P
Factor	1	43.25	43.25	37.85**	0.00
Error	162	185.11	1.14		
Total	163	228.36			

*Note: The statistical significance of the F-values is ** for p<0.01 and * for p<0.05.*

Figure 3.5. Analysis of variance: resource allocator role

Source	DF	SS	MS	F	P
Factor	1	7.95	7.95	8.41**	0.00
Error	160	151.12	0.95		
Total	161	159.07			

*Note: The statistical significance of the F-values is ** for p<0.01 and * for p<0.05.*

project managers in outsourcing projects. The hypothesis is supported (F = 37.85, p = 0.00).

The statistical test of hypothesis H1b is shown in Figure 3.5. As we can see from the data, project managers in internal IT projects emphasize the resource allocator role significantly more than project managers in outsourcing projects. The hypothesis is significant at the 0.01 level of significance (F = 8.41, p = 0.00).

The second main hypothesis (H2) proposed in this section was whether project managers in outsourcing projects are more externally oriented than project managers in internal IT projects. The main hypothesis was de-composed into two sub-hypotheses (H2a and H2b).

The results of the ANOVA analysis of hypothesis H2a are presented in Figure 3.6. The hypothesis is not supported (F = 0.42, p = 0.52).

The results of the testing of hypothesis H2b are shown in Figure 3.7. The results conclude that project managers in outsourcing projects do not emphasize the monitor role significantly more than project managers in internal IT projects. Thus, the hypothesis is not supported (F = 0.95, p = 0.33).

Hypothesis 3 examines whether the spokesman role is more important in internal IT projects than in outsourcing projects. Figure 3.8 displays that this hypothesis did not find support (F = 0.19, p = 0.66).

Figure 3.6. Analysis of variance: liaison role

Source	DF	SS	MS	F	P
Factor	1	0.54	0.54	0.42	0.52
Error	161	208.48	1.30		
Total	162	209.02			

*Note: The statistical significance of the F-values is ** for p<0.01 and * for p<0.05.*

Figure 3.7. Analysis of variance: monitor role

Source	DF	SS	MS	F	P
Factor	1	1.20	1.20	0.95	0.33
Error	161	203.12	1.26		
Total	162	204.32			

*Note: The statistical significance of the F-values is ** for p<0.01 and * for p<0.05.*

Hypothesis 4 examines whether the entrepreneur role is more important in outsourcing projects than in internal IT projects. Figure 3.9 displays that this hypothesis did not find support (F = 0.05, p = 0.82).

To summarize, we have illustrated the importance of each management role in Figure 3.10. The first number is the mean score of project managers in internal IT projects, while the second number is the mean score of project managers in outsourcing projects. The response scale ranged from 1 to 5 (1 = not important and 5 = very important). The statistical significant values are shown with ** for p<0.01 and * for p<0.05.

Figure 3.8. Analysis of variance: entrepreneur role

Source	DF	SS	MS	F	P
Factor	1	0.25	0.25	0.19	0.66
Error	161	205.41	1.28		
Total	162	205.66			

*Note: The statistical significance of the F-values is ** for p<0.01 and * for p<0.05.*

Figure 3.9. Analysis of variance: spokesman role

Source	DF	SS	MS	F	P
Factor	1	0.05	0.05	0.05	0.82
Error	162	164.89	1.02		
Total	163	164.94			

*Note: The statistical significance of the F-values is ** for p<0.01 and * for p<0.05.*

Figure 3.10. Leadership roles (statistical results for internal versus outsourcing projects)

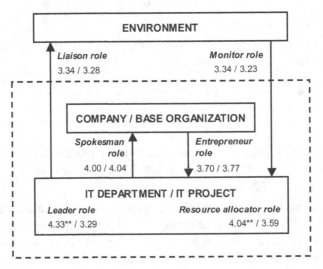

References

Bahli, B., & Rivard, S. (2005). Validating measures of information technology outsourcing risk factors. *Omega, 22,* 175-187.

CSC. (1996). *New IS leaders.* CSC Index Research, Computer Science Corporation, UK: London.

Earl, M. (2000, March-April). Are CIOs obsolete? *Harvard Business Review*, p. 60.

Edum-Fotwe, F. T., & McCaffer, R. (2000). Developing project management competency: Perspectives from the construction industry. *International Journal of Project Management, 18*(2), 111-124.

Frame, J. D. (1995). *Managing projects in organizations.* San Francisco: Jossey-Bass Publishers.

Gottschalk, P. (2005). *Strategic knowledge management technology.* Hershey, PA: Idea Group Publishing.

Gottschalk, P. (2006). *E-business strategy, sourcing and governance.* Hershey, PA: Idea Group Publishing.

Gottschalk, P., & Karlsen, J. T. (2005). A comparison of leadership roles in internal IT projects versus outsourcing projects. *Industrial Management & Data Systems, 105*(9), 1137-1149.

Grover, V., Jeong, S. R., Kettinger, W. J., & Lee, C. C. (1993). The chief information officer: A study of managerial roles. *Journal of Management Information Systems, 10*(2), 107-130.

Kern, T., & Willcocks, L. P. (2002). Exploring relationship in information technology outsourcing: The interaction approach. *European Journal of Information Systems, 11*, 3-19.

Ko, D. G., Kirsch, L. J., & King, W. R. (2005). Antecedents of knowledge transfer from consultants to clients in enterprise system implementations. *MIS Quarterly, 29*(1), 59-85.

Koh, C., Ang, S., & Straub, D. W. (2004). IT outsourcing success: A psychological contract perspective. *Information Systems Research, 15*(4), 356-373.

Lee, J. N., Miranda, S. M., & Kim, Y. G. (2004). IT outsourcing strategies: Universalistic, contingency, and configurational explanations of success. *Information Systems Research, 15*(2), 110-131.

Levina, N., & Ross, J. W. (2003). From the vendor's perspective: Exploring the value proposition in information technology outsourcing. *MIS Quarterly, 27*(3), 331-364.

Maruca, R. F. (2000, March-April). Are CIOs obsolete? *Harvard Business Review*, pp. 55-63.

Mintzberg, H. (1994). Rounding out the manager's job. *Sloan Management Review, 36*(1), 11-26.

Murch, R. (2000). *Project management: Best practices for IT Professionals.* New York: Prentice Hall.

Willcocks, L. P., Hindle, J. L., Feeny, D. F., & Lacity, M. C. (2004, Summer). IT and business process outsourcing: The knowledge potential. *Information Systems Management*, 7-15.

Chapter IV

Theories
of the Firm

Introduction

In this book, we need to develop a general understanding of business firms to enable strategic IS/IT planning. In this chapter, we will present the resource-based theory of the firm, the activity-based theory of the firm, and the firm in terms of its value configuration.

An understanding of firm theories and value configurations is important to later discussions of the topics in the book. The resource-based theory is applied to understand resources needed for e-business, sourcing, and governance. An important resource is knowledge in terms of know-what, know-how, and know-why.

Resource-Based Theory of the Firm

According to the resource-based theory of the firm, performance differences across firms can be attributed to the variance in the firm's resources and capabilities. Resources that are valuable, unique, and difficult to imitate can provide the basis for firms' competitive advantages. In turn, these competitive advantages produce positive returns. According to Hitt, Bierman, Shimizu, and Kochhar. (2001), most of the few empirical tests of the resource-based theory that have been conducted have supported positive, direct effects of resources. An important and often critical resource is IS/IT applications in the firm.

The essence of the resource-based theory of the firm lies in its emphasis on the internal resources available to the firm, rather than on the external opportunities and threats dictated by industry conditions. Firms are considered to be highly heterogeneous, and the bundles of resources available to each firm are different. This is both because firms have different initial resource endowments and because managerial decisions affect resource accumulation and the direction of firm growth as well as resource utilization (Loewendahl, 2000).

The resource-based theory of the firm holds that, in order to generate sustainable competitive advantage, a resource must provide economic value and must be presently scarce, difficult to imitate, non-substitutable, and not readily obtainable in factor markets. This theory rests on two key points. First, resources are the determinants of firm performance. Second, resources must be rare, valuable, difficult to imitate, and non-substitutable by other rare resources. When the latter occurs, a competitive advantage has been created (Priem & Butler, 2001).

Resources can simultaneously be characterized as valuable, rare, non-substitutable, and inimitable. To the extent that an organization's physical assets, infrastructure, and workforce satisfy these criteria, they qualify as resources. A firm's performance depends fundamentally on its ability to have a distinctive, sustainable competitive advantage, which derives from the possession of firm-specific resources (Priem & Butler, 2001).

The resource-based theory is a useful perspective in strategic management. Research on the competitive implications of such firm resources as knowledge, learning, culture, teamwork, and human capital was given a significant boost by resource-based theory — a theory that indicated it was these kinds of resources that were most likely to be sources of sustainable competitive advantage for firms (Barney, 2001).

Firms' resource endowments, particularly intangible resources, are difficult to change except over the long term. For example, although human resources may be mobile to some extent, capabilities may not be valuable for all firms or even for their competitors. Some capabilities are based on firm-specific knowledge, and others are valuable when integrated with additional individual capabilities and specific firm resources. Therefore, intangible resources are more likely than tangible resources to produce a competitive advantage. In particular, intangible, firm-specific resources such as knowledge allow firms to add value to incoming factors of production (Hitt et al., 2001).

Resource-based theory attributes advantage in an industry to a firm's control over bundles of unique material, human, organizational, and locational resources and skills that enable unique value-creating strategies. A firm's resources are said to be a source of competitive advantage to the degree that they are scarce, specialized, appropriable, valuable, rare, and difficult to imitate or substitute.

A special branch of resource-based theory is resource-advantage theory. Resource-advantage theory is a moderately socialized and embedded theory of competition that draws on and is applied by several disciplines including economics, management, and marketing. The theory recognizes social structures and social relations that affect competition and therefore financial performance. It is a general theory of competition that describes the process of competition. Competition is a process, not a result. At its core, resource-advantage theory combines heterogeneous demand theory with the resource-based theory of the firm (Hunt & Arnett, 2003).

We will return to the topic of resources when we discuss the CIO's strategic resource mobilization later in this book.

Activity-Based Theory of the Firm

The resource-based theory of the firm grew out of efforts to explain the growth of firms. Although its origins lay primarily in economics, researchers in strategy have developed the resource-based theory. The main attraction of the resource-based theory is that it focuses on explaining why firms are different and its effect on profitability. The main tenets of the resource-based theory are that firms differ in their resource endowments that these differences are persistent, and that firm-level performance differentials can be explained by analyzing a firm's resource position. Differences in resources are seen to lead to non-replicable efficiency rents.

Sheehan (2002) discussed comparing and contrasting the resource-based theory with the activity-based theory, and his discussion is presented here.

The activity-based theory conceives the firm as a bundle of activities, while the resource-based theory conceives the firm as a bundle of resources. The resource-based theory focuses on explaining why firms create more value than others by examining differences in resource stocks. However, the resource-based theory places little or no emphasis on resource flows. The role of the production function in transforming inputs into end products (other than having the latent ability to transform) is under-conceptualized in the resource-based theory. On the other hand, the activity-based theory focuses on flows of resources in activities. It emphasizes the impact of the firm's production function on creating value, while placing little attention on differences in stocks of resources. It is implicitly assumed that all necessary inputs (resources) can be acquired from the market.

Value Configuration of the Firm

To comprehend the value that information technology provides to organizations, we must first understand the way a particular organization conducts business and how information systems affect the performance of various component activities within the organization. Understanding how firms differ is a central challenge for both theory and practice of management. For a long time, Porter's (1985) value chain was the only value configuration known to managers. Stabell and Fjeldstad (1998) have identified two alternative value configurations. A value shop schedules activities and applies resources in a fashion that is dimensioned and appropriate to the needs of the client's problem, while a value chain performs a fixed set of activities that enables it to produce a standard product in large numbers. Examples of value shops are professional service firms, as found in medicine, law, architecture, and engineering. A value network links clients or customers who are or wish to be interdependent. Examples of value networks are telephone companies, retail banks, and insurance companies.

A value configuration describes how value is created in a company for its customers. A value configuration shows how the most important business processes function to create value for customers. A value configuration represents the way a particular organization conducts business.

The Firm as a Value Chain

The best-known value configuration is the value chain (Porter, 1985). In the value chain, value is created through efficient production of goods and services based on a variety of resources. The company is perceived as a series or chain of activities. Primary activities in the value chain include inbound logistics, production, outbound logistics, marketing and sales, and service. Support activities include infrastructure, human resources, technology development, and procurement. Attention is on performing these activities in the chain in efficient and effective ways. In Figure 4.1, examples of IS/IT are assigned to primary and support activities. This figure can be used to describe the current IS/IT situation in the organization as it illustrates the extent of coverage of IS/IT for each activity.

Figure 4.1. Examples of IS/IT in the value chain

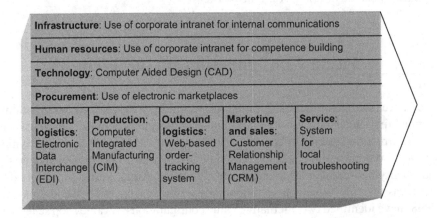

The Firm as a Value Shop

Value cannot only be created in value chains. Value also can be created in two alternative value configurations: value shop and value network (Stabell & Fjeldstad, 1998). In the value shop, activities are scheduled and resources are applied in a fashion that is dimensioned and appropriate to the needs of the client's problem, while a value chain performs a fixed set of activities that enables it to produce a standard product in large numbers. The value shop is a company that creates value by solving unique problems for customers and clients. Knowledge is the most important resource, and reputation is critical to firm success.

Typical examples of value chains are manufacturing industries such as paper and car production, while typical examples of value shops are law firms and medical hospitals. Often, such companies are called professional service firms or knowledge-intensive service firms. Like the medical hospital as a way to practice medicine, the law firm provides a standard format for delivering complex legal services. Many features of its style — specialization, teamwork, continuous monitoring on behalf of clients (patients), and representation in many forums — have been emulated in other vehicles for delivering professional services (Galanter & Palay, 1991).

Knowledge-intensive service firms are typical value shops. Sheehan (2002) defines knowledge-intensive service firms as entities that sell problem-solving services, where the solution chosen by the expert is based on real-time feedback from the client. Clients retain knowledge-intensive service firms to reduce their uncertainty. Clients hire knowledge-intensive service firms precisely because the client believes the firm knows something that the client does not and believes it is necessary to solve their problems.

While expertise plays a role in all firms, its role is distinctive in knowledge-intensive service firms. Expert, often professional, knowledge is at the core of the service provided by the type of firm.

Knowledge-intensive service firms not only sell a problem-solving service, but equally a problem-finding, problem-defining, solution-execution, and monitoring service. Problem-finding is often a key for acquiring new clients. Once the client is acquired and their problem is defined, not all problems will be solved by the firm. Rather, the firm may only clarify that there is no problem (i.e., the patient does not have a heart condition) or that the problem should be referred to another specialist (i.e., the patient needs a heart specialist). If a problem is treated within the firm, then the firm needs to follow up the implementation to ensure that the problem in fact has been solved (i.e., is the patient's heart now working properly?). This follows from the fact that there is often uncertainty in both problem diagnosis and problem resolution.

Sheehan (2002) has created a typology of knowledge-intensive service firms consisting of the following three types. First, knowledge-intensive search firms search for opportunities. The amount of value they create depends on the size of the finding or discovery, where size is measured by quality rather than quantity. Examples of search firms include petroleum and mineral exploration, drug discovery in the pharmaceutical industry, and research in the biotechnology industry. Second, knowledge-intensive diagnosis firms create value by clarifying problems. Once the problem has been identified, the suggested remedy usually follows directly. Examples of diagnosis firms include doctors, surgeons, psychotherapists, veterinarians, lawyers, auditors and tax accountants, and software support. Finally, knowledge-intensive design firms create value by conceiving new ways of constructing material or intangible artifacts. Examples of design firms include architecture, advertising, research and development, engineering design, and strategy consulting.

Knowledge-intensive service firms create value through problem acquisition and definition, alternative generation and selection, implementation of an alternative, and follow-up to see if the solution selected resolves the problem. To reflect this process, Stabell and Fjeldstad (1998) have outlined the value configuration of a value shop.

A value shop is characterized by five primary activities: problem finding and acquisition; problem-solving; choice; execution; control and evaluation (Figure 4.2). Problem-finding and acquisition involves working with the customer to determine the exact nature of the problem or need. It involves deciding on the overall plan of approaching the problem. Problem-solving is the actual generation of ideas and action (or treatment) plans. Choice represents the decision of choosing between alternatives. While the least important primary activity of the value shop in terms of

Figure 4.2. Examples of IS/IT in the value shop

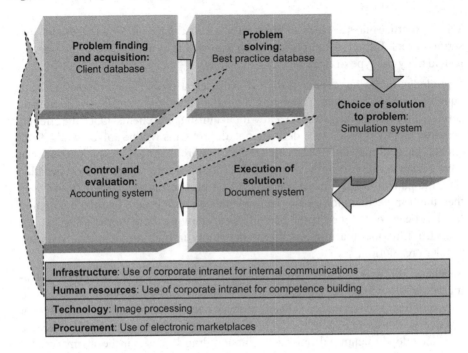

time and effort, it is also the most important in terms of customer value. Execution represents communicating, organizing, and implementing the decision, or performing the treatment. Control and evaluation activities involve monitoring and measurement of how well the solution solved the original problem or met the original need.

This may feed back into the first activity, problem-finding and acquisition, for two reasons. First, if the proposed solution is inadequate or did not work, it feeds back into learning why it was inadequate and begins the problem-solving phase anew. Second, if the problem solution was successful, the firm might enlarge the scope of the problem-solving process to solve a bigger problem related to or dependent upon the first problem being solved (Afuah & Tucci, 2003).

Figure 4.2 can be used to identify current IS/IT in the organization. We let a law firm serve as the example in Figure 4.3. Within each of the five activities, there are many tasks in a law firm. For each task, there may be IS/IT support. For example, problem-solving may consist of the two tasks of case analysis and reference search. Lawyers will be eager to discuss the case and to search more information on similar cases. A system for case-based reasoning may be installed, where the current case can be compared to similar cases handled by the law firm. Also, intelligent search

Figure 4.3. Examples of IS/IT in the value shop

Activities	Tasks	IS/IT
Problem-finding and acquisition	Register client information Register case information	Financial system Case database
Problem-solving	Do case analysis Do reference search	Case-based reasoning Library search engine
Choice	Evaluate alternatives Make recommendation to client	Case-based reasoning Office systems
Execution	Participate at meetings Revise recommendation	Office systems Office systems
Control and evaluation	Register recommendation Check client satisfaction	Case database Financial system

engines with a thesaurus may be available in the law firm to find relevant information on the Internet and in legal databases.

The Firm as a Value Network

The third and final value configuration is the value network. A value network is a company that creates value by connecting clients and customers that are, or want to be, dependent on each other. These companies distribute information, money, products, and services. While activities in both value chains and value shops are done sequentially, activities in value networks occur in parallel. The number and combination of customers and access points in the network are important value drivers in the value network. More customers and more connections create higher value to customers.

Stabell and Fjeldstad (1998) suggest that managing a value network can be compared to managing a club. The mediating firm admits members that complement each other, and in some cases exclude those that do not. The firm establishes, monitors, and terminates direct or indirect relationships among members. Supplier-customer relationships may exist between the members of the club, but to the mediating firm they are all customers.

Examples of value networks include telecommunication companies, financial institutions (e.g., banks and insurance companies), and stockbrokers. Value networks perform three activities (see Figure 4.4):

Figure 4.4. Examples of IS/IT in the value network

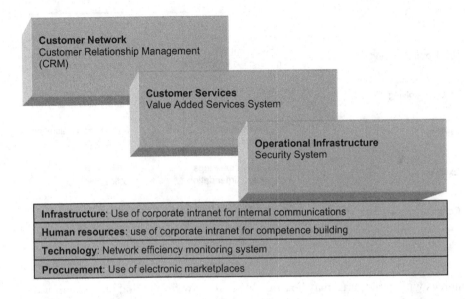

- Development of customer network through marketing and recruiting of new customers, to enable increased value for both existing customers and new customers.
- Development of new services and improvement in existing services.
- Development of infrastructure so that customer services can be provided more efficiently and effectively.

The current IS/IT situation in a value network will mainly be described through the infrastructure that typically will consist of information technology. In addition, many of the new services may be information systems that will be used by customers in their communication and business transactions with other customers. The knowledge component will mainly be found in the services of a value network, as information systems are made available to customers to exchange relevant information.

Comparison of Value Configurations

Value chain, value shop, and value network are alternative value configurations that impact the use of information technology in the company as illustrated in Figure

Figure 4.5. Characteristics of value configurations

Characteristics	Value Chain	Value Shop	Value Network
Value creation	Transformation of input to output	Solving clients and customers problems	Connecting clients and customers to each other
Work form	Sequential production	Integrated and cyclical problem-solving	Monitored and simultaneous connections
Information systems	Making production more efficient	Adding value to the knowledge work	Main value by use of IT infrastructure
Example	Paper factory	Law firm	Telecom company

4.5. While the role of IT is to make production more efficient in a value chain, IT creates added value in the value shop, while IT in the form of infrastructure is the main value in the value network. Some companies have more than one value configuration, but most companies have one dominating configuration.

In the long term, business organizations can choose to change their value configurations. A bank, for example, can be a value shop when it focuses on converting inputs to outputs. The value resides in the output and once you have the output, you can remove the production organization. This removal does not impact on the value of the output. The value shop is a solution provider. It solves problems. The input is a problem. The output is a solution to the problem. A bank that does this would view itself as a financial advisor that also has the ability to provide the money. But what it would do is identify client problems, address those problems, select a solution together with the client, and help to implement it. It would have stringent quality controls. As part of its offering, it would probably supply the client with some cash as a loan or accept some of the client's cash for investment (Chatzkel, 2002).

Or, the bank can be a value network, which is basically the logic of the marketplace. The bank would define its role as a conduit between people that do not have money and those people that do have money. What the bank does is to arrange the flow of cash between them. The bank will attract people with money to make deposits and investments. The bank also will attract people without money to make loans. As a value network, the bank will connect people with opposite financial needs. The network consists of people with different financial needs. Over time, people in the network may change status from money needer to money provider and vice versa (Chatzkel, 2002).

Both as a value shop and as a value network, the business organization can be identified as a bank. But it would have completely different consequences for what it will focus on doing well, what it will focus on doing itself, versus what it would not want to do itself. This provides a kind of strategic systems logic. It asks, "Which strategic system in terms of value configuration are we going to operate in?" Choosing an appropriate value configuration is a long-term decision with long-term consequences.

CIO in Value Configurations

The contingent approach to moving the CIO to the CEO position implies that the CEO candidacy of a CIO is dependent on the situation. One important situational factor is the value configuration of the organization. As indicated in Figure 4.5, the main purpose of information systems in the value chain is to make production more efficient. The CIO must focus on systems such as enterprise resource planning (ERP) to make a significant contribution to firm performance. The CIO becomes an expert at the operational level, including supply chain management. Unfortunately for the CIO, operational expertise will seldom be the critical qualification for the next CEO.

The main purpose of information systems in the value shop is adding value to the knowledge work. When lawyers in a law firm try to solve client problems, they look for answers in previous cases and ideas from colleagues. They search legal databases and client databases, they search electronic yellow pages to find relevant knowledge sources both internally and internally, and they apply case-based reasoning to develop tentative strategies for clients. Lawyers use information systems when they work on client cases to enable tracking by both colleagues and clients in electronic networks that are safe.

Similarly, doctors in a hospital are becoming dependent on electronic sources for medication decisions, treatment decisions, patient history, and resource availability. They accumulate knowledge by interacting with information systems. A final example of a value shop is police investigations, where detectives work on collecting information about a criminal case to develop a likely pattern that can serve as evidence in court.

In the value shop, information systems support knowledge work by adding value to the work. The value of knowledge workers increases as the value of their work increases. In the value shop, the CIO is involved in adding value based on an understanding of how knowledge workers carry out their tasks. The CIO in the value shop is close to knowledge work of professionals by providing support through knowledge management systems. In contrast to CIOs in the value chain, CIOs in the value shop are closer to the people in the organization. The CIO must relate to professionals and executives in their knowledge work. In contrast, CIOs in value chains relate to topics such as logistics, production, supply chains, and projects, which are less person-focused and more task-focused.

At this stage of reasoning about value configurations, it is risky to suggest that a CIO in a value shop is closer to becoming the next CEO, compared to a CIO in a value chain. This is so, because there are so many factors — perhaps even more important factors — that determine the candidacy. Nevertheless, ceteris paribus (everything else constant), there are indeed reasons as already outlined, that support the case that the CIO in a value shop is closer to become the next CEO.

In a well-known law firm, the CIO is also the knowledge manager of the firm. He or she is a trained lawyer. His or her background is from the legal profession, based on which the firm makes money. In addition, he or she is running the knowledge work at the organizational level. It will be no surprise to partners in the firm if this person becomes the next CEO in the firm.

Value network is the third and final alternative for the value configuration of a firm. The main purpose of information systems in a value network is to operate an efficient infrastructure. Infrastructures connect customers in banks, insurance companies, and phone operators. Working on infrastructures requires less understanding of the business compared to working on knowledge management systems, even if the work is concerned with infrastructure services rather than the infrastructure itself.

In summary, it can be argued that a CIO in a value shop is closer to becoming a candidate for the CEO position compared to a CIO in a value chain or a value network.

References

Barney, J. B. (2001). Is the resource-based "view" a useful perspective for strategic management research? Yes. *Academy of Management Review, 26*(1), 41-56.

Chatzkel, J. (2002). A conversation with Göran Roos. *Journal of Intellectual Capital, 3*(2), 96-117.

Galanter, M., & Palay, T. (1991). *Tournament of lawyers. The transformation of the big law firms*. Chicago: The University of Chicago Press.

Hitt, M. A., Bierman, L., Shimizu, K., & Kochhar, R. (2001). Direct and moderating effects of human capital on strategy and performance in professional service firms: A resource-based perspective. *Academy of Management Journal, 44*(1), 13-28.

Hunt, S. D., & Arnett, D. B. (2003, Winter). Resource-advantage theory and embeddedness: Explaining r-a theory's explanatory success. *Journal of Marketing Theory and Practice*, 1-17.

Loewendahl, B. R. (2000). *Strategic management of professional service firms* (2nd ed.). Copenhagen, Denmark: Copenhagen Business School Press.

Porter, M. E. (1985). *Competitive strategy*. New York: The Free Press.

Priem, R. L., & Butler, J. E. (2001). Is the resource-based view a useful perspective for strategic management research? *Academy of Management Review, 26*(1), 22-40.

Sheehan, N. T. (2002, April). *Reputation as a driver in knowledge-intensive service firms*. Series of Dissertations, Norwegian School of Management, Sandvika, Norway.

Chapter V

The CIO's Strategic IT Resources

Introduction

The CIO can be found at different hierarchical levels in the organization. The CEO is assigned as the only member at level 1. Level 2 includes the most senior executives, and a number of them may sit on a firm's board of directors. Their job titles include chief operating officer, chief financial officer, president, and division president. Level 3 includes the next tier of executives, such as senior and executive vice presidents. Level 4 includes higher-level vice presidents.

The CIO is typically found at level 2, 3, or 4. One of the determinants of hierarchical position is resource allocation. Generally, executives in functional positions associated with larger strategic resource allocations will be at a higher executive level than other executives in their firm. They also will receive greater cash compensation (Carpenter & Wade, 2002). Being at a higher executive level makes a CIO a more possible internal candidate for the position of the firm's CEO (Zhang & Rajagopalan, 2003). Hence, the CIO will improve his or her chances of becoming the next CEO by mobilizing strategic resources.

Resource-Based Firm Performance

As introduced earlier in this book, performance differences across firms can be attributed to the variance in the firms' resources and capabilities. The essence of the resource-based theory of the firm lies in its emphasis on the internal resources available to the firm, rather than on the external opportunities and threats dictated by industry conditions. A firm's resources are said to be a source of competitive advantage to the degree that they are scarce, specialized, appropriable, valuable, rare, and difficult to imitate or substitute.

A fundamental idea in resource-based theory is that a firm must continually enhance its resources and capabilities to take advantage of changing conditions. Optimal growth involves a balance between the exploitation of existing resource positions and the development of new resource positions. Thus, a firm would be expected to develop new resources after its existing resource base has been fully utilized. Building new resource positions is important if the firm is to achieve sustained growth. When unused productive resources are coupled with changing managerial knowledge, unique opportunities for growth are created (Pettus, 2001).

The term resource is derived from Latin, *resurgere*, which means "to rise" and implies an aid or expedient for reaching an end. A resource implies a potential means to achieve an end, or as something that can be used to create value. The first strategy textbooks outlining a holistic perspective focused on how resources needed to be allocated or deployed to earn rents. For a long time, the interest in the term was linked to the efficiency of resource allocation, but this focus has later been expanded to issues such as resource accumulation, resource stocks, and resource flows (Haanaes, 1997).

The resource-based theory prescribes that firm resources are the main driver of firm performance. The resources to conceive, choose, and implement strategies are likely to be heterogeneously distributed across firms, which in turn are posited to account for the differences in firm performance. This theory posits that firm resources are rent yielding, when they are valuable, rare, imperfectly imitable, and non-substitutable. Moreover, resources tend to survive competitive imitation because of isolating mechanisms such as causal ambiguity, time-compression diseconomies, embeddedness, and path dependencies (Ravichandran & Lertwongsatien, 2005).

Firms develop firm-specific resources and then renew these to respond to shifts in the business environment. Firms develop dynamic capabilities to adapt to changing environments. According to Pettus (2001), the term dynamic refers to the capacity to renew resource positions to achieve congruence with changing environmental conditions. A capability refers to the key role of strategic management in appropriately adapting, integrating, and reconfiguring internal and external organizational skills, resources, and functional capabilities to match the requirements of a changing environment.

If firms are to develop dynamic capabilities, learning is crucial. Change is costly; therefore, the ability of firms to make necessary adjustments depends upon their ability to scan the environment to evaluate markets and competitors and to quickly accomplish reconfiguration and transformation ahead of competition. However, history matters. Thus, opportunities for growth will involve dynamic capabilities closely related to existing capabilities. As such, opportunities will be most effective when they are close to previous resource use (Pettus, 2001).

According to Johnson and Scholes (2002), successful strategies are dependent on the organization having the strategic capability to perform at the level that is required for success. So, the first reason why an understanding of strategic capability is important is concerned with whether an organization's strategies continue to fit the environment in which the organization is operating and the opportunities and threats that exist. Many of the issues of strategy development are concerned with changing a strategic capability better to fit a changing environment. Understanding strategic capability is also important from another perspective. The organization's capability may be the leading edge of strategic developments, in the sense that new opportunities may be created by stretching and exploiting the organization's capability either in ways which competitors find difficult to match or in genuinely new directions, or both. This requires organizations to be innovative in the way they develop and exploit their capability.

In this perspective, strategic capability is about providing products or services to customers that are valued — or might be valued in the future. An understanding of what customers value is the starting point. The discussion then moves to whether an organization has the resources to provide products and services that meet these customer requirements.

A resource is meant to be anything that could be thought of as a human or non-human strength of a given firm. More formally, a firm's resources at a given time can be defined as those (tangible and intangible) assets that are tied to the firm over a substantial period of time. Examples of resources are brand names, in-house knowledge of technology, employment of skilled personnel, trade contracts, machinery, efficient procedures, capital, and so forth. According to the economic school, resources include human capital, structural capital, relational capital, and financial capital.

Priem and Butler (2001) find it problematic that virtually anything associated with a firm can be a resource, because this notion suggests that prescriptions for dealing in certain ways with certain categories of resources might be operationally valid, whereas other categories of resources might be inherently difficult for practitioners to measure and manipulate. One example of a resource that might be difficult to measure and manipulate is tacit knowledge. Some have argued for tacit knowledge — that understanding gained from experience but that sometimes cannot be expressed to another person and is unknown to oneself — as a source of competitive advantage. In this sense, tacit knowledge is unknown to its owner until it emerges in a situation of knowledge application.

Another example is the "CEO resources." Prescriptions have been made to top managers of poorly performing firms that they are the cause of the problem and should think about voluntarily exiting the firm. This is a case where viewing CEOs as resources would have more prescriptive implications for boards of directors than for the CEOs themselves. Similarly, viewing boards of directors as resources would have more prescriptive implications for the CEOs who appoint boards or the governments that regulate them than the boards themselves. Thus, some resources may be of less interest to strategy than others, depending in part on whether the resource can be manipulated and in part on the group — frequently CEOs — for whom prescriptions are desired. Identifying specific resources that may be particularly effective for certain actors in certain contexts might be a helpful first step in establishing boundaries for (and contributions of) the resource-based view in strategic management (Priem & Butler, 2001).

Characteristics of Strategic Resources

Barney (2002) discusses how value, rarity, non-duplication, and organization can be brought together into a single framework to understand the return potential associated with exploiting any of a firm's resources and capabilities. The framework consists of the following five steps (Barney, 2002):

1. If a resource or capability controlled by a firm is *not valuable*, that resource will not enable a firm to choose or implement strategies that exploit environmental opportunities or neutralize environmental threats. Organizing to exploit this resource will increase a firm's costs or decrease its revenues. These types of resources are weaknesses. Firms will either have to fix these weaknesses or avoid using them when choosing and implementing strategies. If firms do exploit these kinds of resources and capabilities, they can expect to put themselves at a competitive disadvantage compared to firms that either do not possess these non-valuable resources or do not use them in conceiving and implementing strategies. Firms at a competitive disadvantage are likely to earn below-normal economic profits.

2. If a resource or capability is *valuable but not rare*, exploiting this resource in conceiving and implementing strategies will generate competitive parity and normal economic performance. Exploiting these valuable-but-not-rare resources will generally not create above-normal economic performance for a firm, but failure to exploit them can put a firm at a competitive disadvantage. In this sense, valuable-but-not-rare resources can be thought of as organizational strengths.

3. If a resource or capability is *valuable and rare but not costly to imitate (duplicate)*, exploiting this resource will generate a temporary competitive advantage for a firm and above-normal economic profits. A firm that exploits this kind of resource is, in an important sense, gaining a first-mover advantage, because it is the first firm that is able to exploit a particular resource. However, once competing firms observe this competitive advantage, they will be able to acquire or develop the resources needed to implement this strategy through direct duplication or substitution at no cost disadvantage compared to the first-moving firm. Over time, any competitive advantage that the first mover obtained would be competed away as other firms imitate (duplicate or replicate) the resources needed to compete. However, between the time a firm gains a competitive advantage by exploiting a valuable and rare but imitable resource or capability, and the time that competitive advantage is competed away through imitation, the first-moving firm can earn above-normal economic performance. Consequently, this type of resource or capability can be thought of as an organizational strength and distinctive competence.

4. If a resource is *valuable, rare, and costly to imitate*, exploiting this resource will generate a sustained competitive advantage and above-normal economic profits. In this case, competing firms face a significant cost disadvantage in imitating a successful firm's resources and capabilities, and thus cannot imitate this firm's strategies. This advantage may reflect the unique history of the successful firm, causal ambiguity about which resources to imitate, or the socially complex nature of these resources and capabilities. In any case, attempts to compete away the advantages of firms that exploit these resources will not generate above-normal or even normal performance for imitating firms. Even if these firms are able to acquire or develop the resources and capabilities in question, the very high costs of doing so would put them at a competitive disadvantage compared to the firm that already possessed the valuable, rare, and costly to imitate resources. These kinds of resources and capabilities are organizational strengths and sustainable distinctive competencies.

5. The question of organization operates as an adjustment factor in the framework. If a firm with a resource that is *valuable, rare, and costly to imitate is disorganized*, some of its potential above-normal return could be lost. If the firm completely fails to organize itself to take advantage of this resource, it could actually lead the firm that has the potential for above-normal performance to earn normal or even below-normal performance.

Barney (2001) discusses how value and rarity of resources can be determined. *Value* is a question of conditions under which resources will and will not be valuable. Models of the competitive environment within which a firm competes can determine value. Such models fall into two large categories: (1) efforts to use structure-conduct-performance-based models to specify conditions under which different firm resources will be valuable; (2) efforts to determine the value of firm resources that apply other models derived from industrial organization models of perfect and imperfect competition.

As an example of resource value determination, Barney (2001) discusses the ability of a cost leadership strategy to generate sustained competitive advantage. Several firm attributes may be associated with cost leadership, such as volume-derived economies of scale, cumulative volume-derived learning curve economies, and policy choices. These firm attributes can be shown to generate economic value in at least some market settings. The logic used to demonstrate the value of these attributes is a market structure logic that is consistent with traditional microeconomics. After identifying the conditions under which cost leadership can generate economic value, it is possible to turn to the conditions under which cost leadership can be a source of competitive advantage (i.e., rare) and sustained competitive advantage (i.e., rare and costly to imitate).

The resource-based theory postulates that some resources will have a higher value for one firm than for other firms. The reasons why the value of resources may be firm-specific are multiple and include the experience of working together as a team, the firm possessing superior knowledge about its resources, the bundling of the resources, and the existence of co-specialized or complementary assets (Haanaes, 1997).

The value of a given resource may change over time as the market conditions change, for example, in terms of technology, customer preferences, or industry structure. Thus, it is often argued that firms need to maintain a dynamic, as opposed to static, evaluation of the value of different resources.

Rarity is a question of how many competing firms possess a particular valuable resource. If only one competing firm possesses a particular valuable resource, then that firm can gain a competitive advantage, that is, it can improve its efficiency and effectiveness in ways that competing firms cannot. One example of this form of testable assertion is mentioned by Barney (2001). The example is concerned with organizational culture as a source of competitive advantage. If only one competing firm possesses a valuable organizational culture (where the value of that culture is determined in ways that are exogenous to the firm), then that firm can gain a competitive advantage, that is, it can improve its efficiency and effectiveness in ways that competing firms cannot. Both these assertions are testable. If a firm uniquely possesses a valuable resource and cannot improve its efficiency and effectiveness in ways that generate competitive advantages, then these assertions are contradicted. One could test these assertions by measuring the extent to which a firm uniquely possesses valuable resources, for example, valuable organizational culture, measuring the activities that different firms engage in to improve their efficiency and effectiveness, and then seeing if there are some activities a firm with the unique culture engages in to improve its effectiveness and efficiency – activities not engaged in by other competing firms.

Efficient firms can sustain their competitive advantage only if their resources can neither be extended freely nor imitated by other firms. Hence, in order for resources to have the potential to generate rents, they must be rare. Valuable, but common, resources cannot by themselves represent sources of competitive advantage because competitors can access them. Nobody needs to pay extra for obtaining a resource that is not held in limited supply.

In addition to value and rarity, inimitability has to be determined. *Inimitability* can be determined through barriers to imitation and replication. The extent of barriers and impediments against direct and indirect imitation determine the extent of inimitability. One effective barrier to imitation is that competitors fail to understand the firm's sources of advantage. The lack of understanding can be caused by tacitness, complexity, and specificity that form bases for competitive advantage (Haanaes, 1997).

Several authors have categorized resources. A common categorization is tangibles versus intangibles. Tangibles are relatively clearly defined and easy to identify. Tangible resources include plants, technology, land, geographical location, access to raw materials, capital, equipment, and legal resources. Tangible resources tend to be property-based and also may include databases, licenses, patents, registered designs and trademarks, as well as other property rights that are easily bought and sold.

Intangibles are more difficult to define and also to study empirically. Intangible resources encompass skills, knowledge, organizational capital, relationships, capabilities, and human capital, as well as brands, company and product reputation, networks, competences, perceptions of quality, and the ability to manage change. Intangible resources are generally less easy to transfer than tangible resources, as the value of an intangible resource is difficult to measure (Haanaes, 1997).

Strategic IT Resources

The resource-based view started to appear in IT research one decade ago. Now IT resources can be compared to one another and, perhaps more importantly, can be compared with non-IT resources. Thus, the resource-based view promotes cross-functional studies through comparisons with other firm resources.

In the beginning of resource-based studies of IT resources, IT was divided into three assets, which together with processes contributed to business value. These three IT assets were labeled human assets (e.g., technical skills, business understanding, problem-solving orientation), technology assets (e.g., physical IT assets, technical platforms, databases, architectures, standards), and relationship assets (e.g., partnerships with other divisions, client relationships, top management sponsorship, shared risk, and responsibility). IT processes were defined as planning ability, cost-effective operations and support, and fast delivery. This categorization was later modified to include IT infrastructure, human IT resources, and IT-enabled intangibles.

Wade and Hulland (2004) presented a typology of IT resources, where the IT resources held by a firm can be sorted into three types of processes: inside-out, outside-in, and spanning. Inside-out resources are deployed from inside the firm in response to market requirements and opportunities, and tend to be internally focused. In contrast, outside-in resources are externally oriented, placing an emphasis on anticipated market requirements, creating durable customer relationships, and understanding competitors. Finally, spanning resources, which involve both internal and external analysis, are needed to integrate the firm's inside-out and outside-in resources.

Inside-out resources include IS infrastructure, IS technical skills, IS development, and cost-effective IS operations:

- **IT infrastructure:** Many components of the IT infrastructure (such as off-the-shelf computer hardware and software) convey no particular strategic benefit due to lack of rarity, ease of imitation, and ready mobility. Thus, the types of IT infrastructure of importance are either proprietary or complex and hard to imitate. Despite research attempts to focus on the non-imitable aspects of IT infrastructure, the IT infrastructure resource has generally not been found to be a source of sustained competitive advantage for firms.

- **IT technical skills:** IT technical skills are a result of the appropriate, updated technology skills, relating to both systems hardware and software that are held by the IS/IT employees of a firm. Such skills do not include only current technical knowledge, but also the ability to deploy, use, and manage that knowledge. Thus, this resource is focused on technical skills that are advanced, complex, and, therefore, difficult to imitate. Although the relative mobility of IS/IT personnel tends to be high, some IS skills cannot be easily transferred, such as corporate-level knowledge assets and technology integration skills, and, thus, these resources can become a source of sustained competitive advantage.

- **IT development:** IT development refers to the capability to develop or experiment with new technologies, as well as a general level of alertness to emerging technologies and trends that allow a firm to quickly take advantage of new advances. Thus, IT development includes capabilities associated with managing a systems development life cycle that is capable of supporting competitive advantage, and should therefore lead to superior firm performance.

- **Cost-effective IT operations:** This resource encompasses the ability to provide efficient and cost-effective IS operations on an ongoing basis. Firms with greater efficiency can develop a long-term competitive advantage by using this capability to reduce costs and develop a cost leadership position in their industry. In the context of IS operations, the ability to avoid large, persistent cost overruns, unnecessary downtime, and system failure is likely to be an important precursor to superior performance. Furthermore, the ability to develop and manage IT systems of appropriate quality that function effectively can be expected to have a positive impact on performance.

Outside-in resources include external relationship management and market responsiveness:

- **External relationship management:** This resource represents the firm's ability to manage linkages between the IT function and stakeholders outside the firm. It can manifest itself as an ability to work with suppliers to develop appropriate systems and infrastructure requirements for the firm, to manage relationships with outsourcing partners, or to manage customer relationships by providing solutions, support, and/or customer service. Many large IT departments rely on external partners for a significant portion of their work. The ability to work with and manage these relationships is an important organizational resource leading to competitive advantage and superior firm performance.
- **Market responsiveness:** Market responsiveness involves both the collection of information from sources external to the firm as well as the dissemination of a firm's market intelligence across departments and the organization's response to that learning. It includes the abilities to develop and manage projects rapidly and to react quickly to changes in market conditions. A key aspect of market responsiveness is strategic flexibility, which allows the organization to undertake strategic change when necessary.

Spanning resources include IS-business partnerships and IS planning and change management:

- **IS-business partnerships:** This capability represents the processes of integration and alignment between the IS function and other functional areas or departments of the firm. The importance of IS alignment, particularly with business strategy, has been well documented. This resource has variously been referred to as synergy, assimilation, and partnerships. All of these studies recognize the importance of building relationships internally within the firm between the IS function and other areas or departments. Such relationships help to span the traditional gaps that exist between functions and departments, resulting in superior competitive position and firm performance. An element of this resource is the support for collaboration within the firm.

- **IS planning and change management:** The capability to plan, manage, and use appropriate technology architectures and standards also helps to span these gaps. Key aspects of this resource include the ability to anticipate future changes and growth, to choose platforms (including hardware, network, and software standards) that can accommodate this change, and to effectively manage the resulting technology change and growth. This resource has been defined variously in previous research as "understanding the business case," "problem-solving orientation," and "capacity to manage IT change." It includes the ability of IS managers to understand how technologies can and should be used, as well as how to motivate and manage IS personnel through the change process.

From a resource-based perspective, Ravichandran and Lertwongsatien (2005) argue that IS resources that are inimitable and valuable can be rent yielding. Technology assets such as networks and databases are unlikely to be rent yielding, since they could be easily procured in factor markets. However, combining hardware and software assets to create a flexible and sophisticated IT infrastructure can be non-imitable, because creating such an infrastructure requires carefully melding technology components to fit firm needs and priorities. Skilled human resources, relationships between IS department and user department, and IS managerial knowledge are valuable resources that are posited to be rent yielding in addition to sophisticated IT infrastructure.

In order to explore the usefulness of the resource-based theory for IT resources, it is necessary to explicitly recognize the characteristics and attributes of resources that lead them to become strategically important. Although firms possess many resources, only a few of these have the potential to lead the firm to a position of sustained competitive advantage. What is it, then, that separates regular resources from those that confer a sustainable strategic benefit?

According to Wade and Hulland (2004), resource-based theorists have approached this question by identifying sets of resource attributes that might conceptually influence a firm's competitive position. Under this view, only resources exhibiting all of these attributes can lead to a sustained competitive advantage for the firm. We have already mentioned Barney's (2001) attributes of value, rareness, inimitability, non-substitutability, combination, and exploration.

In addition, an important seventh attribute is immobile. Once a firm establishes a competitive advantage through the strategic use of resources, competitors will likely attempt to amass comparable resources in order to share in the advantage. A primary source of resources is factor markets. If firms are able to acquire the resources neces-

Figure 5.1. IT resources in terms of strategic importance based on attributes

Attributes / Resources	Valuable	Rare	Exploitable	Inimitable	Non-substitutable	Combinable	Immobile	TOTAL
IT infrastructure	4	2	5	5	2	5	4	27
IT technical skills	4	2	3	3	4	4	3	23
IT development	4	3	3	3	4	3	2	22
Cost- effective IT operations	4	2	3	2	4	3	1	19

sary to imitate a rival's advantage, the rival's advantage will be short-lived. Thus, a requirement for sustained competitive advantage is that resources be imperfectly mobile or non-tradable.

To govern IT resources efficiently and effectively, it is necessary to understand the strategic attributes of each resource. Figure 5.1 shows an example of how strategic IT resources can be identified. The scale from 1 (little extent) to 5 (great extent) is applied.

In this example, we see that IT infrastructure is the IT resource with the greatest potential to lead to sustained competitive advantage, which would contradict that the IT infrastructure resource has generally not been found to be a source of sustained competitive advantage for firms. On the other hand, cost-effective IT operations have the least potential.

Wade and Hulland (2004) suggest that some of the resources create competitive advantage, while others sustain that advantage. A distinction is made between resources that help the firm attain a competitive advantage and those that help the firm to sustain the advantage. These two types of resource attributes can be thought of as, respectively, ex ante and ex post limits to competition.

Ex ante limits to competition suggest that prior to any firm establishing a superior resource position, there must be limited competition for that position. If any firm wishing to do so can acquire and deploy resources to achieve the position, it cannot by definition be superior. Attributes in this category include value, rarity, and appropriateness.

Ex post limits to competition mean that subsequent to a firm gaining a superior position and earning rents, there must be forces that limit competition for those rents. Attributes in this category include replicate ability, substitutability, and mobility.

Damianides (2005) applied a different approach to identify resources. He defined the following naturally grouped processes of IT resources: plan and organize, acquire and implement, deliver and support, and monitor and evaluate. He also developed an IT governance checklist, listing questions to ask to uncover IT issues, questions to ask to find out how management addresses the IT issues, and questions to self-assess IT governance practices.

Melville, Kraemer, and Gurbaxani (2004) developed an integrative model of IT business value to link information technology and organizational performance. In a resource-based perspective, they found that IT is a valuable resource, but the extent and dimensions are dependent upon internal and external factors, including complementary organizational resources of the firm and its trading partners, as well as the competitive and macro environment.

Similarly, Santhanam and Hartono (2003) applied resource-based theory to link information technology capability to firm performance. Their results indicate that firms with superior IT capability indeed exhibit superior current and sustained firm performance when compared to average industry performance, even after adjusting for effects of prior firm performance.

Aligning IT Resources to the Organization's Strategy

Strategic alignment includes enterprise-wide strategic planning, practical strategic planning, and the importance of the CIO's involvement as a full participant in the strategic planning process and strategic resource management. Once the executive team agrees on the strategic plan, it is the CIO's responsibility to see that the IT resources are aligned with those strategies. The CIO works to align resources to strategy on two levels: within the IT organization and its strategies, and those of the IT organization within the company as a whole. Once the strategic plan for the IT organization is in alignment with the overall company's strategic plan, the CIO aligns the IT resources to the IT organization's strategic plan and validates that alignment with the strategic plans of the peers and partners. Real alignment means that all local strategic plans support the achievement of company strategy. As an enabler of local and global strategy, the CIO and the IT organization figure as one of the company's primary strategic resources (Schubert, 2004).

Alignment is the capacity to demonstrate a positive relationship between information technologies and accepted measures of performance. The means by which alignment takes place is the allocation of resources. Understanding which and how many resources are needed and how much time is required to accomplish goals and meet commitments is key to a CIO's success and to the success of the IT organization (Schubert, 2004).

When information technology human capital is a strategic resource, its effective management represents a significant organizational capability. Ferratt, Agarwal, Brown, and Moore (2005) applied configuration theory to examine organizational practices related to the management of IT human capital. Organizations manage human capital by instituting a variety of human resource and work practices. Such practices typically include activities associated with recruiting workers with desired competencies, providing training and development opportunities, designing jobs and performance appraisal processes, developing compensation systems, and the like. Collectively, this set of practices for managing workers is an organization's configuration of human resource management (HRM) practices and is a proximal determinant of significant outcomes, such as employee turnover, job performance, job satisfaction, and firm performance.

Ferratt et al. (2005) ask the question: Given the potentially bewildering variety in practices that organizations can implement, how do CIOs make strategic choices about IT HRM practices? There are at least three choices here. One theoretical perspective, the universalistic approach, argues that there is a set of HRM practices that is effective across multiple organizational contexts regardless of situational contingencies. This best practice or high performance work system approach exhorts all firms to implement specific practices for managing workers (e.g., extensive training and incentive pay) to realize desired outcomes. A second perspective, the contingency approach, suggests that the effects of HRM practices on outcomes are moderated by a variety of contingency variables such as firm strategy. Finally, the configuration perspective focuses attention on patterns of HRM practices that exhibit nonlinear, synergistic effects on outcomes. Therefore, configuration theories focus on the identification of sets of practices, recognizing that the benefit of adopting one practice may increase with the adoption of other complementary practices.

Building on the theoretical foundation of configuration analysis and previous research in management of human capital, Ferratt et al. (2005) empirically investigated predictions about the relationship between different bundles of human resource practices and IT staff turnover rates. They developed two hypotheses regarding the relationship of IT HRM configurations to turnover. They tested these hypotheses based on a field survey of more than 100 IT organizations.

The first hypothesis suggested that organizations with a human capital-focused configuration for managing IT professionals will have significantly lower IT staff turnover rates than organizations with a task-focused configuration for managing IT professionals. This hypothesis was confirmed in the empirical study.

The second hypothesis suggested that firms with intermediate IT HRM configurations will have IT staff turnover rates higher than those firms with a human capital-focused configuration and lower than those firms with a task-focused configuration.

Intermediate configurations represent strategies for IT professionals between the extremes of short-term and long-term investment strategies. This hypothesis was not confirmed in the empirical study.

Effect of IT Resources on Firm Performance

Ravichandran and Lertwongsatien (2005) drew on resource-based theory to examine how information systems resources and capabilities affect firm performance. A basic premise was that a firm's performance could be explained by how effective the firm is in using information technology to support and enhance its core competencies. It was assumed that it is the targeted use of IS assets that is likely to be rent yielding.

Ravichandran and Lertwongsatien (2005) developed the theoretical underpinnings of this premise and proposed a model that interrelates IS resources, IS capabilities, IT support for core competencies, and firm performance. The model was empirically tested using data collected from 129 firms in the United States. The results provide strong support for the research model and suggest that variation in firm performance could be explained by the extent to which IT is used to support and enhance a firm's core competencies. The results also support the proposition that an organization's ability to use IT to support its core competencies is dependent on IS functional capabilities, which, in turn, are dependent on the nature of human, technology, and relationship resources of the IS department.

Core competencies are the basis for firms to compete in the market. Core competencies can be categorized into market-access, integrity-related, and functionality-related competencies. Market-access competencies include all those that allow a firm to be in close proximity to its customers, identify their needs effectively, and respond in a timely manner to shifts in customer needs and tastes. Examples of market-access competency include capabilities to segment and target markets precisely and tailor offerings to match the demands of customers. Integrity-related competencies include those that allow a firm to offer reliable products and services at competitive prices and deliver them with minimal inconvenience. Efficient manufacturing operations, streamlined supply chains, and integrated business processes are some indicators of integrity-related competencies. Finally, functionality-related competencies are those that enable a firm to offer unique products and services with distinctive customer benefits. This competency reflects strengths in product development and the innovation potential of an organization (Ravichandran & Lertwongsatien, 2005).

Firm competencies are developed over a period of time and reflect choices made by the organization about resource acquisition and deployment. All firms have limited IT resources and have to make choices about how these resources are deployed.

Choices that result in embedding IT within areas of critical importance to the organization are likely to yield resource bundles that are dissimilar to those of the competitors, which in turn, can be rent yielding. Embedding IT within areas of core competence makes the IS assets inimitable by making it difficult for competitors to create similar bundles of complementary IS and organizational assets as well as understand the contributions of IS assets to firm performance. Thus, other things being equal, firms that target IS initiatives toward core competencies are likely to realize greater value from their IS assets than those that are less focused in their IT deployment (Ravichandran & Lertwongsatien, 2005).

Using IT to improve activities that are integral to a firm's core competencies results in resource bundles that are unlikely to be easily imitated by competitors because of isolating mechanisms such as causal ambiguity and resource connectedness. For example, Wal-Mart's ability to perform better than most of its competitors in the retail industry is partly due to the complementarities between its business practices and its use of IT. Despite attempts by other retailers to copy Wal-Mart's IT systems, they fail to replicate its success in reaping returns from IT investment because of difficulties in understanding how IT and business capabilities interact to affect Wal-Mart's performance (Ravichandran & Lertwongsatien, 2005).

Ravichandran and Lertwongsatien's (2005) findings about causal relationship between IS capabilities and IT support for core competencies and those between IS resources and IS functional capabilities highlight the path and time dependencies involved in using IT in pursuit of firm strategies. Organizations that have successfully used IT to gain competitive advantage have been able to do so because of a history of choices about the acquisition and deployment of IS resources.

Ravichandran and Lertwongsatien's (2005) research model is illustrated in Figure 5.2. This model can serve as a basis for IS performance evaluation. By providing empirical evidence that IT support for core competencies has a positive effect on firm performance, their study highlights that CIOs have to do more than invest in the latest technologies or develop a strong IT department. The results indicate that CIOs have to clearly understand the strategic thrust of the organization and institute mechanisms to ensure that IS capabilities are channeled toward areas of importance to the organization. Among other things, this requires close interactions with business managers and the CEO to play an active role in IT deployment decisions.

Figure 5.2. Model for effect of information systems resources on firm performance

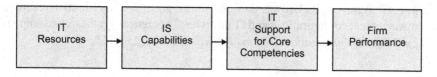

CIO in Resource Positions

A CIO trying to prepare for the CEO position will find the resource-based perspective useful. While the CEO is in the business of mobilizing strategic resources for the firm, the CIO is in a similar business of mobilizing strategic IT resources for the firm. In a law firm, the CEO is dependent on strategic knowledge resources in terms of valuable, rare, non-replicable, non-transferable, combinable, and applicable legal knowledge for firm success. Similarly, the CIO is dependent on strategic knowledge management systems based on valuable, rare, non-replicable, non-transferable, combinable, and applicable information technology resources for IT success in the firm.

Both CEO and CIO will develop resource-based strategies. For the CEO, the resource-based strategy for the firm will describe how the firm is mobilizing and combining its resources so that competitive goods and services can be produced and sold. Similarly, the CIO develops a resource-based IT strategy, which describes how information technology infrastructure and architecture enables the production of competitive goods and services for the firm.

In the resource-based theory, it is less important to understand the end products, and it is more important to understand what enables production of end products in terms of resources. In this perspective, the job of the CIO is not very different from the job of the CEO. Based on an understanding of similarities of executive positions, the CIO will find it easier to position himself or herself for the CEO job.

References

Barney, J. B. (2001). Is the resource-based "view" a useful perspective for strategic management research? Yes. *Academy of Management Review, 26*(1), 41-56.

Barney, J. B. (2002). *Gaining and sustaining competitive advantage.* Upper Saddle River, NJ: Prentice Hall.

Carpenter, M. A., & Wade, J. B. (2002). Microlevel opportunity structures as determinants of non-CEO executive pay. *Academy of Management Journal, 45*(6), 1085-1103.

Damianides, M. (2005). Sarbanse-Oxley and IT governance: New guidance on IT control and compliance. *Information Systems Management, 22*(1), 77-85.

Ferratt, T. W., Agarwal, R., Brown, C. V., & Moore, J. E. (2005). IT human resource management configurations and IT turnover: Theoretical synthesis and empirical analysis. *Information Systems Research, 16*(3), 237-255.

Haanaes, K. B. (1997). *Managing resource mobilization: Case studies of Dynal, Fiat Auto Poland and Alcatel Tecom Norway.* PhD series 9.97, Copenhagen Business School, Copenhagen, Denmark.

Johnson, G., & Scholes, K. (2002). *Exploring corporate strategy.* Harlow, Essex, UK: Pearson Education, Prentice Hall.

Melville, N., Kraemer, K., & Gurbaxani, V. (2004). Information technology and organizational performance: An integrative model of IT business value. *MIS Quarterly, 28*(82), 283-322.

Pettus, M. L. (2001). The resource-based view as a development growth process: Evidence from the deregulated trucking industry. *Academy of Management Journal, 44*(4), 878-896.

Priem, R. L., & Butler, J. E. (2001). Is the resource-based view a useful perspective for strategic management research? *Academy of Management Review, 26*(1), 22-40.

Ravichandran, T., & Lertwongsatien, C. (2005). Effect of information systems resources and capabilities on firm performance: A resource-based perspective. *Journal of Management Information Systems, 21*(4), 237-276.

Santhanam, R., & Hartono, E. (2003). Issues in linking information technology capability to firm performance. *MIS Quarterly, 27*(19), 125-153.

Schubert, K. D. (2004). *CIO survival guide: The roles and responsibilities of the chief information officer.* Hoboken, NJ: John Wiley & Sons.

Wade, M., & Hulland, J. (2004). The resource-based view and information systems research: Review, extension, and suggestions for future research. *MIS Quarterly, 28*(1), 107-142.

Zhang, Y., & Rajagopalan, N. (2003). Explaining new CEO origin: Firm versus industry antecedents. *Academy of Management Journal, 46*(3), 327-338.

Chapter VI

Corporate Strategic Management

Introduction

Over the last several decades, strategy researchers have devoted attention to the question of how corporate elites (i.e., corporate executives and directors) affect corporate strategy. The CEO as a person in position shapes the scope of the firm, while the CIO as a person in another position shapes the scope of IT in the firm. Jensen and Zajac (2004) proposed and tested the notion that while differences in individual characteristics of corporate elites may imply different preferences for particular corporate strategies such as diversification and acquisitions, these basic preferences, when situated in different agency contexts (e.g., CIO, CEO), generate very different strategic outcomes.

Strategy can simply be defined as principles, a broad-based formula, to be applied in order to achieve a purpose. These principles are general guidelines guiding the daily work to reach business goals. Strategy is the pattern of resource allocation decisions made throughout the organization. These encapsulate both desired goals and beliefs about what are acceptable and, most critically, unacceptable means for achieving them.

While the business strategy is the broadest pattern of resource allocation decisions, more specific decisions are related to information systems and information technology. IS must be seen both in a business and an IT context. IS is in the middle because IS supports the business while using IT. This will be discussed later in this book in terms of IT governance as strategic alignment.

Why is strategic IS/IT planning undertaken within business organizations? Hann and Weber (1996) see IS/IT planning as a set of activities directed toward achieving the following objectives:

1.   Recognizing organizational opportunities and problems where IS/IT might be applied successfully.

2.   Identifying the resources needed to allow IS/IT to be applied successfully to these opportunities and problems.

3.   Developing strategies and procedures to allow IS/IT to be applied successfully to these opportunities and problems.

4.   Establishing a basis for monitoring and bonding IT managers so their actions are more likely to be congruent with the goals of their superiors.

5.   Resolving how the gains and losses from unforeseen circumstances will be distributed among senior management and the IT manager.

6.   Determining the level of decision rights to be delegated to the IT manager.

Empirical studies of information systems/information technology planning practices in organizations indicate that wide variations exist. Hann and Weber (1996) found that organizations differ in terms of how much IS/IT planning they do, the planning methodologies they use, the personnel involved in planning, the strength of the linkage between IS/IT plans and corporate plans, the focus of IS/IT plans (e.g., strategic systems versus resource needs), and the way in which IS/IT plans are implemented.

It has been argued that the Internet renders strategic planning obsolete. In reality, it is more important than ever for companies to do strategic planning (Porter, 2001, p. 63):

> *Many have argued that the Internet renders strategy obsolete. In reality, the opposite is true. Because the Internet tends to weaken industry profitability without providing proprietary operational advantages, it is more important than ever for companies to distinguish themselves through strategy. The winners will be those that view the Internet as a complement to, not a cannibal of, traditional ways of competing.*

The Y model provides a coherent step-by-step procedure for development of an IS/IT strategy.

Strategic Planning

Often, strategy development is equated with strategic planning procedures. They represent the design approach to managing strategy. Such procedures may take the form of highly systematized, step-by-step, chronological procedures involving many different parts of the organization. For example, the annual strategic planning cycle in a company may follow a procedure like this:

1.   **May:** Broad strategic direction.

2.   **June:** Review of current strategy.

3.   **August:** Goals for business units.

4.   **September:** Strategies for business units.

5.   **October:** Board meeting to agree strategic plan.

6.   **November:** Board meeting to agree operational plan and budget.

Some of the key concepts in strategic planning are future thinking, controlling the future, decision-making, integrated decision-making, and a formalized procedure to produce an articulated result in the form of an integrated process of decisions. Strategic planning is the process of deciding on the projects that the organization will undertake and the approximate amount of resources that will be allocated to each program over the next several years.

Planning represents the extent to which decision-makers look into the future and use formal planning methodologies. Planning is something we do in advance of taking action, it is anticipatory decision-making. We make decisions before action is required. The focus of planning revolves around objectives, which are the heart of a strategic plan. According to Mintzberg (1994), planning has the following characteristics:

- **Planning is future thinking:** It is taking the future into account. Planning denotes thinking about the future. Planning is action laid out in advance.

- **Planning is controlling the future:** It is not just thinking about it but achieving it — enacting it. Planning is the design of a desired future and of effective ways of bringing it about. It is to create controlled change in the environment.

- **Planning is decision-making:** Planning is the conscious determination of courses of action designed to accomplish purposes. Planning are those activities which are concerned specifically with determining in advance what actions and/or human and physical resources are required to reach a goal. It includes identifying alternatives, analyzing each one, and selecting the best ones.

- **Planning is integrated decision-making:** It means fitting together ongoing activities into a meaningful whole. Planning implies getting somewhat more organized, it means making a feasible commitment around which already available courses of action get organized. This definition may seem close to the preceding one. But, because it is concerned not so much with the making of decisions as with the conscious attempt to integrate different ones, it is fundamentally different and begins to identify a position for planning.

- **Planning is a formalized procedure to produce an articulated result, in the form of an integrated system of decisions:** What captures the notion of planning above all — most clearly distinguishes its literature and differentiates its practice from other processes — is its emphasis on formalization, the systemization of the phenomenon to which planning is meant to apply. Planning is a set of concepts, procedures, and tests. Formalization here means three things: (a) to decompose, (b) to articulate, and (c) to rationalize the process by which decisions are made and integrated in organizations.

Given that this is planning, the question becomes — why do it? Mintzberg (1994) provides the following answers:

- Organizations must plan to coordinate their activities.
- Organizations must plan to ensure that the future is taken into account.
- Organizations must plan to be rational in terms of formalized planning.
- Organizations must plan to control.

Strategy is both a plan for the future and a pattern from the past, it is the match an organization makes between its internal resources and skills (sometimes collectively called competencies) and the opportunities and risks created by its external environments. Strategy is the long-term direction of an organization. Strategy is a course of action for achieving an organization's purpose. Strategy is the direction and scope of an organization over the long term, which achieves advantage for the organization through its configuration of resources within a changing environment and to fulfill stakeholder expectations (Johnson & Scholes, 2002).

Strategy as a plan is a direction, a guide, or course of action into the future, a path to get from here to there. Strategy as a pattern is a consistency in behavior over time. Strategy as a position is the determination of particular products in particular markets. Strategy as perspective is an organization's way of doing things (Mintzberg, 1994).

Strategic planning does not attempt to make future decisions, as decisions can be made only in the present. Planning requires that choices be made among possible events in the future, but decisions made in their light can be made only in the present. Once made, these decisions may have long-term, irrevocable consequences. Strategic planning has many benefits for an organization (Johnson & Scholes, 2002, p. 61):

- It can provide a structured means of **analysis and thinking** about complex strategic problems, at its best requiring managers to **question and challenge** the received wisdom they take for granted.

- It can encourage a **longer-term view** of strategy than might otherwise occur. Planning horizons vary of course. In a fast-moving consumer goods company, three- to five-year plans may be appropriate. In companies which have to take very long-term views on capital investment, such as those in the oil industry, planning horizons can be as long as 14 years (in Exxon) or 20 years (in Shell).

- It can be used as a means of **control** by regularly reviewing performance and progress against agreed objectives or previously agreed strategic direction.

- It can be a useful means of **coordination**, for example, by bringing together the various business unit strategies within an overall corporate strategy, or ensuring that resources within a business are coordinated to put strategy into effect.

- Strategic planning also may help to **communicate** intended strategy.

- It can be used as a way of involving people in strategy development, therefore, perhaps helping to create **ownership** of the strategy.

- Planning systems may provide a sense of security and logic for the organization and, in particular, management who believe they *should* be proactively determining the future strategy and exercising control over the destiny of the organization.

In the strategic planning perspective on strategy formation, strategies are intentionally designed, much as an engineer designs a bridge. Building a bridge requires a long formulation phase, including extensive analysis of the situation, the drawing up of a number of rough designs, evaluation of these alternatives, choice of a preferred design, and further detailing in the form of a blueprint. Only after the design phase has been completed do the construction companies take over and build according to plan. Characteristic of such a planning approach to producing bridges and strategies is that the entire process can be disassembled into a number of distinct steps that need to be carried out in a sequential and orderly way. Only by going through these steps in a conscious and structured manner will the best results be obtained (Wit & Meyer, 2004).

The whole purpose of strategizing is to give organizations direction, instead of letting them drift. Organizations cannot act rationally without intentions — if you do not know where you are going, any behavior is fine. By first setting a goal and then choosing a strategy to get there, organizations can get organized. A structure can be chosen, tasks can be assigned, responsibilities can be divided, budgets can be allotted, and targets can be set. Not unimportantly, a control system can be created to measure results in comparison to the plan, so that corrective action can be taken (Wit & Meyer, 2004).

Another advantage of the planning approach to strategy formation is that it allows for the formalization and differentiation of strategy tasks. Because of its highly structured and sequential nature, strategic planning lends itself well to formalization. The steps of the strategic planning approach can be captured in planning procedures to enhance and organize the strategy formation process. In such planning procedures, not all elements of strategy formation need to be carried out by one and the same person, but can be divided among a number of people. The most important division of labor is often between those formulating the plans and those implementing them (Wit & Meyer, 2004).

In many large companies the managers proposing the plans are also the ones implementing them, but deciding on the plans is passed up to a higher level. Often, other tasks are spun off as well, or shared with others, such as diagnosis (strategy department or external consultants), implementation (staff departments), and evaluation (corporate planner and controller). Such task differentiation and specialization can lead to better use of management talent, much as the division of labor has improved the field of production. At the same, having a formalized procedure allows for sufficient coordination and mutual adjustment, to ensure that all specialized elements are integrated back into a consistent organization-wide strategy (Wit & Meyer, 2004).

An important advantage of strategic planning is that it encourages long-term thinking and commitment. Strategic planning directs attention to the future. Managers making strategic plans have to take a more long-term view and are stimulated to prepare for, or even create, the future. Instead of just focusing on small steps, planning challenges managers to define a desirable future and to work toward it. Instead of wavering and opportunism, strategic planning commits the organization to a course of action and allows for investments to be made at the present that may only pay off in the long run (Wit & Meyer, 2004).

Corporate strategy is concerned with the strategic decisions at the corporate level of organizations; these decisions may affect many business units. At this level, managers are acting on behalf of shareholders, or other stakeholders, to provide services and, quite possibly, strategic guidance to business units which, themselves, seek to generate value by interacting with customers. In these circumstances, a key

Figure 6.1. Corporate strategy above other levels

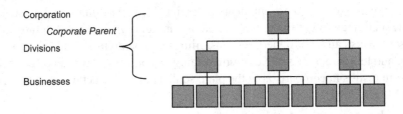

question is to what extent and how might the corporate level add value to what the businesses do; or at the least, how it might avoid destroying value (Johnson & Scholes, 2002).

A multi-business company structure may consist of a number of business units grouped within divisions and a corporate center or head office providing, perhaps, legal services, financial services, and the staff of the chief executive. There are different views as to what is meant by corporate strategy and what represents corporate at distinct from business-level strategy. Johnson and Scholes (2002) argue that anything above the business unit level represents corporate activity.

The levels of management above that of business units are often referred to as the corporate parent. So, for example, the divisions within a corporation which look after several businesses act in a corporate parenting role. The corporate parenting role can be as (Johnson & Scholes, 2002):

- **The portfolio manager:** A corporate parent acting as an agent on behalf of financial markets and shareholders with a view to enhancing the value attained from the various businesses in a more efficient or effective way than financial markets could. Their role is to identify and acquire undervalued assets or businesses and improve them.

- **The restructurer:** A corporate parent identifying restructuring opportunities in businesses and having the skills to intervene to transform performance in those businesses. They may well hold a diverse range of businesses within their portfolio. However, they do have a limited role at business-unit level, which is to identify ways in which businesses can be turned around or fitness improved and to manage the restructuring period.

- **The synergy manager:** Synergy is often seen as the main reason for the existence of the corporate parent. Potentially, synergy can occur in situations where two or more activities or processes complement each other, to the extent that their combined effect is greater than the sum of the parts. In terms of corporate strategy, the logic is that value can be enhanced across business units. This can be done in a number of ways: activities might be shared, and there may exist common skills or competences across businesses.

- **The parental developer:** A corporate parent seeks to employ its own competences as a parent to add value to its businesses. Here, the issue is not so much about how it can help create or develop benefits across business units or transference between business units, as in the case of managing synergy. Rather, parental developers have to enhance the potential of business units.

In our strategic planning perspective, corporate strategy will depend on the main role of the corporate parent. The portfolio manager is not directly intervening in the strategies of business units. Rather, they are setting financial targets, making central evaluations about the well-being and future prospects of such businesses, and investing or divesting accordingly. The restructurer is directly intervening in business units as it is likely that the business restructuring opportunities that will be sought will be those that match the skills of the corporate center. The synergy manager will initiate activities and develop resources that are shared across business units. Managers in the businesses have to be prepared to co-operate in such transference and sharing (Johnson & Scholes, 2002).

Finally, the parental developer has to enhance the potential of business units in various ways. Suppose, for example, it has a great deal of experience in globalizing domestically based businesses, or a valuable brand that may enhance the performance of image of a business, or perhaps specialist skills in financial management, brand marketing, or research and development. If such parenting competences exist, corporate managers then need to identify a parenting opportunity — a business or businesses which are not fulfilling their potential but where improvement could be made by the application of the competences of the parent (Johnson & Scholes, 2002).

Strategic management includes understanding the strategic position of an organization, strategic choices for the future, and turning strategy into action. Understanding the strategic position is concerned with the impact on strategy of the external environment, internal resources and competences, and the expectations and influence of stakeholders. Strategic choices involve understanding the underlying bases for future strategy at both the corporate and business unit levels and the options for developing strategy in terms of both the directions in which strategy might move and the methods of development. Translating strategy into action is concerned with ensuring that strategies are working in practice. A strategy is not just a good idea, a statement, or a plan. It is only meaningful when it is actually being carried out (Johnson & Scholes, 2002).

Generally, there are some characteristics of strategic decisions that are usually associated with the word strategy (Johnson & Scholes, 2002):

- Strategy is likely to be concerned with long-term direction of an organization.

- Strategic decisions are normally about trying to achieve some advantage for the organization over competition.

- Strategic decisions are likely to be concerned with the scope of an organization's activities.

- Strategy can be seen as the matching of the resources and activities of an organization to the environment in which it operates.

- Strategy also can be seen as building on or expanding an organization's resources and competences to create opportunities or to capitalize on them.

- Strategies may require major resource changes for an organization.

- Strategic decisions are likely to affect operational decisions.

- The strategy of an organization is affected not only by environmental forces and resource availability, but also by the values and expectations of those who have power in and around the organization.

The notion of *strategic fit* is developing strategy by identifying opportunities in the business environment and adapting resources and competences so as to take advantage of these. The correct *positioning* of the organization is important, for example, in terms of the extent to which it meets clearly identified market needs. *Strategic position* is concerned with the impact on strategy of the external environment, internal resources and competences, and the expectations and influence of stakeholders (Johnson & Scholes, 2002).

Strategy development is here equated with strategic planning procedures. They represent the design approach to managing strategy, which views strategy development as the deliberate positioning of the organization through a rational, analytic, structured, and directive process. *Strategy as design* is an important strategy lens. Alternative and supplementing lenses are strategy as experience and strategy as ideas. *Strategy as experience* suggests that strategies develop in an adaptive fashion and change gradually. Strategy is here understood in terms of continuity; once an organization has adopted a particular strategy, it tends to develop from and within that strategy, rather than fundamentally changing direction. *Strategy as ideas* sees strategy as the emergence of order and innovation from the variety and diversity that exists in and around an organization. New ideas and therefore innovation may come from anywhere in an organization or from stimuli in the world around it (Johnson & Scholes, 2002).

In addition to strategic planning, strategy development and strategy formation is also concerned with concepts such as strategic leadership, organizational politics, strategic incrementalism, the learning organization, imposed strategy, and multiple processes of strategy development. A *strategic leader* is an individual upon whom strategy development and change are seen to be dependent. Managers often suggest that the strategy being followed by the organization is really the outcome of *organizational politics* in terms of the bargaining and power politics that go on between important executives. Managers may have a view of where they want the organization to be in years to come and try to move toward this position incrementally, where *strategic incrementalism* can be thought of as the deliberate development of strategy by learning through doing over time. The concept of the *learning organization* and strategy as a learning process implies continual regeneration of strategy from the variety of knowledge, experience, and skills of individuals with a culture, which encourages mutual questioning and challenge around a shared purpose or vision. Forces or agencies external to the organization may cause *imposed strategy* that the organization has to follow. Different lenses and different strategy development processes may cause *multiple processes of strategy development*, since there is no right way in which strategies are developed (Johnson & Scholes, 2002).

At the beginning of this section on strategic planning, strategy was defined as a course of action for achieving an organization's purpose. Where managers have a clear understanding of their organization's purpose, this can provide strong guidance during processes of strategic thinking, strategy formation, and strategic change. The *organizational purpose* can function as a fundamental principle, against which strategic options can be evaluated. Organizational purpose can be defined as the reason for which an organization exists. The broader set of fundamental principles giving direction to strategic decision-making, of which organizational purpose is the central element, is referred to as the *corporate mission*. The corporate mission may have elements such as organizational beliefs, organizational values, and business definition (Wit & Meyer, 2004).

Some authors distinguish between deliberate strategy and emergent strategy as two alternative processes of strategy formulation. According to Christensen and Raynor (2003), *deliberate strategy*, such as strategic planning, is the appropriate tool for organizing action if three conditions are met. First, the strategy must encompass and address correctly all of the important details required to succeed, and those responsible for implementation must understand each important detail in management's deliberate strategy. Second, if the organization is to take collective action, the strategy needs to make as much sense to all employees as they view the world from their own context as it does to top management, so that they will all act appropriately and consistent. Finally, the collective intentions must be realized with little unanticipated influence from outside political, technological, and market forces.

Emergent strategy bubbles up from within the organization and is the cumulative effect of day-to-day prioritization and investment decisions made by middle managers, engineers, salespeople, and financial staff. These tend to be tactical, day-to-day operating decisions that are made by people who are not in a visionary, futuristic, or strategic state of mind (Christensen & Raynor, 2003).

Some authors distinguish between intended strategy and realized strategy. *Intended strategy* is an expression of desired strategic direction deliberately formulated and planned by managers. *Realized strategy* is the strategy actually being followed by an organization in practice. *Strategic drift* occurs when an organization's strategy gradually moves away from relevance to the forces at work in its environment. (Johnson & Scholes, 2002).

As we will see throughout this book, strategic planning procedures apply methods for analysis, choice, and implementation. A general method is available in terms of strategy maps as defined by Kaplan and Norton (2004), which represent interesting perspectives on strategy development and strategy formation. Strategy maps are used to describe how the organization creates value, and they were developed for the balanced scorecard. The strategy map is based on several principles:

- **Strategy balances contradictory forces:** Investing in intangible assets for long-term revenue growth usually conflicts with cutting costs for short-term financial performance.

- **Strategy is based on a differentiated customer value proposition:** Satisfying customers is the source of sustainable value creation.

- **Value is created through internal business processes:** The financial and customer perspectives in strategy maps and balanced scorecards describe the outcomes, that is, what the organization hopes to achieve.

- **Strategy consists of simultaneous, complementary themes:** Operations management, customer management, innovation, regulations, and societal expectations deliver benefits at different points in time.

- **Strategic alignment determines the value of intangible assets:** Human capital, information capital, and organization capital are intangible assets.

Understanding the strategic position of an organization and considering the strategic choices open to it are of little value unless the strategies managers wish to follow and can turn it into organizational action. Strategies cannot take effect until they take shape in action. Such action takes form in the day-to-day processes and relationships that exist in organizations; and these need to be managed, desirably in line with the intended strategy (Johnson & Scholes, 2002).

Translating strategies into action is no simple task. First, it is important to organize for success by introducing appropriate structure, processes, relationships, and boundaries. Second, it is important to enable success by managing people, managing information, managing finance, managing technology, and integrating resources. Finally, strategic change has to be managed by diagnosing the change situation, applying relevant styles and roles, and implementing levers for managing strategic change, such as organizational routines and symbolic processes (Johnson & Scholes, 2002).

The design school of strategic planning is built on the belief that strategy formation is a process of conception — the use of a few basic ideas to design strategy. Of these, the most essential is that of congruence, or fit, between external and organizational factors. A number of premises underlie the design school (Mintzberg, 1994):

1. Strategy formation should be a controlled, conscious process of thought.
2. Responsibility for the process must rest with the chief executive officer; that person is *the* strategist.
3. The model of strategy formation must be kept simple and informal.
4. Strategies should be unique; the best ones result from a process of creative design.
5. Strategies must come out of the design process fully developed.
6. The strategies should be made explicit and, if possible, articulated, which means they have to be kept simple.
7. Finally, once these unique, full-blown, explicit, and simple strategies are fully formulated, they must then be implemented.

Strategic Planning and Firm Performance

Numerous researchers and executives advocate strategic planning. They argue that an explicit planning process rather than haphazard guesswork results in the collection and interpretation of data critical to creating and maintaining organization-environment alignment. They argue that planning generally produces better alignment and financial results than does trial-and-error learning (Miller & Cardinal, 1994).

Despite the intuitive appeal of these arguments, several researchers have countered that explicit strategic planning is dysfunctional, or at best irrelevant. One of the most widely circulated criticisms is that planning yields too much rigidity. Proponents of the rigidity hypothesis maintain that a plan channels attention and behavior to an unacceptable degree, driving out important innovations that are not part of the plan. Given that the future parameters of even relatively stable industries are difficult to predict, these theoreticians consider any reduction in creative thinking and action dysfunctional (Miller & Cardinal, 1994).

Miller and Cardinal (1994) developed a model that might explain the inconsistent planning-performance findings reported in previous research. Results from the model suggest that strategic planning positively influences firm performance. Researchers who have concluded that planning does not generally benefit performance appear to have been incorrect.

Measurement of Competitive Strategy

The measurement of competitive strategy is an important issue in strategic management. Porter (1985) first defined three generic competitive strategies — cost leadership, differentiation, and focus. Attempts to measure these strategies seek to capture differences in the extent to which firms emphasize various competitive dimensions. Competitive strategy is traditionally measured at the business level. Yet, businesses often consist of product portfolios in which a different competitive strategy is used for each product. Thus, business-level measures may not be good indicators of product-level competitive strategy. Further, business-level analyses have found combined cost-leadership and differentiation strategies. But if competitive strategies are formulated at the product level, it is unclear whether combined strategies exist at that level.

Nayyar (1993) examined these issues. He found that business-level measures are not good indicators of product-level competitive strategies. He also found no evidence supporting the existence of combined competitive strategies at the product level. He found that cost-leadership and differentiation are mutually exclusive at the product level. They do not appear to be two dimensions of any strategy. Previously used business-level measures tend to identify combined competitive strategies, a result that may reflect the existence of product portfolios rather than combined competitive strategies.

These findings suggest a need for a re-examination of the concept of competitive strategies. It appears that firms use competitive strategies for products and then construct product portfolios to obtain overall cost, differentiation, and pre-emption advantages. Within any industry, different firms may construct different product portfolios.

In his measurement of competitive strategy, Nayyar (1993) used the following competitive dimensions associated with a cost-leadership strategy: operating efficiency, cost control, pricing below competitors, managing raw materials cost and availability, trade sales promotion, manufacturing process improvements and innovation, and product cost reduction. The following competitive dimensions were associated with a differentiation strategy: new product development; extensive customer service; building and maintaining brand equity; marketing innovation; influence over distribution channels; targeting high-priced segment(s); advertising, building, and maintaining the firm's reputation; providing product(s) with many features; and premium product quality. The following competitive dimensions were associated with a focus strategy: serving special market segment(s) and manufacturing and selling customized products.

Instead of measuring competitive strategy in terms of alternative strategies, Julien and Ramangalahy (2003) measured competitive strategy in terms of intensity. The more competitive a strategy is, the more intense the competitive strategy. The intensity was measured in terms of marketing differentiation, segmentation differentiation, innovation differentiation, and products service. Marketing differentiation is based on competitive pricing, brand development, control over distribution, advertising, and innovation in terms of marketing techniques. Segmentation differentiation relies on the ability to offer specialized products to specific customer groups. Innovation differentiation is based on the ability to offer new and technologically superior products. Product service is based on the quality of the products and services provided by customers.

Competitive strategy must drive other strategies in the firm, such as knowledge strategy. Executives must be able to articulate why customers buy a company's products or services rather than those of its competitors. What value do customers expect from the company? How does knowledge that resides in the company add value for customers? Assuming the competitive strategy is clear, managers will want to consider three further questions that can help them choose a primary knowledge management strategy (Hansen, Nohria, & Tierny, 1999):

- **Do you offer standardized or customized products?** Companies that follow a standardized product strategy sell products that do not vary much, if at all. A knowledge management strategy based on reuse fits companies that are creating standardized products.

- **Do you have a mature or innovative product?** A business strategy based on mature products typically benefits most from a reuse of existing knowledge.

- **Do your people rely on explicit or tacit knowledge to solve problems?** Explicit knowledge is knowledge that can be codified, such as simple software code and market data.

Strategic planning in a turbulent environment is challenging. The challenge of making strategy when the future is unknowable forced reconsideration of both the process of strategy formulation and the nature of organizational strategy. Attempts to reconcile systematic strategic planning with turbulent, unpredictable business environments included the following (Grant, 2003):

- **Scenario planning:** Multiple scenario planning seeks not to predict the future but to envisage alternative views of the future in the form of distinct configurations of key environmental variables. Abandoning single-point forecasts in favor of alternative futures implies forsaking single-point plans in favor of strategy alternatives, emphasizing strategic flexibility that creates option values.

- **Strategic intent and the role of vision:** If uncertainty precludes planning in any detailed sense, then strategy is primarily concerned with establishing broad parameters for the development of the enterprise with regard to domain selection and domain navigation. Uncertainty requires that strategy is concerned less with specific actions and more with establishing clarity of direction within which short-term flexibility can be reconciled with overall coordination of strategic decisions.

- **Strategic innovation:** If established companies are to prosper and survive, new external environments require new strategies. Strategic planning may be a source of institutional inertia rather than innovation. Yet, systematic approaches to strategy can be encouraging to managers to explore alternatives beyond the scope of their prior experiences. Strategic inertia may have more to do with the planners than of planning per se.

- **Complexity and self-organization:** Often faced with a constantly changing fitness landscape, maximizing survival implies constant exploration, parallel exploration efforts by different organizational members, and the combination of incremental steps. A key feature of strategic processes is the presence of semi-structures that create plans, standards, and responsibilities for certain activities, while allowing freedom elsewhere. One application of the semi-structure concept to strategy formulation concerns the use of simple rules that permit adaptation while establishing bounds that can prevent companies from falling off the edge of chaos.

Hopkins and Hopkins (1997) investigated relationships among managerial, environmental, and organizational factors, strategic planning intensity, and financial performance in US banks. The results suggested that the intensity with which banks engage in the strategic planning process has a direct, positive effect on banks' financial performance, and mediates the effects of managerial and organizational factors on banks' performance. Results also indicated a reciprocal relationship between strategic planning intensity and performance. That is, strategic planning intensity causes better performance, and, in turn, better performance causes greater strategic planning intensity.

Strategic planning takes many different forms in different organizations. However, Boyd and Reuning-Elliott's (1998) study of strategic planning provide strong support for the measurement properties of the strategic planning construct. In particular, the study results indicate that strategic planning is a construct that can be reliably measured through seven indicators: mission statement, trend analysis, competitor analysis, long-term goals, annual goals, short-term action plans, and ongoing evaluation. This evidence is important because previous researchers rarely tested for dimensionality of the planning construct, nor did most studies report tests of the reliability of their measures.

A small, entrepreneurial start-up may operate without any explicit strategy. The firm's strategy is likely to exist only in the head of the founder, and apart from being articulated through verbal communication with employees, suppliers, and other interested parties, may have been made explicit only when a business plan was required by outside investors. Most corporations with an established management structure tend to have some form of strategic planning process, though in small, single-business companies the strategy process may be highly informal, with no regular cycle, and may result in little documentation. Most larger companies, especially those with multiple businesses, have more systematic strategic planning processes, the outcome of which is a documented plan that integrates the business plans of the individual divisions (Grant, 2003).

Whether formal or informal, systematic or ad hoc, documented or not, the strategy formulation process is an important vehicle for achieving coordination within a company. The strategy process occupies multiple roles within the firm. It is in part a coordination device encouraging consistency between the decisions being made at different levels and in different parts of the organization. It also is in part a mechanism for driving performance by establishing consensus around ambitious long-term targets and by inspiring organizational members through creating vision, and a sense of mission. In these roles, the strategy process can be important in achieving both coordination and cooperation (Grant, 2003).

The system through which strategy is formulated varies considerably from company to company. Even after the entrepreneurial start-up has grown into a large company, strategy making may remain the preserve of the chief executive. Medium-sized, single-business companies typically have simple strategic planning processes where functional managers provide key inputs such as financial projections and market analysis, but the key elements of strategy — goals, new business developments, capital investment, and key competitive initiatives — are decided by the chief executive (Grant, 2003).

The more systematized strategic planning processes typical of large companies with separate divisions or business units traditionally follow an annual cycle. Strategic plans tend to be for three to five years and combine top-down initiatives (indications of performance expectations and identification of key strategic initiatives) and bottom-up business plans (proposed strategies and financial forecasts for individual divisions and business units). After discussion between the corporate level and the individual businesses, the business plans are amended and agreed and integrated into an overall corporate plan that is presented to and agreed by the board of directors (Grant, 2003).

The resulting strategic plan typically comprises the following elements (Grant, 2003):

- A statement of the goals the company seeks to achieve over the planning period with regard to both financial targets and strategic goals.

- A set of assumptions or forecasts about key developments in the external environment to which the company must respond.

- A qualitative statement of how the shape of the business will be changing in relation to geographical and segment emphasis, and the basis on which the company will be establishing and extending its competitive advantage.

- Specific action steps with regard to decisions and projects, supported by a set of mileposts stating what is to be achieved by specific dates.

- A set of financial projections, including a capital expenditure budget and outline operating budgets.

Although directed toward making decisions that are documented in written strategic plans, the important elements of strategic planning form the strategy process: the dialog through which knowledge is shared and ideas communicated, the establishment of consensus, and the commitment to action and results (Grant, 2003).

The Y Model for Strategy Work

In all kinds of strategy work, there are three steps. The first step is concerned with analysis. The second step is concerned with choice (selection and decision), while the final step is concerned with implementation.

We now introduce a model for strategy work. This is illustrated in Figure 6.2. The model consists of seven stages covering analysis, choice, and implementation. The stages are as follows (Gottschalk, 2005):

1. **Describe current situation:** The current IS/IT situation in the business can be described using several methods. The benefits method identifies benefits from use of IS/IT in the business. Distinctions are made between rationalization benefits, control benefits, organizational benefits, and market benefits. Other methods include the three-era model, management activities, and stages of growth.

2. **Describe desired situation:** The desired business situation can be described using several methods. Examples of methods are value configuration, com-

petitive strategy, management strategy, business process redesign, knowledge management, the Internet and electronic business, and information technology benefits (Gottschalk, 2005).

3. **Analyze and prioritize needs for change:** After descriptions of the current situation and the desired situation, needs for change can be identified. The gap between desired and current situation is called needs for change. Analysis is to provide details on needs, what change is needed, and how changes can take place. *What*-analysis will create an understanding of vision and goals, knowledge strategy, market strategy, and corporate problems and opportunities. *How*-analysis will create an understanding of technology trends and applications. These analyses should result in proposals for new IS/IT in the organization.

4. **Seek for alternative actions:** When needs for change have been identified and proposals for filling gaps have been developed, alternative actions for improving the current situation can be developed. New IS/IT can be developed, acquired, and implemented in alternative ways. For example, an information system can be developed in-house by company staff, it can be purchased as a standard application from a vendor, or it can be leased from an application systems provider (ASP).

5. **Select actions and make an action plan:** When needs for change and alternative actions have been identified, several choices have to be made and documented in an action plan. Important issues here include development process, user involvement, time frame, and financial budget for IS/IT projects.

6. **Implement plan and describe results:** This is the stage of action. Technical equipment such as servers, PCs, printers, and cables are installed. Operating systems are installed. Application packages, software programs, programming tools, end-user tools, and database systems are installed. Development projects are organized. Management and user training takes place. Document results over time.

7. **Evaluate results:** Implementation results are compared with needs for change. It is determined to what extent gaps between desired and current situation have been closed. This is the beginning of the IS/IT strategy revision process, where a new process through the Y model takes place. Typically, a new IS/IT strategy process should take place every other year in business organizations.

Stages 1 to 3 cover *analysis*, Stages 4 and 5 cover *choice*, and Stages 6 and 7 cover *implementation*. In some strategy models, Stage 2 is listed as the first stage. It is recommended to do Stage 1 before Stage 2. It is easier to describe the ideal situation when you know the current situation. If you start out with Stage 2, it often feels difficult and abstract to describe what you would like to achieve. Having done Stage 1 first makes the work more relevant. Stage 3 is a so-called gap analysis,

Figure 6.2. The Y model for IS/IT strategy work

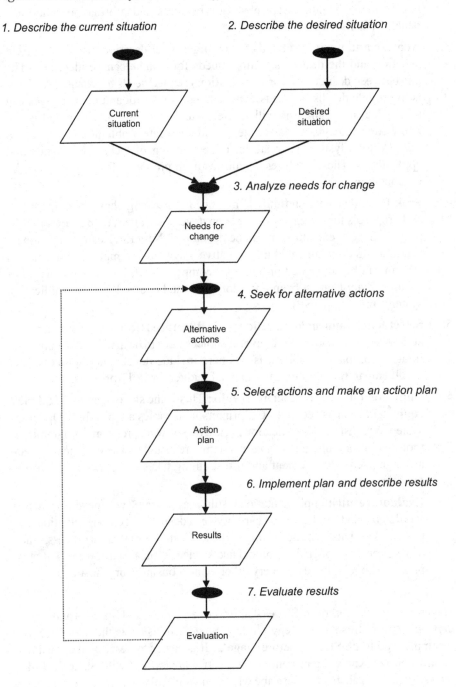

looking at the difference between the desired and actual situation. This stage also includes prioritizing. Stage 4 is a creative session as it calls for ideas and proposals for alternative actions. Stages 5 and 6 are typical planning stages. The final stage is important because we can learn from performing an evaluation.

A graphical representation of the Y model is shown in Figure 6.2, using the description technique provided earlier in this book. It is called the Y model as it looks like the letter Y. There is one feedback-arrow to compare the evaluation with the desired situation.

Resource-Based Strategy

Strategic management models traditionally have defined the firm's strategy in terms of its product/market positioning — the products it makes and the markets its serves. The resource-based approach suggests, however, that firms should position themselves strategically, based on their unique, valuable, and inimitable resources and capabilities, rather than the products and services derived from those capabilities. Resources and capabilities can be thought of as a platform from which the firm derives various products for various markets. Leveraging resources and capabilities across many markets and products, rather than targeting specific products for specific markets, becomes the strategic driver. While products and markets may come and go, resources and capabilities are more enduring.

According to Hitt, Bierman, Shimizu, and Kochhar (2001), scholars argue that resources form the basis of firm strategies and are critical in the implementation of those strategies as well. Therefore, firm resources and strategy seem to interact to produce positive returns. Firms employ both tangible resources (e.g., buildings and financial resources) and intangible resources (e.g., human capital and brand equity) in the development and implementation of strategy. Outside of natural resource monopolies, intangible resources are more likely to produce a competitive advantage because they are often rare and socially complex, thereby making them difficult to imitate.

According to Barney (2001), resource-based theory includes a very simple view about how resources are connected to the strategies a firm pursues. It is almost as though once a firm becomes aware of the valuable, rare, costly to imitate, and non-substitutable resources it controls, the actions the firm should take to exploit these resources will be self-evident. That may be true some of the time. For example, if a firm possesses valuable, rare, costly to imitate, and non-substitutable economies of scale, learning curve economies, access to low-cost factors of production, and technological resources, it seems clear that the firm should pursue a cost leadership strategy.

However, the link between resources and the strategy of a firm often will not be so obvious. Resource-based strategy has to determine when, where, and how resources may be useful. Such strategy is not obvious, since a firm's resources may be consistent with several different strategies, all with the ability to create the same level of competitive advantage. In this situation, how should a firm decide which of these several different strategies it should pursue? According to Barney (2001), this and other questions presented by Priem and Butler (2001) concerning the resource-based theory of the firm indicate that the theory is still a theory in many respects, and that more conceptual and empirical research has to be conducted to make the theory more useful to business executives who develop resource-based strategies for their firms.

Resource-based strategy is concerned with the mobilization of resources. Since perceived resources merely represent potential sources of value-creation, they need to be mobilized to create value. Conversely, for a specific resource to have value, it has to increase or otherwise facilitate value-creation. The activity whereby tangible and intangible resources are recognized, combined, and turned into activities with the aim of creating value is called resource mobilization. The term *resource mobilization* is appropriate, as it incorporates the activity-creation based on both individual and organizational resources, as well as tangibles and intangibles. According to Haanaes (1997), alternative terms such as resource allocation, resource leveraging, or resource deployment are appropriate when describing the value-creation based on tangible resources, but less so for intangibles. For example, a competence cannot be allocated, as the person controlling it has full discretion over it. Moreover, the competence can be used in different ways. An engineer can choose to work for a different organization and to work with varying enthusiasm. Also, the same engineer can choose not to utilize his or her competence at all. Thus, the term resource mobilization is meant to cover the value-creation based on all types of resources, and it recognizes that all activity creation has a human aspect.

In strategic management and organization theory, much attention has been given to the importance for the firm to reduce uncertainty and its dependence on key resources that it cannot fully control. If a large part of the resource accumulation takes place in terms of increased competences that key professionals could easily use for the benefit of other employers, priorities must be set in terms of linking these individually controlled resources to the firm. Loewendahl (2000) suggests three alternative strategies. The simplest strategy, which may be acceptable to some firms, involves minimizing the dependence on individual professionals and their personal competence. In this sense, the firm chooses to avoid the dependence on individual tangibles. A second strategy is that of linking the professionals more tightly to the firm and reducing the probability of losing them. The third alternative strategy involves increasing the organizationally controlled competence resources without reducing the individually controlled resources. Such a strategy leads to a reduction in the relative impact of individual professionals on total performance, without reducing the absolute value of their contributions. Firms that have been able to develop a high degree of organizationally controlled resources, including relational resources that are linked to the firm rather than to individual employees, are likely to be less concerned about the exit and entry of individual professionals and more concerned about the development and maintenance of their organizational resource base.

According to Maister (1993), there is a natural, but regrettable, tendency for professional firms, in their strategy development process, to focus on new things: What new markets does the firm want to enter? What new clients does the firm want to target? What new services does the firm want to offer? This focus on new services and new markets is too often a cop-out. A new specialty (or a new office location) may or may not make sense for the firm, but it rarely does much (if anything) to affect the profitability or competitiveness of the vast bulk of the firm's existing practices.

On the other hand, an improvement in competitiveness in the firm's core businesses will have a much higher return on investment since the firm can capitalize on it by applying it to a larger volume of business. Enhancing the competitiveness of the existing practice will require changes in the behavior of employees. It implies new methods of operating, new skill development, and new accountabilities. Possible strategies for being more valuable to clients can be found in answers to the following questions (Maister, 1993):

- Can we develop an innovative approach to **hiring** so that we can be more valuable to clients by achieving a higher caliber of staff than the competition?

- Can we **train** our people better than the competition in a variety of technical and counseling skills so that they will be more valuable on the marketplace than their counterparts at other firms?

- Can we develop innovative **methodologies** for handling our matters (or engagements, transactions, or projects) so that our delivery of services becomes more thorough and efficient?

- Can we develop systematic ways of helping, encouraging, and ensuring that our people are skilled at client **counseling** in addition to being top suppliers?

- Can we become better than our competition at accumulating, disseminating, and building our firm-wide expertise and experience, so that each professional becomes more valuable in the marketplace by being **empowered** with a greater breadth and depth of experience?

- Can we organize and **specialize** our people in innovative ways, so that they become particularly skilled and valuable to the market because of their focus on a particular market segment's needs?

- Can we become more valuable to our clients by being more systematic and diligent about **listening** to the market: collecting, analyzing, and absorbing the details of their business more than our competition?

- Can we become more valuable to our clients by investing in research and **development** on issues of particular interest to them?

In resource-based strategy, there has to be consistency between resources and business. The logic behind this requirement is that the resources should create a competitive advantage in the business in which the firm competes. To meet this requirement, corporate resources can be evaluated against key success factors in each business. When doing so, it is important to keep in mind that to justify retaining a business, or entering a business, the resources should convey a substantial advantage. Merely having pedestrian resources that could be applied in an industry is seldom sufficient to justify entry or maintain presence in an attractive industry (Collis & Montgomery, 1997).

Moreover, managers must remember that, regardless of the advantage of a particular corporate resource appears to yield, the firm also must compete on all the other resources that are required to produce and deliver the product or service in each business. One great resource does not ensure a successful competitive position, particularly if a firm is disadvantaged on other resource dimensions (Collis & Montgomery, 1997).

Activity-Based Strategy

The goal of strategy formulation in the resource-based theory is to identify and increase those resources that allow a firm to gain and sustain superior rents. Firms owning strategic resources are predicted to earn superior rents, while firms possessing no or few strategic resources are thought to earn industry average rents or below-average rents. The goal of strategy formulation in the activity-based theory is to identify and explore drivers that allow a firm to gain and sustain superior rents. Drivers are a central concept in the activity-based theory. To be considered drivers, firm-level factors must meet three criteria: They are structural factors at the level of activities; they are more or less controllable by management; and they impact the cost and/or differentiation position of the firm. The definition of drivers is primarily based on what drivers do. Drivers are abstract, relative, and relational properties of activities. For example, scale of an activity is a driver, as the size of the activity relative to competitors may represent a competitive advantage.

The analytical focus of the resource-based theory is potentially narrower than that of the activity-based theory. While the activity-based theory takes the firm's entire activity set as its unit of analysis, the resource-based theory focuses on individual resources or bundles of resources. Having a narrower focus means that the resource-based theory may not take into account the negative impact of resources, how a resource's value may change as the environment changes, or the role of non-core resources in achieving competitive advantage.

The activity-based and resource-based theories are similar as they both attempt to explain how firms attain superior positions through factors that increase firm differentiation or lower firm cost. While drivers and resources share a common goal of achieving and sustaining superior positions, the manner by which they are seen to reach a profitable position is different. With the resource-based theory, it is the possession or control of strategic resources that allows a firm to gain a profitable position. On the other hand, drivers within the activity-based theory are not unique to the firm. They are generic, structural factors, which are available to all firms in the industry, in the sense that they are conceptualized as properties of the firm's activities. A firm gains a profitable position by configuring its activities using drivers. It is this position that a firm may own, but only if it is difficult for rivals to copy the firm's configuration.

The sustainability of superior positions created by configuring drivers or owning resources is based on barriers to imitation. The sustainability of competitive advantage as per the activity-based theory is through barriers to imitation at the activity level. If the firm has a competitive advantage, as long as competitors are unable to copy the way activities are performed and configured through the drivers, the firm should be able to achieve above-average earnings over an extended period. The sustainability of superior profitability in the resource-based theory is through barriers to imitation of resources and immobility of resources. If resources are easily copied or substituted, then the sustainability of the position is suspect.

Sheehan (2002) concludes his discussion by finding similarities between the resource-based theory and the activity-based theory. Resources in the resource-based theory are similar to drivers in the activity-based theory as both are based on earning efficiency rents. Furthermore, capabilities in the resource-based theory are similar to activities in the activity-based theory as both imply action.

Strategic Alignment

Alignment between business strategy and IT strategy is widely believed to improve business performance (Sabherwal & Chan, 2001). Therefore, strategic alignment is both a top management concern and also an important characteristic of the attributes of effective CIOs.

While the business strategy is the broadest pattern of resource allocation decisions, more specific decisions are related to information systems and information technology. IS must be seen both in a business and an IT context. IS is in the middle because IS supports the business while using IT.

Business strategy is concerned with achieving the mission, vision, and objectives of a company, while IS strategy is concerned with use of IS/IT applications, and IT strategy is concerned with the technical infrastructure. A company typically has several IS/IT applications. The connection between them is also of great interest, as interdependencies should prevent applications from being separate islands. Furthermore, the arrows in the illustration in Figure 6.3 are of importance. Arrows from business strategy to IS strategy and from IS to IT strategy represent the alignment perspective, they illustrate the *what* before *how*. Arrows from IT to IS strategy and from IS to business strategy represent the extension from *what* to *how* to *what*. This is the impact perspective, representing the potential impacts of modern information technology on future business options.

Necessary elements of a *business strategy* include mission, vision, objectives, market strategy, knowledge strategy, and our general approach to the use of information, information systems, and information technology.

Mission describes the reason for firm existence. For example, the reason for law firm existence is client's needs for legal advice. The mission addresses the organizations basic question of "What business are we in?" This single, essential sentence should include no quantification, but must unambiguously state the purpose of the organization and should just as carefully define what the organization does not do. The mission is an unambiguous statement of what the organization does and its long-term, overall purpose. Its primary role is to set a direction for everyone to follow. It may be short, succinct, and inspirational, or contain broad philosophical

Figure 6.3. Relationships between strategies at three levels

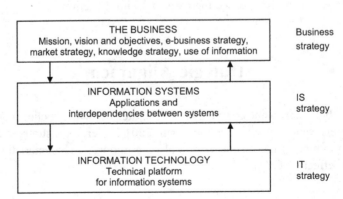

statements that tie an organization to certain activities and to economic, social, ethical, or political ends. Values also are frequently stated alongside the mission. Three differing examples of missions are: to help people move from one place to another; to provide medical treatment to sick people; and to enable electronic communication between people.

Vision describes what the firm wants to achieve. For example, the law firm wants to become the leading law firm in Norway. The vision represents the view that senior managers have for the future of the organization; so it is what they want it to become. This view offers a way to judge the appropriateness of all potential activities that the organization might engage in. The vision gives a picture, frequently covering many aspects that everyone can identify with, of what the business will be in the future, and how it will operate. It exists to bring objectives to life and to give the whole organization a destination that it can visualize so that every stakeholder has a shared picture of the future aim.

Objectives describe where the business is heading. For example, the law firm can choose to merge with another law firm to become the leading law firm in Norway. Objectives are the set of major achievements that will accomplish the vision. These are usually small in number, but embody the most important aspects of the vision, such as financial returns, customer service, manufacturing excellence, staff morale, and social and environmental obligations.

Market strategy describes market segments and products. For example, the law firm can focus on corporate clients in the area of tax law.

Necessary elements of an *IS strategy* include future IS/IT applications, future competence of human resources (IS/IT professionals), future IS/IT organizational structure, and control of the IS/IT function. An important application area is knowledge management systems (KMS). The future applications are planned according to priorities, how they are to be developed or acquired (make or buy), how they meet user requirements, and how security is achieved. The future competence is planned by types of resources needed, motivation and skills needed (managers, users, IS/IT professionals), salaries, and other benefits. The future IS/IT organization defines tasks, roles, management, and possibly outsourcing.

Necessary elements of an *IT strategy* include selection of IT hardware, basic software, and networks, as well as how these components should interact as a technological platform and how required security level is maintained. The IT platform consists of hardware, systems software, networks and communications, standards, and support from selected vendors.

An *IS/IT strategy* is a combined strategy including business context, the IS in a narrow sense, and the technological platform. Necessary elements of an IS/IT strategy include business direction and strategy (mission, vision, objectives, knowledge strategy), applications (knowledge management systems), people (future com-

Figure 6.4. IS/IT strategy elements and interdependencies

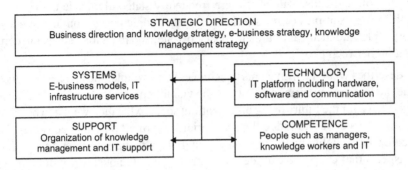

petence of human resources), organization (future organization and control of IT function), and IT platform (future technical infrastructure). Hence, IS/IT is quite a broad term. The term is broad to take care of all connections and interdependencies in a strategy, as changes in one element will have effect on all other elements, as illustrated in Figure 6.4.

The same thinking is represented in a famous model called Leavitt's Diamond (Gottschalk, 2005). Everything is connected and changes in one element affect all the others as illustrated in Figure 6.5. Tasks are performed using systems, structure is important for support functions, and people represent the competence. The Diamond can only create change in desired strategic business direction if all interdependencies between elements are taken care of over time.

Most large companies in the United States and Europe have long struggled with the need for tighter relationships between IT and business management. This perennial management problem is echoed once again in a study of how French CEOs and CIOs view the performance of information systems within their organizations. Insights from the study suggest that CEOs are growing keener to find a solution — and that both CIOs and the leaders of business units may soon be held more accountable for business ownership of IT (Monnoyer, 2003).

Figure 6.5. Leavitt's Diamond of elements and interrelationships

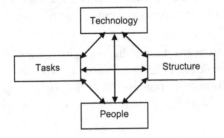

In the survey, CEOs say that IT is not meeting their (admittedly high) performance expectations, particularly in providing systems and tools to support managerial decision-making and in gaining the scale advantages of deploying common systems and processes across business units. CEOs attribute the gap between expected and actual performance mainly to the insufficient involvement of business units in IT projects, to the weak oversight and management of these projects, and to IT's inadequate understanding of their business requirements (Monnoyer, 2003).

CIO in Strategic Management

When the CEO and the top management team develops corporate strategy, they apply methods such as SWOT analysis (strengths, weaknesses, opportunities, and threats), value configuration analysis, competitive forces analysis, marketing analysis, and product portfolio analysis.

Similarly, the CIO applies the same kind of methods when developing IS/IT strategy. For example, results of a SWOT analysis will trigger questions such as:

- How can IS/IT be applied to exploit strengths?
- How can IS/IT be applied to minimize consequences of weaknesses?
- How can IS/IT be applied to explore opportunities?
- How can IS/IT be applied to avoid threats?

In the case of product portfolio analysis, the CEO will be concerned with the distribution of products among wild cats, stars, cash cows, and dead dogs. The CEO would like to see more wild cats developing into stars, and more stars developing into and staying on as cash cows. Similarly, the CIO will avoid new IS/IT projects that support dead dogs. Rather, the CIO will identify new IS/IT to enable wild cats to develop into stars and new IS/IT that enable stars to continue their life as cash cows.

The positions of CEO and CIO have more similarities at the level of strategic management, than at the level of operational management. In strategic management, competitive forces are just as important to the CEO as they are to the CIO when developing strategy. While the CEO may want to form alliances with customers to reduce customer power, the CIO may want to form supply chains with customers to improve the relative power of the firm even more.

Based on this chapter, in general, and the Y model, in particular, CIOs can derive practical insight about how to perform their jobs, interact with other senior managers and the CEO, or position their organizations to obtain maximum strategic impact. For example, the Y model provides insight into the various phases and stages that executives go through when developing strategy. Identifying these phases and stages and matching IS/IT strategy messages in the process will enable the CIO to become a natural part of corporate strategic management in the firm.

References

Barney, J. B. (2001). Is the resource-based "view" a useful perspective for strategic management research? Yes. *Academy of Management Review, 26*(1), 41-56.

Boyd, B. K., & Reuning-Elliott, E. (1998). A measurement model of strategic planning. *Strategic Management Journal, 19,* 181-192.

Christensen, C. M., & Raynor, M. E. (2003). *The innovator's solution.* Boston: Harvard Business School Press.

Collis, D. J., & Montgomery, C. A. (1997). *Corporate strategy — resources and the scope of the firm.* Chicago: Irwin, McGraw-Hill.

Gottschalk, P. (2005). *Strategic knowledge management technology.* Hershey, PA: Idea Group Publishing.

Haanaes, K. B. (1997). *Managing resource mobilization: Case studies of Dynal, Fiat Auto Poland and Alcatel Tecom Norway.* PhD series 9.97, Copenhagen Business School, Copenhagen, Denmark.

Hann, J., & Weber, R. (1996). Information systems planning: A model and empirical tests. *Management Science, 42*(7), 1043-1064.

Hansen, M. T., Nohria, N., & Tierny, T. (1999, March-April). What's your strategy for managing knowledge? *Harvard Business Review*, 106-116.

Hitt, M. A., Bierman, L., Shimizu, K., & Kochhar, R. (2001). Direct and moderating effects of human capital on strategy and performance in professional service firms: A resource-based perspective. *Academy of Management Journal, 44*(1), 13-28.

Hopkins, W. E., & Hopkins, S. A. (1997). Strategic planning — financial performance relationships in banks: A causal examination. *Strategic Management Journal, 18*(8), 635-652.

Jensen, M., & Zajac, E. J. (2004). Corporate elites and corporate strategy: How demographic preferences and structural position shape the scope of the firm. *Strategic Management Journal, 25,* 507-524.

Julien, P. A., & Ramangalahy, C. (2003, Spring). Competitive strategy and performance of exporting SMEs: An empirical investigation of the impact of their
export information search and competencies. *Entrepreneurship Theory and
Practice,* 227-245.

Kaplan, R. S., & Norton, D. P. (2004). *Strategy maps.* Boston: Harvard Business
School Press.

Loewendahl, B. R. (2000). *Strategic management of professional service firms* (2nd
ed.). Copenhagen, Denmark: Copenhagen Business School Press.

Maister, D. H. (1993). *Managing the professional service firm.* New York: Free
Press.

Miller, C. C., & Cardinal, L. B. (1994). Strategic planning and firm performance:
A synthesis of more than two decades of research. *Academy of Management
Journal, 37*(6), 1649-1665.

Mintzberg, H. (1994). Rounding out the manager's job. *Sloan Management Review,
36*(1), 11-26.

Monnoyer, E. (2003). What CEOs really think about IT. *McKinsey Quarterly, 3,*
80-82.

Nayyar, P. R. (1993). On the measurement of competitive strategy: Evidence from
a large multiproduct U.S. firm. *Academy of Management Journal, 36*(6),
1652-1669.

Porter, M. E. (1985). *Competitive strategy.* New York: The Free Press.

Porter, M. E. (2001, March). Strategy and the Internet. *Harvard Business Review,*
63-78.

Priem, R. L., & Butler, J. E. (2001). Is the resource-based view a useful perspective for strategic management research? *Academy of Management Review,
26*(1), 22-40.

Sabherwal, R., & Chan, Y. E. (2001). Alignment between business and IS strategies: A study of prospectors, analyzers, and defenders. *Information Systems
Research, 12*(1), 11-33.

Sheehan, N. T. (2002, April). *Reputation as a driver in knowledge-intensive service
firms.* Series of Dissertations, Norwegian School of Management, Sandvika,
Norway.

Wit, B. D., & Meyer, R. (2004). *Strategy — process, content, context* (3rd ed.).
London: Thomson Learning.

Chapter VII

The CIO Developing E-Business

Introduction

As companies expand their use of the Internet from electronic commerce to electronic business, the CIO emerges as the most important executive for performance improvements when selecting business models.

Electronic Commerce

Electronic commerce (EC) is an important concept that describes the process of buying, selling, or exchanging products, services, and information, via computer networks, including the Internet (Turban, King, Lee, Warkentin, & Chung, 2002). From a communications perspective, EC is the delivery of goods, services, information, or payments over computer networks or by any other electronic means. From a business process perspective, EC is the application of technology toward the automation of business transactions and workflow. From a service perspective, EC is a tool that addresses the desire of firms, consumers, and management to cut service costs while improving the quality of goods and increasing the speed of service delivery. From an online perspective, EC provides the capability of buying and selling products and information on the Internet and other online services. From a collaboration perspective, EC is the framework for inter- and intra-organizational collaboration. From a community perspective, EC provides a gathering place for community members, to learn, transact, and collaborate.

Electronic commerce over large ubiquitous networks will soon be conducted in routine fashion. While some may question the time frame involved, few will question its imminence. In this transient phase of rapid technological change, it is difficult to see the real implications of these changes for both business and society. Recent writings have elaborated on the power of information technologies to reduce the costs of coordination and transactions, consequently to influence governance structures between buyers and sellers. Much of the popular press is also fairly aggressive in providing anecdotes of innovative companies that have leveraged Web-based technologies by expanding, improving, or modifying product and service offerings. A subliminal theme in all this hyperbole is the notion that these technologies are good and will provide the consumer with many more options, services, and advantages. Grover and Ramanlal (1999) challenged this theme by presenting alternative scenarios in which these technologies did not necessarily work in the best interest of the customer. For example, product customization, enabled by IT networks, can allow sellers to exploit buyers rather than benefit buyers.

The emergence of e-commerce is creating fundamental change to the way that business is conducted. These changes are altering the way in which every enterprise acquires wealth and creates shareholder value. The myriad of powerful computing and communications technology enabling e-commerce allows organizations to streamline their business processes, enhance customer service, and offer digital products and services. This shift underlying marketing fundamentals is now the driving force that is luring many organizations to embrace e-commerce. However, as they are learning, organizations must proceed with caution, as the road to e-commerce is littered with failed initiatives (Chang, Jackson, & Grover, 2003).

While engaging in e-commerce undoubtedly has substantial benefits, this marketplace also is quite competitive. E-commerce reduces customer search and switching costs, has the ability to distribute information on new products, access new sales channels, and reduce entry-level capital requirements, thereby lowering barriers to entry. Companies which exhibit a market orientation, by being vigilant regarding the needs of customers and the actions of competitors, tend to achieve better performance. Over-emphasizing one dimension at the cost of the other tend to lead to sub-optimization in an environment that rewards the ability to sense and respond to a variety of information cues (Chang et al., 2003).

Figure 7.1. E-commerce is part of e-business

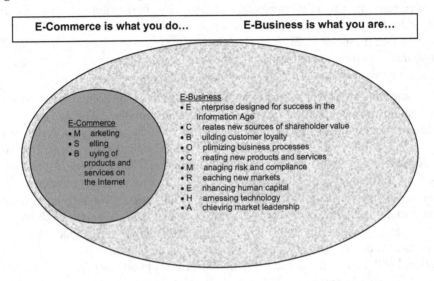

Electronic Business

The term commerce is defined by some as describing transactions conducted between business partners. When this definition of commerce is used, some people find the term electronic commerce to be fairly narrow. Thus, many use the term e-business. E-business refers to a broader definition of EC, not just the buying and selling of goods and services, but also servicing customers, collaborating with business partners, and conducting electronic transactions within an organization (Turban et al., 2002).

E-commerce is part of e-business, as illustrated in Figure 7.1. The difference can be demonstrated using a business example. The business example is concerned with handling of customer complaints. As long as customers do not complain, then e-commerce may be sufficient for electronic transactions with customers. The front end of the business is electronic, and this front end is the only contact customers have with the business.

However, if a customer complains, then other parts of the business may have to get involved. For example, if the customer has received a computer which is found deficient, then the customer gets in touch with the vendor. The vendor has to decide whether the complaint is justified. If it is, then the vendor has to decide whether to (a) fix the product, (b) replace the product, or (c) refund the money paid for the product.

Figure 7.2. Customer complaint-handling business process in company with e-commerce but no e-business

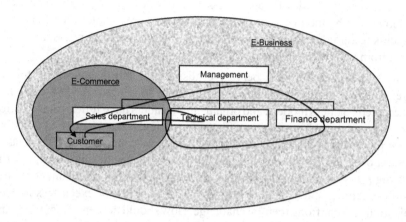

This kind of decision-making will typically involve other departments in addition to marketing and sales departments. These other departments may be the technical department, the production department, and the finance department. While the marketing and sales departments have electronic communication with the customer using information systems, other departments may not be connected to the same information systems.

In this situation, the internal handling of a customer complaint in the business is not transparent to and accessible for the customer. The customer may experience time passing by, without any information from the vendor. A complaining customer was angry already at the time of the complaint. The anger and frustration are rising as the customer receives no response. The customer is unable to obtain information from the vendor by electronic means, since the vendor is doing e-commerce, not e-business.

If the vendor would be an e-business, then the business process of customer complaints handling would be an integrated information system to which the customer has access. Then it is possible for the customer to follow the complaint-handling process, and it is possible for other departments than marketing and sales to stay in direct contact with the complaining customer to resolve the issues. This business process is illustrated in Figure 7.2.

Weill and Vitale (2001) use the following working definition of e-business: marketing, buying, selling, delivering, servicing, and paying for products, services, and information across (nonproprietary) networks linking an enterprise and its prospects, customers, agents, suppliers, competitors, allies, and complementors. The essence of this definition is the conduct of business and business processes over computer networks based on nonproprietary standards. The Internet is the exemplar of a nonproprietary network used today for e-business. Given its low cost and universal access, the Internet will be the major infrastructure for the foreseeable future. However, new access technologies already on the horizon (e.g., use of wireless application protocol from mobile telephones) will supplement the Internet.

E-business embodies the most pervasive, disruptive, and disconcerting form of change: It leaves no aspect of managing organizations untouched, it challenges long-accepted business models, and organization leaders have little to draw on from their past experience to manage its effects. In particular, its capacity to transform business processes is no longer in dispute. The new technologies at the heart of e-business open up myriad possibilities not just to reconsider the re-engineering of existing processes but also to design, develop, and deploy fundamentally new ways of conceiving and executing business processes. Senior executives in every organization thus confront a central challenge: How should they endeavor to capture, analyze, and project the transformational impact of e-business on their organization's most critical or core processes? Later in this book, we put forward that knowledge management provides one useful vehicle for doing so (Fahey, Srivastava, Sharon, & Smith, 2001).

In spite of its pervasiveness, visibility, and impact, e-business often remains a poorly understood phenomenon in many industries. E-business constitutes the ability of a firm to electronically connect many organizations, in multiple ways, both internal and external, for many different purposes. It allows an organization to execute electronic transactions with any individual entity along the value creation — suppliers, logistics providers, wholesalers, distributors, service providers, and end customers. Increasingly, e-business allows an organization to establish real-time connections simultaneously among numerous entities for some specific purpose, such as optimizing the flow of physical items (raw materials, components, finished products) through the supply chain (Fahey et al., 2001).

E-business raises a number of critical business issues, each of which in turn generates distinct knowledge issues and challenges specific to the e-business transformation of processes. First, e-business is transforming the *solutions* available to customers in almost every industry, that is, the breadth of solutions and how the solutions are obtained and experienced. Consumers can now buy books, food, clothing, and a lot of other goods over the Internet in ways that allow distinct forms of customization. Industrial purchasers can now use the Internet to scour the offerings of many providers and procure components and supplies in combinations, prices, and delivery schedules that dramatically lower the costs of search, speed delivery, and reduce prices. These new solutions open up possibilities for customer value creation and delivery that were simply unimaginable few years ago (Fahey et al., 2001).

Second, the creators and purveyors of the new customer value propositions represent new types of *rivals*. Traditional booksellers are confronted by *amazon.com*;

Merrill Lunch faces E*TRADE. These new entities recast the profile of rivals in many industries and, partly as a consequence, reshape the contours and boundaries of most traditional competitive spaces or industries (Fahey et al., 2001).

Third, in part due to the competitive context changes just noted, the nature and content of *strategy*, and by implication, the dynamics of marketplace rivalry, are undergoing profound change. No longer can most firms rely on making modest, incremental changes to long-established strategy success formulas. Strategy in product domains as diverse as financial services, household furnishings, computers, automobiles, and industrial components, increasingly revolves around inventing new product solutions and/or new ways of interacting with customers in designing, developing, and delivering these solutions. In fact, organizations are adjusting their strategies according to the new notion of the customer where customer intimacy, customer relationship management, one-to-one marketing, and the concept of the customer as opposed to the product as the new asset of the organization and real carrier of value dominate. In short, e-business offers the platform for new forms of marketplace strategy models — a significant element of any firm's business model — that will change the competitive rules of the game (Fahey et al., 2001).

Fourth, e-business requires firms to refocus and reconfigure almost every type of tangible and intangible asset. It places an especially heavy premium on developing and leveraging intangible assets, including many different types of new skills, new forms of integrated and intensive relationships with external entities, new sets of perceptions held by customers, channels, and suppliers, and significant new knowledge (Fahey et al., 2001).

Fifth, e-business is dramatically reshaping every traditional business process: from developing new products and managing customer relationships to acquiring human resources and procuring raw materials and components. By enabling major new tasks to be added to individual processes, e-business broadens their scope, content, and value-generating capability. For example, customer relationship management has been essentially reinvented through e-business's ability to access large bodies of heretofore unavailable data, massage and mine such data in radical new ways, and customize the outputs of such analysis to customer segments and, in many cases, to individual customers. By integrating traditionally largely separate processes, e-business in effect creates what might well be described as new business processes (Fahey et al., 2001).

Competitive Strategy

A study conducted by Chang et al. (2003) proposed that e-commerce initiatives are important strategic initiatives and that firms with a stronger e-commerce market orientation will be more successful. Content analysis of CEO's letter to shareholders of 145 Fortune 500 firms was conducted to evaluate the importance of e-commerce and strategic orientation. The results provide support to the studies proposition and indicate that e-commerce must be pursued carefully as a strategic initiative rather than as an appendage to an existing organization.

Strategy is an ongoing process of evaluating purpose as well as questioning, verifying, and redefining the manner of interaction with the competitive environment. Complexity of the strategy process can be simplified by searching for patterns of behavior in organizations. These patterns of emergent behavior can be used to describe the underlying processes of organizational adaptation. Basic strategic orientation of organizations can be described in terms of a typology of defenders, prospectors, analyzers, and reactors. Each orientation differs with respect to risk disposition, innovativeness, and operational efficiencies. Strategic orientation such as low cost or differentiation are means of altering the firm's position vis-à-vis competitors and suppliers. Strategy involves mustering resources and creating capabilities that are difficult to imitate by competitors, resulting in superior rents. Strategic orientation is both an issue of how firms position themselves with respect to competitors and an issue of how firm-specific resources are exploited (Grover & Saeed, 2004).

Much strategic management literature has been devoted to identifying attributes or dimensions of a company's strategic orientation. Internet-based businesses include portals, travel sites, e-tailers, and providers of financial and informational services. These businesses attempt to leverage the Internet infrastructure and digital economics in order to gain strategic positioning within the marketplace. For Internet-based businesses, four major dimensions of strategic orientation are particularly pertinent: risk disposition, innovativeness, operational efficiency, and marketing intensity (Grover & Saeed, 2004).

Internet Strategy

Many of the pioneers of Internet business, both dot-coms and established companies, have competed in ways that violate nearly every precept of good strategy. For a long time there was an absence of strategy. According to Porter (2001), the time has come to take a clearer view of the Internet. It is necessary to move away from rhetoric — such as Internet industries, e-business strategies, and a new economy — and see the Internet for what it is. It is an enabling technology, a powerful set of tools that can be used, wisely or unwisely, in almost any industry and as part of almost any strategy.

Strategy is neither the quest for the universally best way of competing nor an effort to be all things to every customer. It defines a way of competing that delivers unique value in a particular set of uses or for a particular set of customers. To establish and maintain a distinctive strategic positioning, a company needs to follow six fundamental principles (Porter 2001):

- It must start with the **right goal**: superior long-term return on investment. Only by grounding strategy in sustained profitability will real economic value be generated. Economic value is created when customers are willing to pay a price for a product or service that exceeds the cost of producing it.

- A company's strategy must enable it to deliver a **value proposition**, or set of benefits, different from those that competitors offer.

- Strategy needs to be reflected in a **distinctive value configuration**. To establish a sustainable competitive advantage, a company must perform different activities than rivals or perform similar activities in different ways.

- Robust strategies involve **trade-offs**. A company must abandon or forgo some product features, services, or activities in order to be unique at others.

- Strategy defines how all the elements of what a company does **fit** together. A strategy involves making choices throughout the value configuration that are independent; all a company's activities must be mutually reinforcing.

- Strategy involves **continuity** of direction. A company must define a distinctive value proposition that it will stand for, even if that means forgoing certain opportunities.

The absence of strategy in may pioneering Internet businesses has misled them to focus on revenues rather than profits, indirect values rather than real value, every conceivable product rather than trade-offs, activities of rivals rather than tailoring the value configuration, and a rash of partnerships rather than build control. To capitalize on the Internet's strategic potential, executives and entrepreneurs alike will need to develop a strategy that exploits this potential. In some industries, the use of the Internet represents only a modest shift from well-established practices. Virtual activities do not eliminate the need for physical activities, but often amplify their importance. The complementarity between Internet activities and traditional activities arises for a number of reasons. First, introducing Internet applications in one activity often places greater demands on physical activities elsewhere in the value configuration. Second, using the Internet in one activity can have systemic consequences, requiring new or enhanced physical activities that are often unanticipated. Third, most Internet applications have some shortcomings in comparison with conventional methods, such as customers being unable to physically examine products (Porter, 2001).

E-Business Models

A business model can be defined as the method by which a firm builds and uses its resources to offer its customers better value than its competitors and to make money doing so. It details how a firm makes money now and how it plans to do so in the long run. The model is what enables a firm to have a sustainable competitive advantage, to perform better than its rivals in the long term. A business model can be conceptualized as a system that is made up of components, linkages between the components, and dynamics (Afuah & Tucci, 2003).

Weill and Vitale (2001) define an e-business model as a description of the roles and relationships among a firm's consumers, customers, allies, and suppliers that identifies the major flows of product, information, and money, and the major benefits to participants.

There are many different ways to describe and classify e-business models. Weill and Vitale (2001) propose that there are a finite number of atomic e-business models, each of which captures a different way to conduct e-business. Firms can combine atomic e-business models as building blocks to create tailored e-business models and initiatives, using their competencies as their guide. Weill and Vitale (2001) identified eight atomic e-business models, each of which describes the essence of conducting business electronically.

1. **Direct to customer:** The distinguishing characteristic of this model is that buyer and seller communicate directly, rather than through an intermediary. The seller may be a retailer, a wholesaler, or a manufacturer. The customer may be an individual or a business. Examples of the direct-to-customer model are Dell Computer Corporation (www.dell.com) and Gap, Inc. (www.gap.com).

    *   **Infrastructure:** The direct-to-customer model requires extensive electronic connection with the customer, including online payment systems. Many direct-to-customer implementations include an extranet to allow customized Web pages for major B2B customers. Operating a direct-to-customer e-business requires significant investment in the equivalent of the store, that is, the Web site. Direct-to-customer businesses spend millions of dollars developing easy-to-navigate and easy-to-use Web sites with the goal of improving the B2B or B2C shopping experience online. Lands End (www.landsend.com) has devised a feature by which women can build and store a three-dimensional model of themselves to "try on" clothes electronically.

        In their field research, Weill and Vitale (2001) found that firms with e-business initiatives containing the direct-to-customer e-business model needed and were investing more heavily in three areas of infrastructure services: application infrastructure, communications, and IT management.

Direct-to-customer firms particularly needed payment transaction processing to process online customer payments, enterprise-wide resource planning (ERP) to process customer transactions, workflow infrastructure to optimize business process performance, communication network services linking all points in the enterprise to each other and the outside world (often using TCP/IP protocol), the installation and maintenance of workstations and local area networks supporting the large number of people required to operate a direct-to-customer model, and service-level agreements between the business and the IT group or outsourcer to ensure, monitor, and improve the systems necessary for the model.

- **Sources of revenue:** The main source of revenue in the direct-to-customer model is usually direct sales to customers. Supplemental revenues come from advertising, the sale of customer information, and product placement fees.

- **Critical success factors:** Critical success factors are the things a firm must do well to flourish. The following list shows the critical success factors for the direct-to-customer model: create and maintain customer awareness, in order to build a critical mass of users to cover the fixed cost of building an electronic presence; reduce customer acquisition costs; strive to own the customer relationship and understand individual customer needs; increase repeat purchases and average transaction size; provide fast and efficient transaction processing, fulfillment, and payment; ensure adequate security for the organization and its customers; and provide interfaces that combine ease of use with richness of experience, integrating multiple channels.

2. **Full-service provider:** A firm using the full-service provider model provides total coverage of customer needs in a particular domain, consolidated via a single point of contact. The domain could be any major area of customer needs requiring multiple products and services, for example, financial services, health care, or industrial chemicals. The full-service provider adds value by providing a full range of products, sourced both internally and externally, and consolidated them using the channel chosen by the customer. Examples of the full-service provider are the Prudential Advisor (www.prusec.com) and GE Supply Company (www.gesupply.com).

    - **Infrastructure:** Virtually all businesses aspire to get 100% of their customers' business, or at least to getting as much of that business as they can profitably handle. Yet the number of full-service providers remains small. Part of the reason for this is required infrastructure. The missing piece of infrastructure in many businesses is often a database containing information about the customer and the products that the customer owns. Without owning these data, a provider does not own the customer relationship, and therefore some of the customer's transactions are likely to take place directly with other providers. All of the important interactions with customers occurring across any channel or business unit must be recorded in the firm-wide customer database.

In their field research, Weill and Vitale (2001) identified databases and data warehouses as some of the most important infrastructure services associated with the full-service provider model. Other important infrastructure services included the following: the ability to evaluate proposals for new information systems initiatives to coordinate IT investments across a multi-business-unit firm with the goal of a single point of contact for the customer; centralized management of IT infrastructure capacity to integrate across multiple business units within the firm and third-party providers; installation and maintenance of workstations and local area networks to operate the online business linking all the business units and third-party providers; electronic support for groups to coordinate the cross-functional teams required to implement this model; and the identification and testing of new technologies to find cost-effective ways to deliver this complex business model to the customer across multiple channels.

- **Sources of revenue:** A full-service provider gains revenues from selling its own products and those of others, and possibly also from annual membership fees, management fees, transaction fees, commissions on third-party products, advertising or listing fees from third-party providers, and fees for selling aggregated data about customers.

- **Critical success factors:** One important critical success factor is the brand, credibility, and trust necessary for a customer to look to the firm for its complete needs in an area. Another is owning the customer relationship in one domain and integrating and consolidating the offering of many third parties into a single channel or multiple channels. A third factor is owning more of the customer data in the relevant domain than any other player. A final factor is enforcement of policies to protect the interests of internal and external suppliers, as well as customers.

3. **Whole of enterprise:** The single point of contact for the e-business customer is the essence of the whole-of-enterprise atomic business model. Although many of this model's breakthrough innovations have occurred in public-sector organizations, the model is applicable in both the for-profit and the public sectors. An example of this model is the Australian state of Victoria with its Business Channel (www.business.channel.vic.gov.au) and Health Channel (www.betterhealth.vic.gov.au).

- **Infrastructure:** For the whole-of-enterprise model, infrastructure needs to link the different systems in the various business units and provide a firm-wide perspective for management. The field research by Weill and Vitale (2001) revealed that the following infrastructure services are the most important for implementing this model: centralized management of infrastructure capacity to facilitate integration and capture economies of scale; identification and testing of new technologies to find new ways to integrate the often different systems in many business units into a single point of customer contact; management of key data independent of applications and the creation of a centralized repository for firm-wide information; electronic means of summarizing data from different applications and platforms to manage the complexity arising from a single point of contact for multiple business units; development of an ERP service to process the transactions instigated by customers interacting with several different business units, often requiring consolidating or linking several ERPs in the firm; payment transaction processing, either on a firm-wide basis or by linking several systems across the business units; large-scale data-processing facilities to process transactions from multiple business units, often centralized to achieve economies of scale; and integrated mobile computing applications, which provide another channel to the customer.

- **Sources of revenue:** In the for-profit sector, revenues are generated by provision of goods and services to the customer by the business units. There also may be the opportunity to charge an annual service or membership fee for this level of service. In the government sector, the motivation is usually twofold: improved service and reduced cost. Service to the community is improved through continuous, round-the-clock operation and faster service times. Government costs can potentially be reduced by sharing more infrastructure and eliminating the need to perform the same transaction in multiple agencies.

- **Critical success factors:** The following list details the critical success factors for the whole-of-enterprise model: changing customer behavior to make use of the new model, as opposed to the customer continuing to interact directly with individual units; reducing costs in the individual business units as the direct demands on them fall and managing the transfer pricing issues that will inevitably arise; altering the perspective of the business units to take an enterprise-wide view, which includes broad product awareness, training, and cross-selling; in the integrated implementation, re-engineering the business processes to link into life events at the front end and existing legacy processes and systems at the back end; and finding compelling and practical life events that customers can use as triggers to access the enterprise.

4.   **Intermediaries:** such as portals, agents, auctions, aggregators, and other intermediaries. E-business is often promoted as an ideal way for sellers and buyers to interact directly, shortening old-economy value chains by disintermediating some of their members. Yet, some of the most popular sites on the Internet, both for consumers and for business users, are in fact intermediaries —sites that stand between the buyer and the seller. The services of intermediaries include search (to locate providers of products and services), specification (to identify important product attributes), price (to establish the price, including optional extras such as warranties), sale (to complete the sales transaction, including payment and settlement), fulfillment (to fulfill the purchase by delivering the product or service), surveillance (to conduct surveillance of the activities of buyers and sellers in order to report aggregate activity and prices and to inform and regulate the market), and enforcement (to enforce proper conduct by buyers and sellers). Examples of intermediaries are electronic malls, shopping agents, specialty auctions, electronic markets, electronic auctions, and portals.

   - **Infrastructure:** Intermediaries generate value by concentrating information and bringing together buyers and sellers, operating entirely in space and thus relying on IT as the primary infrastructure. Weill and Vitale (2001) found in their field interviews that the most important infrastructure services for firms pursuing the intermediary atomic business model are the following: knowledge management, including knowledge databases and contact databases that enable the codification and sharing of knowledge in this highly information-intensive business; enforcing Internet and e-mail policies to ensure proper and consistent use of electronic channels to buyers, sellers, and intermediaries; workstation networks to support the products and services of this all-electronic business model; centralized management of e-business applications, ensuring consistency and integration across product offerings; information systems planning to identify the most effective uses of IT in the business; and information systems project management to ensure that business value is achieved from IT investments.

   - **Sources of revenue:** An intermediary may earn revenues from buyers, sellers, or both. Sellers may pay a listing fee, a transaction fee, a sales commission, or some combination. Similarly, buyers may pay a subscription fee, a success fee, or a sales commission.

   - **Critical success factors:** The chief requirement for survival as an intermediary is sufficient volume of usage to cover the fixed costs of establishing the business and the required infrastructure. Attracting and retaining a critical mass of customers is therefore the primary critical success factor. Another important critical success factor is building up infrastructure just quickly enough to meet demand as it increases.

5.   **Shared infrastructure:** The firm provides infrastructure shared by its owners. Other suppliers, who are users of the shared infrastructure but not owners, can also be included. Customers who access the shared infrastructure directly are given a choice of suppliers and value propositions. The owner and the non-owner suppliers are generally represented objectively. In some situations, goods or services flow directly from the shared infrastructure to the customer. In other situations, a message is sent by the shared infrastructure to the supplier, who then completes the transaction by providing the goods or services to the customer.

An example illustrating the features of the shared-infrastructure business model is the system from 2000 by America's largest automakers, some of their dealers, and IBM, Motorola, and Intel. The initiative was named Covisint (collaboration vision integrity). General Motors, Ford, and DaimlerChrysler see stronger potential benefits from cooperating on supply-chain logistics than from competing.

- **Infrastructure:** The shared-infrastructure business model requires competitors to cooperate by sharing IT infrastructure and information. This level of cooperation requires agreement on high-level IT architectures as well as operational standards for applications, data communications, and technology. Effective implementation of the shared-infrastructure model also requires enforcement of these standards, and most shared-infrastructure models have a joint committee to set and enforce standards. Another role of these committees is to implement the policies of the shared infrastructure about what information, if any, is shared and what information is confidential to partner firms. Weill and Vitale (2001) found in their field research that the most important infrastructure services required by firms implementing the shared-infrastructure atomic business model all concerned architectures and standards: specification and enforcement of high-level architectures for data, technology, applications, communications, and work that are agreed to by alliance partners; and specification and enforcement of detailed standards for the high-level architectures.

- **Sources of revenue:** Revenues can be generated both from membership fees and from transaction fees. The alliance may be run on a nonprofit basis or on a profit-making basis. Not-for-profit shared infrastructures are typically open to all eligible organizations and distribute any excess revenues back to their members. The for-profit models are typically owned by a subset of the firms in a given segment, which split up any profits among themselves.

- **Critical success factors:** Critical success factors for the shared-infrastructure model include the following: no dominant partner that gains more than any other partner; an unbiased channel and objective presentation of product and service information; critical mass of both alliance partners and customers; management of conflict among the ongoing e-business initiatives of the alliance partners; compilation and delivery of accurate and timely statements of the services and benefits provided to each member of the alliance; and interoperability of systems.

6. **Virtual community:** Virtual communities deserve our attention, not only because they are the clearest, and perhaps the last, surviving embodiment of the original intent of the Internet. By using IT to leverage the fundamental human desire for communication with peers, virtual communities can create significant value for their owners as well as for their members. Once established, a virtual community is less susceptible to competition by imitation than any of the other atomic business models. In this business model, the firm of interest — the sponsor of the virtual community — sits in the center, positioned between members of the community and suppliers. Fundamental to the success of this model is that members are able, and in fact are encouraged, to communicate with one another directly. Communication between members may be via e-mail, bulletin boards, online chat, Web-based conferencing, or other computer-based media, and it is the distinguishing feature of this model. Examples of this model are Parent Soup (www.parentsoup.com), a virtual community for parents, and Motley Fool (www.motleyfool.com), a virtual community of investors.

- **Infrastructure:** Virtual communities depend on IT to exist. In particular, the creation and continual enhancement of an Internet site is essential if a virtual community is to survive. Many virtual-community sites include not just static content and links, but also tools of interest to potential members. Weill and Vitale (2001) found in their field research that the infrastructure services most important for the virtual-community business model are the following: training in the use of IT for members of the community; application service provision (ASP) to provide specialized systems virtual communities needs such as bulletin boards, e-mail, and ISP access; IT research and development, including infrastructure services for identifying and testing new technologies and for evaluating proposals for new information systems initiatives; information systems planning to identify and prioritize potential investments in IT in this completely online business; and installation and maintenance of workstations and local area networks to support the electronic world of the virtual community.

- **Sources of revenue:** A sponsoring firm can gain revenue from membership fees, direct sales of goods and services, advertising, clickthroughs, and sales commissions. A firm sponsoring a virtual community as an adjunct to its other activities may receive no direct revenue at all from the virtual community. Rather, the firm receives less tangible benefits, such as customer loyalty and increased knowledge about its customer base.

- **Critical success factors:** The critical success factors for a virtual community include: finding and retaining a critical mass of members; building and maintaining loyalty with an appropriate mix of content and features; maintaining privacy and security for member information; balancing commercial potential and members' interests; leveraging member profile information with advertisers and merchants; and engendering a feeling of trust in the community by its members.

7. **Value net integrator:** Traditionally, most firms operate simultaneously in two worlds: the physical and the virtual. In the physical world, goods and services are created in a series of value-adding activities connecting the supply side (suppliers, procurement, and logistics) with the demand side (customers, marketing, and shipping). In the virtual world, information about the members of the physical value chain are gathered, synthesized, and distributed along the virtual value chain. E-business provides the opportunity to separate the physical and virtual value chains. Value net integrators take advantage of that split and attempt to control the virtual value chain in their industries by gathering, synthesizing, and distributing information. Value net integrators add value by improving the effectiveness of the value chain by coordinating information. A pure value net integrator operates exclusively in the virtual value chain, owning a few physical assets. To achieve the gathering, synthesizing, and distributing of information, the value net integrator receives and sends information to all other players in the model. The value net integrator coordinates product flows from suppliers to allies and customers. The product flows from the suppliers to customers may be direct or via allies. In some cases, the value net integrator may sell information or other products to the customer. The value net integrator always strives to own the customer relationship with the other participants in the model, thus knowing more about their operations than any other player. Examples of value net integrators are Seven-Eleven Japan and Cisco Systems (www.cisco.com).

  - **Infrastructure:** The value net integrator succeeds in its role by gathering, synthesizing, and distributing information. Thus, for a value net integrator, data and electronic connectivity with allies and other players are very important assets. Field research carried out by Weill and Vitale (2001) suggests that the most important infrastructure services required for a value net integrator include: middleware, linking systems on different platforms across the many players in the value net; a centralized data warehouse that collects and summarizes key information for analysis from decentralized databases held by several players across the value net; specification and enforcement of high-level architectures and detailed standards for data, technology, applications, and communications to link together different technology platforms owned by different firms; call centers to provide advice and guidance for partners and allies in getting the most value from the information provided by the value net generator; and high-capacity communications network service to support the high volumes of information flowing across the value net.

- **Sources of revenue:** In this model, revenues are generally earned by fees or margins on the physical goods that pass through the industry value net. By using information about consumers, the value net integrator is able to increase prices by meeting consumer demand. By using information about suppliers, the value net integrator reduces costs by cutting inventories and lead times.

- **Critical success factors:** The critical success factors for the value net integrator atomic business model are as follows: reducing ownership of physical assets while retaining ownership of data; owning or having access to the complete industry virtual value chain; establishing a trusted brand recognized at all places in the value chain; operating in markets where information can add significant value, such as those that are complex, fragmented, regulated, multilayered, inefficient, and large with many sources of information; presenting the information to customers, allies, partners, and suppliers in clear and innovative ways that provide value; and helping other value chain participants capitalize on the information provided by the value net integrator.

8. **Content provider:** Like many terms associated with e-business, content provider has different meanings to different people. We define content provider as a firm that creates and provides content (information, products, or services) in digital form to customers via third parties. The physical-world analogy of a content provider is a journalist, recording artist, or stock analyst. Digital products such as software, electronic travel guides, and digital music and video are examples of content. A virtual-world example of a content provider is weather forecasters such as Storm Weather Center (www.storm.no).

- **Infrastructure:** Content providers must excel at tailoring and manipulating their core content to meet the specific needs of customers. Content providers must categorize and store their content in well-indexed modules so it can be combined and customized to meet customer needs via a wide variety of channels. Customers and transactions tend to be relatively few, at least compared with the number of end consumers and their transactions. Often complex and unique IT infrastructures are needed to support the particular needs of the specialized professionals employed by the content provider. Field research by Weill and Vitale (2001) identified the most important infrastructure services: multimedia storage farms or storage area network infrastructures to deal with large amounts of information; a strong focus on architecture, including setting and enforcing standards particularly for work; detailed data architectures to structure, specify, link manipulate, and manage the core intellectual property; workstation network infrastructures to enable the fundamentally online business of a content provider; and a common systems development environment to provide compatible and integrated systems, ensuring the systems can provide content across multiple channels to their customers.

- **Sources of revenue:** The primary source of revenue for a content provider is fees from its third parties or allies. These fees may be based on a fixed price per month or year, or on the number of times the third party's own customers access the content. In some situations, the fees paid are lower for content branded by the provider, and higher for unbranded content, which then appears to the customer to have been generated by the third party itself.

- **Critical success factors:** To succeed, a content provider must provide reliable, timely content in the right format and at the right price. The critical success factors for this model include the following: branding (the value of content is due in part to reputation), recognized as best in class (the business of content provision will be global and competitive), and network (establishing and maintaining a network of third parties through which content is distributed).

One way of comparing these e-business models is to analyze to what extent each model creates integration with customers and to what extent each model creates integration with partners. As illustrated in figure 7.3, the business model of Direct

Figure 7.3. E-business models integration with customers vs. partners

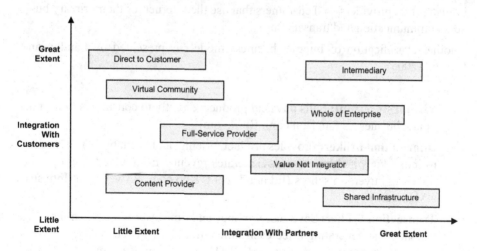

to Customer mainly creates integration with customers, while Shared Infrastructure mainly creates integration with partners.

Determining Appropriate Models

Despite works by Weill and Vitale (2002) and others, how an e-business model must be defined and specified is largely an open issue. Business decision-makers tend to use the notion in a highly informal way, and usually there is a big gap between the business view and that of IT developers.

The electronic business landscape is confusing for many new entrants, and many of them face the paradox that hesitation would run the risk of being left behind, but rushing in and making an incorrect choice regarding electronic business initiatives could have dire consequences for organizations. According to Hayes and Finnegan (2005), Internet-only or "dot-com" models have proven particularly vulnerable. For example, the dot-com implosion of Spring 2000 led to a large number of high-profile collapses including boo, ClickMango, and eToys. "Clicks and mortar" strategies have also met with mixed success (e.g., Wall Street Journal Interactive and Fyffes' World-of-Fruit).

The Internet age has produced many Internet business models. For example, Afuah and Tucci (2003) distinguish between the following nine: brokerage model, advertising model, infomediary model, merchant model, manufacturing model, affiliate model, community model, subscription model, and utility model. An Internet business model — sometimes labeled b-Web — is a business on the Internet that represents a distinct system of suppliers, distributors, commerce service providers, infrastructure providers, and customers that use the Internet for their primary business communication and transactions.

Another classification of Internet business models is presented by Laudon and Laudon (2005):

- **Virtual storefront:** Sells physical products directly to consumers or to individual businesses (amazon.com, EPM.com)

- **Information broker:** Provides product, pricing, and availability information to individuals and businesses. Generates revenue from advertising or from directing buyers to sellers (Edmunds.com, Kbb.com, Insweb.com, IndustrialMall.com)

- **Transaction broker:** Saves users money and time by processing online sales transactions, generating a fee each time a transaction occurs. Also provides information on rates and terms (E*TRADE.com, Expedia.com)

- **Online marketplace:** Provides a digital environment where buyers and sellers can meet, search for products, display products, and establish prices for those products (eBay.com, Priceline.com, ChemConnect.com, Pantellos.com)

- **Content provider:** Creates revenue by providing digital content, such as digital news, music, photos, or video, over the Web (WSJ.com, CNN.com, TheStreet.com, Gettyimages.com, MP3.com)

- **Online service provider:** Provides online service for individuals and businesses. Generates revenue from subscription or transaction fees, from advertising, or from collecting marketing information from users (@Backup.com, Xdrive.com, Employease.com, Salesforce.com)

- **Virtual community:** Provides an online meeting place where people with similar interests can communicate and find useful information (Motocross.com, iVillage.com, Sailnet.com)

- **Portal:** Provides initial point of entry to the Web along with specialized content and other services (Yahoo.com, MSN.com, StarMedia.com)

Hayes and Finnegan (2005) present several classifications of e-business models. One classification includes e-shop, e-mall, e-procurement, third-party marketplace, e-auction, virtual community, collaboration platform, value chain service provider, value chain integration, information brokerage, and trust services. Another classification includes aggregation, agora/open market, alliance, and value chain. Next classification includes catalogue hubs, other hubs, yield managers, exchanges, forward aggregator, and reverse aggregator. A final classification consists of a long list including "clicks and mortar" merchant model, virtual merchant, catalogue merchant, virtual mall, metamediary, distributor, manufacturer model, buy/sell fulfillment, market exchange, bounty broker, auction broker, reverse auction, vertical Web community, specialized portal, knowledge networks, open source model, content services, trust services, and transaction broker.

Electronic business poses significant challenges for organizations as it affects both how organizations relate to external parties (customers, suppliers, partners, competitors, and markets) and how they operate internally in managing activities, processes, and systems. Porter (2001) argues that the companies that succeed with e-business will be those that use the Internet in conjunction with their traditional business models and activities.

Hayes and Finnegan (2005) argue that business models are possibly the most discussed, yet least understood, area of electronic business. They refer to how consultants, executives, researchers, and journalists have abused the phrase business model but have rarely given a precise definition of what they exactly meant by using it, and that this has led to the loss of credibility of the concept.

A business model can be understood as a blend of three streams: value, revenue, and logistics. The value stream is concerned with the value proposition for buyers, sellers, and market makers. The revenue stream identifies how the organizations will earn revenue, and the logistics stream involves detailing how supply chain issues will affect the organizations involved (Hayes & Finnegan, 2005).

A business model also can be understood as an architecture for product, service, and information flows, incorporating a description of the sources of revenue, the actors involved, their roles, and the benefits to them. An electronic business model is comprised of components, linkages, and dynamics. Components are factors such as customer scope, product (goods and services) scope, customer value, pricing, revenue sources, connected activities, implementation, capabilities of the firm, and sustainability. Linkages exist when one activity affects another in terms of cost-effectiveness, and trade-offs and optimization are sought to find the right blend to achieve competitive advantage. The dynamics represent how a firm reacts to or initiates change to attain a new competitive advantage, or to sustain an existing one, to have sustainable competitive advantage and to perform better than its rivals in the long term (Hayes & Finnegan, 2005).

While the atomic business models by Weill and Vitale (2002) were distinguished along dimensions such as infrastructure, sources of revenue, and critical success factors, we can think of other criteria to classify an e-business model. For example, three major areas that impact on the sustainability and growth of an e-business are revenue streams, value streams, and logistical streams. These three elements are interrelated with changes in any one impacting on the other. Furthermore, e-business models can be classified in terms of integration with customers versus integration with partners, as illustrated in Figure 7.3.

At the moment, there is no single, comprehensive, and cogent taxonomy of the Web business models. Businesses face questions as to what is their appropriate business model. This is made more difficult when we consider that companies in the same industry often pursue different Internet business models. For example, companies in the automobile industry have industry consortia models such as shared infrastructure, while others have virtual community models.

As a result, determining and employing an appropriate Internet business model has become a major business issue. The problem is that there is no well-developed or complete framework to aid the decision of choosing a model.

In addition to outlining the components of a business model, some authors offer a set of business model representation tools. Weill and Vitale (2001) have developed a formalism to assist analyzing e-business initiatives, which they call e-business model schematic. The schematic is a pictorial representation, aiming to highlight a business model's important elements. This includes characteristics of the firm of interest, its suppliers and allies, the major flows of product, information, and money, and finally the revenues and other benefits each participant receives.

In determining an appropriate e-business model, several criteria can be used, such as:

- **Involved parties**, such as business-to-business, business-to-consumer, and/or consumer-to-consumer.

- **Revenue sources**, such as transaction fee, product price, and/or exposure fee.

- **Value configuration**, such as value chain, value shop, and/or value network.

- **Integration** with customers and/or partners.

- **Relationships**, such as one-to-many, many-to-many, and/or many-to-one.

- **Knowledge**, such as know-how, know-what, and know-why.

Unfortunately, e-business models still fall under open and weak theory domains. An open domain is one that cannot be realistically modeled. A weak theory domain is a domain in which relationships between important concepts are uncertain. General knowledge in such domains is theoretically uncertain, incomplete, and subject to changes. Methods that rely on deductive proofs are not readily applicable. Concepts and statements in Internet business models are more or less plausible, stronger or weaker supported, rather than true or false.

Fortunately, new research on e-business models is emerging. For example, Hayes and Finnegan (2005) present different approaches to understanding e-business models. One approach is the e-business model *ontology*, which can be defined as a rigorous definition of the e-business issues and their interdependencies in a company's business model. The e-business model ontology focuses on four aspects of the organization: product innovation, infrastructure management, customer relationship, and financials.

Dimensions of product innovation are target customer segment, value proposition, and capabilities. Dimensions of customer relationship are information strategy, feel and serve, and trust and loyalty. Dimensions of infrastructure management are resources, activity configuration, and partner network, while dimensions of financials are revenue model, cost structure, and profit/loss.

Architectures for business models can be identified through the deconstruction and reconstruction of the value configuration. Value configuration elements are identified as well as the possible ways that information can be integrated in the value configuration and between the respective value configurations of the parties that are interacting.

As we have seen, decision-makers are faced with an enormous range of electronic business models from which to choose. The process of fully researching each of these models can prove daunting. Such research is a feature of what has been termed the intelligence phase of decision-making. This phase is important as options excluded at this stage do not get considered at a later stage. Hayes and Finnegan (2005) developed a framework for use at the intelligence phase to exclude models that are incompatible with prevailing organizational and supply chain characteristics.

The framework assesses the following characteristics: economic control, supply chain integration, functional integration, innovation, and input sourcing:

- **Economic control** refers to the degree to which a market is hierarchical or self-organizing. This characteristic can be measured in terms of the extent of regulatory bodies, government policy, customers, asset specificity, switching costs, proprietary products, capital requirements, and access to necessary inputs for new entrants in this industry.

- **Supply chain integration** is considered to be a measure of the degree to which the business functions and processes of an organization are integrated with those of their supply chain partners. This characteristic can be measured in terms of shipping scheduling, transportation management, tax reporting, negotiating customer credit terms, negotiating supplier credit terms, determining freight charges and terms, resource planning, and inventory control.

- **Functional integration** refers to the degree to which multiple functions are integrated in a business model. In order to measure the degree to which functions within an organization are integrated, a scale that considers a detailed list of processes can be applied. Examples of process integrations are purchase order processing with servicing functions, shipping scheduling with manufacturing, transportation management with financial functions, tax reporting with financial functions, negotiating customer credit terms with distribution, and negotiating supplier credit terms with distribution.

- **Innovation** is the degree of innovation of an e-business model, which can be defined as the extent to which processes can be performed via the Internet that were not previously possible. Innovation can be divided into internal and external components based on the firm's ability (internal) to innovate or assimilate innovations within the innovative environment of the industrial sector (external).

- **Sourcing** refers to the way in which inputs are sourced by the organization, either systematically from a long-term supplier or through spot markets. The issue of sourcing raw materials is more straightforward as manufacturing and operating inputs are either sourced systematically or on spot markets.

Hayes and Finnegan (2005) believe that their framework has the potential to help decision-makers by providing a method of excluding from consideration those electronic business models that are unsuitable given prevailing organizational and environmental characteristics. Business models are excluded based on scale ratings for items measuring economic control, supply chain integration, functional integration, innovation, and sourcing. For each scale, the decision-maker needs to determine the number of attributes that are applicable to their organization.

Infrastructure Capabilities

As firms integrate e-business into their existing business, they migrate from traditional physical business models to combined physical and virtual models. This shift increases the role of the information technology infrastructure because information and online transaction processing become more important. However, the large number of infrastructure investment options can easily overwhelm senior management. To help, Weill and Vitale (2002) classified e-business initiatives by the building blocks they use (which are called atomic e-business models), and they examined the main IT infrastructure services that these models need. The business models require surprisingly different IT infrastructure services, so categorization should help executives prioritize their IT infrastructure investments based on their business goals. At the heart of this prioritization process is the firm's IT governance process, which should ensure that IT knows of upcoming IT infrastructure needs early in the strategizing process.

Weill and Vitale (2002) define a firm's information technology portfolio as its total investment in computing and communications technology. The IT portfolio thus includes hardware, software, telecommunications, electronically stored data, devices to collect and represent data, and the people who provide IT services.

IT Infrastructure

The foundation of an IT portfolio is the firm's information technology infrastructure. This internal IT infrastructure is composed of four elements: IT components (the technologist's view of the infrastructure building blocks), human IT infrastructure (the intelligence used to translate the IT components into services that users can draw upon), shared IT services (the user's view of the infrastructure), and shared and standard applications (fairly stable uses of the services) as illustrated in Figure 7.4.

- **IT components:** At the base of the internal infrastructure are the technical components, such as computers, printers, database software packages, op-

Figure 7.4. The hierarchy of IT infrastructure

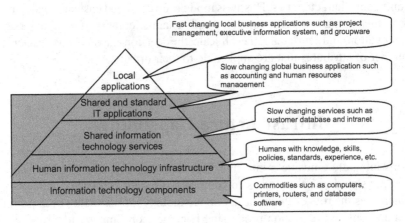

erating systems, and scanners. These components are commodities and are readily available in the marketplace. Traditionally, IT infrastructures have been described in terms of these components. Unfortunately, while technologists understand the capabilities of these components, business people do not — components are not business language to them. Thus, technologists and business people have had difficulty discussing infrastructure needs and business models because they have not had a common language (Weill & Vitale, 2002).

- **Human IT infrastructure:** Describing IT components in business terms requires a translation. That translation is handled by people and is performed in this layer which builds on the IT components layer. The human IT infrastructure layer consists of knowledge, skills, standards, and experience. These tools are used to bind IT components into reliable services, which are services business people can understand (Weill & Vitale, 2002).

- **Shared IT services:** This layer views the infrastructure as a set of services that users can understand, draw upon, and share, to conduct their business. For example, to link with customers and partners, they can draw on channel management services. To manage data, they can draw on data management services. To handle security, they can draw on security and risk services. In all, Weill and Vitale (2002) identified nine service areas needed by IT-enabled business models — with 70 services in all. Therefore, describing IT infrastructure as a set of reliable services allows business people and technologists to discuss business models and their underlying infrastructure needs because the two parties speak the same language.

- **Shared and standard applications:** The top piece of the IT infrastructure consists of stable applications, such as human resource management, budgeting, and accounting. In the last five to seven years, there has been a significant trend by multi-business firms to standardize their common business processes and the associated IT applications. The driver for some firms was improving and reengineering their business processes; for others, it was implementation of large enterprise resource planning (ERP) systems. As a result, shared and standard applications have been added to the typical firm's IT infrastructure (Weill & Vitale, 2002).

Based on these layers, a firm's IT infrastructure capability is its integrated set of reliable IT infrastructure services available to support both existing applications and new initiatives.

The time required to implement a new e-business initiative depends in part on the firm's infrastructure capability. For example, in building a new Web-based housing loan system, a large bank needed to use the following information technology infrastructure services: mainframe and server processing, customer databases, both local area and national communications networks, and security procedures and systems. Having most of these infrastructure services already in place significantly reduced the time and cost to build the loan system (Weill & Vitale, 2002).

Infrastructure Services

Weill and Vitale (2002) identified nine service areas with 70 services needed by IT-enabled e-business models. The service areas were (number of services in parenthesis): applications infrastructure (13), communications (7), data management (6), IT management (9), security (4), architecture and standards (20), channel management (7), IT research and development (2), and IT education (2):

Applications Infrastructure

1. Internet policies such as employee access

2. Enforce Internet policies

3. E-mail policies such as inappropriate and personal mail, harassment policies, filtering policies

4. Enforce e-mail policies

5. Centralized management of e-business applications such as common standards

6. Centralized management of infrastructure capacity such as server traffic

7. Integrated mobile computing applications such as access for internal users

8. ERP (enterprise resource planning) services

9.   Middleware linking systems on different platforms

10.   Wireless applications such as Web applications for wireless devices

11.   Application services provision to business units

12.   Workflow applications such as groupware

13.   Payment transaction processing such as EFT (electronic funds transfer)

Communications

14.   Communications network services

15.   Broadband communication services

16.   Intranet capabilities to support publishing, directories, etc.

17.   Extranet capabilities to support information and applications

18.   Workstation networks

19.   EDI (electronic data interchange) linkages to customers and suppliers

20.   Electronic support to groups

Data Management

21.   Manage key data independent of applications

22.   A centralized data warehouse that summarizes key information from decentralized databases

23.   Data management advice and consultancy

24.   Electronic provision of management information

25.   Storage farms or storage area networks

26.   Knowledge management in terms of contract database, information databases, and communities of practice

IT Management

27.   Large-scale data processing facilities

28.   Server farms including mail server, Web servers, and printer servers

29.   Installation and maintenance of workstations and LANs (local area networks)

30.   Information systems planning for strategy

31.   Information systems project management

32.   Negotiate with suppliers and outsourcers

33.   Service level agreements

34. Common systems development environment
35. Pilot e-business initiatives such as pilot Web shop fronts

Security

36. Security policies for use of information systems
37. Enforce security policies for information systems
38. Disaster planning for business applications
39. Firewall on secure gateway services

Architecture and Standards

40. Specify architectures for data by setting high-level guidelines for data use and integration
41. Specify architectures for technology by setting high-level guidelines for technology use and integration
42. Specify architectures for communications by setting high-level guidelines for communications use and integration
43. Specify architectures for applications by setting high-level guidelines for applications use and integration
44. Specify architectures for work by setting high-level guidelines for the way work will be conducted
45. Enforce architectures for data
46. Enforce architectures for technology
47. Enforce architectures for communications
48. Enforce architectures for applications
49. Enforce architectures for work
50. Specify architecture standards for data
51. Specify architecture standards for technology
52. Specify architecture standards for communications
53. Specify architecture standards for applications
54. Specify architecture standards for work
55. Enforce architecture standards for data
56. Enforce architecture standards for technology
57. Enforce architecture standards for communications
58. Enforce architecture standards for applications
59. Enforce architecture standards for work

Channel Management

60. Electronic file transfer protocols
61. Kiosks
62. Web sites
63. Call centers
64. IVRs
65. Mobile phones
66. Mobile computing

IT Research and Development

67. Identify and test new technologies for business purposes
68. Evaluate proposals for new information systems initiatives

IT Education

69. Training and use of IT
70. Management education for generating value from IT use

These 70 infrastructure services were identified by Weill and Vitale (2002) when they studied IT infrastructure services and e-business. They studied 50 e-business initiatives in 15 firms. Based on their study, they identified eight atomic business models, nine infrastructure areas with 70 infrastructure services. The nine infrastructure areas were defined as follows:

- **Applications infrastructure**. An application is a software program that resides on a computer for the purpose of translating electronic input into meaningful form. Applications management includes purchasing software, developing proprietary applications, modifying applications, providing installation and technical support, and other tasks related to ensuring that applications are meeting the needs of the organization.

- **Communications**. Technology that facilitates digital communication both within the organization and with the outside world is relevant here. It includes the management of hardware and software to facilitate communication via computer, telephone, facsimile, pagers, mobile phones, and other communication and messaging services. It includes the cabling and any other communication linkages required to create an effective communications network, in addition to the necessary hardware and applications to meet the needs of the organization.

- **Data management**. This refers to the way the organization structures and handles its information resources. Data may be sourced from internal or external databases. Data management includes data collection, database design, sorting and reporting information, creating links to external databases, ensuring data compatibility, and other activities surrounding the effective management of electronic information.

- **IT management**. Information technology management includes many of the professional and strategic activities of the information technology group including negotiation, IS planning, project management, and other tasks. IS project management is defined as the coordination and control of all of the activities required to complete an information systems project.

- **Security**. To protect data, equipment, and processing time, organizations restrict access to certain data and protect data and applications from manipulation and contamination. Recovery refers to the need for a plan to maintain computer operations and information should a disaster occur.

- **Architecture and standards**. Information technology architecture is a set of policies and rules that govern the use of information technology and plot a migration path to the way business will be done in the future. In most firms, it provides technical guidelines rather than rules for decision-making. Architecture has to cope with both business uncertainty and technological change, making it one of the most difficult tasks for a firm. A good architecture evolves over time and is documented and accessible to all managers in the firm. Each architecture decision needs a sound business base to encourage voluntary agreement and compliance across the business. A standard is a detailed definition of the technical choices to implement an architecture. Five elements of architectures and standards are important: data, technology, communications, applications, and work. It can be distinguished between specifying architecture or standards and enforcement.

- **Channel management**. New and emerging technologies allow direct connections or distribution channels to customers.

- **IT research and development**. The information systems market develops rapidly, particularly with the rise of new e-business technologies. Thus, it is necessary to continually test applications and hardware to assist with planning decisions. IT research and development includes identifying and testing new technologies for business purposes and evaluating proposals for new information systems initiatives.

- **IT education**. Training and education in the use of IT can be defined as formal classes, individual training, and technology-based self-training programs for users ensuring hands-on computer proficiency levels meeting corporate requirements. IS management education can be defined as education aimed at senior levels in the firm designed to generate value from IT use.

Our presentation of Weill and Vitale's (2002) work on infrastructure services indicate the number and complexity of services that constitute the IT infrastructure in an organization to enable electronic business. Successfully implementing e-business initiatives depends on having the necessary IT infrastructure in place. E-business initiatives can be decomposed into their underlying atomic e-business models, which can have quite different IT infrastructure requirements.

For example, the most critical IT infrastructure service for the first business model of content provider might be storage farms or storage area networks, which is a data management service number 25 on the list. Here, it can be argued that as a content provider, the quality, quantity, and availability of content by electronic means is the most critical service. For the next e-business model of direct to customer, getting paid in an efficient way might be the most critical factor for success, leading to the need for IT infrastructure service number 13 which is payment transaction processing.

Strategic Agility

Companies need to build IT infrastructure for strategic agility. Strategic agility is defined by the set of business initiatives an enterprise can readily implement. Many elements contribute to agility, including customer base, brand, core competence, infrastructure and employees' ability to change. Organizing and coordinating those elements into an integrated group of resources results in an enterprise capability, which, if superior to that of competitors, becomes a distinctive competence. Research conducted by Weill, Subramani, and Broadbent (2002) demonstrated a significant correlation between strategic agility and IT infrastructure capability. This suggests that if managers can describe their desired strategic agility, they then can identify the IT infrastructure service clusters that need to be above the industry average — and thus can create a distinctive competence.

Strategic agility is the ability of a firm to continually sense and explore customer and marketplace enrichment opportunities and respond with the appropriate configurations of capabilities and capacities to exploit these opportunities with speed, surprise, and competitive success. According to Sambamurthy and Zmud (2004), enriching customers, leveraging capabilities and capacities, nurturing inter-organizational cooperation, and mastering change and uncertainty are the four building blocks of strategic agility.

Enriching customers can include the following activities:

- **Solution-centricity:** deliver total solutions for current and anticipated customer needs. Solutions are customizable bundles of products and services.

- **Customer-centricity:** heighten customer convenience, including space, time, speed, and personalized convenience.

- **Accelerate solution and product innovation** to continually refresh customer offerings: portfolio of incremental, architectural, and radical innovation projects.

- **Co-opt customers in the innovation process:** Customers are sources of ideas for product and solution offerings. Customers are co-creators of innovative ideas.

Leveraging capabilities and capacities is the next building block. First, an ecosystem of capabilities has to be built. The ecosystem might consist of customer relationship management, selling chain management, supply-demand synchronization, manufacturing management, financial engineering, brand management, human capital management, and information technology management. Next, world-class excellence has to be nurtured. This implies focus on a balanced set of metrics, such as adaptiveness, responsiveness, speed, cost, effectiveness, and quality. This also implies applying continuous improvement methods for capability enhancement and investing in and developing enabling information infrastructures and services platforms.

Nurturing inter-organizational cooperation is concerned with value net concept, value net posture, and value net integration. In the context of strategic agility, value nets are configurations of sourcing and partnership structures for building the extended enterprise. This definition is different from our main definition of value network as a value configuration in this book. In the context of strategic agility, value nets are architected to leverage other firms' capabilities and assets that complement core capabilities and assets within a firm. Value net posture is concerned with the governance of the value net, which can be either prescriptive or collaborative. Value net integration requires focus on the value net and expertise replication or expertise integration. In addition, the following actions are important in nurturing inter-organizational cooperation:

- Identify and certify potential partners with regard to desired competencies (assets, capabilities) and their financial solvency.

- Develop and continually assess working relationships with partners.

- Develop abilities to work with partners through a variety of contractual mechanisms.

- Develop competencies to quickly establish (and remove) the technology, process, and managerial interfaces needed when initiating business arrangements with new partners.

Mastering change and uncertainty is the fourth and final building block of strategic agility. It requires strategic foresight, strategic insight, and organizational learning. The following actions are important in mastering change and uncertainty:

- Sense, anticipate, and exploit trends, opportunities, and threats.
- Quickly and seamlessly marshal the combinations of capabilities necessary in shaping innovative moves.
- Quickly reconfigure capabilities necessary in shaping innovative moves.
- Execute and learn from strategic experiments and from strategic actions.

The evidence from leading enterprises indicates that implementing different types of electronic business initiatives based on atomic e-business models requires different high-capability IT infrastructures. Strategic agility requires time, money, leadership, and focus — an understanding of which distinct patterns of high-capability infrastructures are needed where. Investing in IT infrastructure is like buying an option. If used successfully, infrastructure enables faster time to market; if not, it will prove an unnecessary cost. To ensure that investments in IT infrastructure support the organization's strategic goals and business initiatives, Weill et al. (2002) consider it critical for the enterprise's most senior executives to understand which specific IT infrastructure capabilities are needed for which kinds of initiatives. That way, they can have some assurance that the investments they make today will serve the strategies of tomorrow.

One approach to improving strategic agility is utility computing. Utility computing proposes to allow clients to buy computing capacity as they do electricity — just by plugging in. For clients, the cost is variable and based on the actual capacity they demand, rather than a fixed cost for a capacity they only use during peak periods. They can get the capacity they need whenever they need it, without expending resources and effort to regularly monitor and upgrade capacity (Ross & Westerman, 2004)

The vision of utility computing goes beyond traditional outsourcing of IT services. It includes all potential combinations of sourcing options, as we shall see in the second part of this book. Vendors are promising to offer applications and business processes, including computing, applications, and expert staff, in an on-demand format, just as many firms now buy call center and payroll processes (Ross & Westerman, 2004).

Utility computing relies on several important technical capabilities to deliver these promised services. First, grid computing enables a network of processors to provide shared processing capacity by seamlessly accessing unused capacity elsewhere. Second, autonomic computing technology enables a network to be self-healing, and thus provides higher reliability across a system than is currently available. Third, Web services provide technical standards that facilitate integration across systems.

In combining these three capabilities in a one-to-many business model, vendors expect to offer on-demand computing capacity and a wide range of plug-and-play technology and process components (Ross & Westerman, 2004).

Another approach to improving strategic agility is organizational architecture work. Organizations often relegate the job of aligning business needs and technology support to IT or operations, but with the strategic uncertainties of e-business, Sauer and Willcocks (2002) find that a separate coordinating role of organizational architect may be the only solution.

The shifting competitive landscape is creating a larger gap between strategists and technologists. Executives are busy creating and refining visions and have little time to focus on technology. Technologists are busy keeping the platform current and have little time to understand the business in depth. Without a mechanism to force communication, each group retreats into its specialty.

Among companies that were successfully aligning business and technology in e-business, Sauer and Willcocks (2002) identified a series of bridging activities that amounted to the creation of what they call organizational architect. An organizational architect is someone who is neither all strategist nor all technologist, who guides the translation of a strategic vision to a flexible, integrated platform. Organizational architects sustain a dialogue between visionaries and technologists as they define and design the right combination of structures, processes, capabilities, and technologies. This combination has a greater chance of improving strategic agility by being responsive to shifting organizational goals.

Sauer and Willcocks (2002) surveyed chief executive officers and chief information officers at 97 companies in the United States, Europe, and Australia that had moved or were moving to e-business. Most were responding to an increasingly volatile business environment by shrinking their development and planning cycles. Half of the companies did not extend their plans beyond one year, and half of those with infrastructure plans updated them quarterly.

Lacking some mechanism to bridge the interests of strategists and technologists, information technology cannot prepare for change, and senior business executives end up guiding and funding short-term technology initiatives. Organizational architects work with both strategists and technologists to identify and grow the organizational and technical capabilities needed to see a vision through to its supporting platform. The architect sees the vision through three main translation phases (Sauer & Willcocks, 2002):

- **Phase 1. From vision to organization:** The organizational architect sets design parameters for the organizational structures, processes, and capabilities that make the vision possible.

- **Phase 2. From organization to technology requirements:** The architect now works to map the organizational needs to platform characteristics.

- **Phase 3. From technology requirements to actual platform:** The architect is now ready to get a fix on reality by talking with technology experts about what they can actually do.

An organizational architect is a significant investment for a business, so it will be important to underwrite the position even though it is essentially a staff function with no immediately visible commercial benefits. Sauer and Willcocks (2002) argue that persistence will be required particularly in difficult economic times.

Sambamurthy and Zmud (2004) define the evolution toward strategic agility in terms of four generations. The first generation was total quality management, while the second was lean management and mass customization,then, followed organizational adaptiveness before strategic agility emerged. Each generation of corporate transformation has emphasized specific types of capabilities and performance enhancement. Path-dependent progression through each of these waves is essential as the learning that occurs within each wave produces necessary changes in orientation and capacity.

Total quality management had efficiency as its competitive base, while lean management and mass customization had customer centricity and product variety as its base. Organizational adaptiveness was characterized by flexibility and partnerships, while strategic agility has entrepreneurial sense-making and improvisation as its competitive base. Furthermore, strategic agility has the design objective of innovation and disruption and the decision architecture of external-internal collaboration.

The evolution toward agility in terms of information architecture started with data and metrics rationalization (total quality management), moved on to process rationalization and data integration (lean management and mass customization), then to meta process rationalization and meta data integration (organizational adaptiveness), and finally to information visibility and information probing (strategic agility).

According to Sambamurthy and Zmud (2004), information technologies can enable agility in several ways. First, the strategic role of IT can shift to fluid decision, authority, and collaboration structures. Second, the IT architecture can shift to modular form. Next, key technologies will be Web services, objects, intelligent agents, and distributed collaboration technologies. Fourth, key IT partnerships will include partners' market experts. Finally, IT investment focus will no longer be cost reduction, productivity improvement, time-to-market, or product life cycle refreshment. Rather, IT investment will focus on real options, market prototyping, time-to-solution, and relationship capital.

Of critical importance is IT investment in IT infrastructure. Strategic agility requires a distinct pattern of high-capability infrastructures. Getting the right balance is difficult. Under-investing reduces strategic agility and slows time-to-market. Also, infrastructure investments must be made before investments in business applications because doing both at the same time results in infrastructure fragmentation. But if the infrastructure is not used or is the wrong kind, a company is over-investing and wasting resources (Weill et al., 2002).

Sambamurthy and Zmud (2004) provide the following managerial guidelines for strategic agility:

- Adaptiveness enables competitive success in the digital economy.
- Strategic agility enables competitive leadership.
- Adaptiveness requires the co-integration of customer- and solution-centricity, capabilities built around information, process, and information technology infrastructures, and value net architectures.
- Additionally, strategic agility requires the mastery of change and uncertainty through entrepreneurial orientation and sensing capabilities.
- Strategic agility is nurtured at multiple levels: competitive agility, innovation agility, and functional agility.
- The evolution toward strategic agility occurs through the learning gained by prior investments in total quality management, lean management, and value net integration.
- Information technology management facilitates strategic agility as a digital options generator by representing a platform for process innovation, for value net integration, and for innovation and strategic experimentation.
- Attention must be focused on significant transformations of the IT function, such as IT architecture, IT investment, IT partnerships, and organizing logic.

Strategic agility is an emerging concept that needs research concerning both organizational and technology issues. Organizational issues include competency development and organizational architecture as demonstrated by the need for organizational architects. Technology issues include distributed intelligence, interfacing intelligent agents and humans, knowledge discovery technologies and processes, rapid start-up and integration initiatives, meta data and process architectures, and end-to-end value chain information visibility (Sambamurthy & Zmud, 2004).

One approach to organizational actions for strategic agility is organization capital readiness. Kaplan and Norton (2004) define organization capital as the ability of the organization to mobilize and sustain the process of change required to execute strategy. Organization capital provides the capability for integration so that individual intangible human and information capital assets, as well as tangible physical and financial assets, are not only aligned to the strategy, but are all integrated and working together to achieve the organization's strategic objectives. An enterprise with high organization capital has a shared understanding of vision, mission, values and strategy, is strongly led, has created a performance culture around the strategy, and shares knowledge across the organization.

If managers can describe their desired strategic agility, they then can identify the IT infrastructure services that need to be above the industry average — and thus can create a distinctive competence. Although none of the enterprises Weill et al. (2002) evaluated had all 70 infrastructure services presented earlier, those with the highest degree of strategic agility had more services in each of the 10 clusters, broader implementations of each service, and more demanding service-level agreements.

Important drivers of strategic agility are strategy, sourcing and governance. Strategy describes paths to the desired future, sourcing describes access to resources for the desired future, while governance describes management mechanisms to lead into the desired future.

References

Afuah, A., & Tucci, C. L. (2003). *Internet business models and strategies* (2nd ed.). New York: McGraw-Hill.

Chang, K., Jackson, J., & Grover, V. (2003). E-commerce and corporate strategy: An executive perspective. *Information & Management, 40,* 663-675.

Fahey, L., Srivastava, R., Sharon, J. S., & Smith, D. E. (2001). Linking e-business and operating processes: The role of knowledge management. *IBM Systems Journal, 40*(4), 889-907.

Grover, V., & Ramanlal, P. (1999). Six myths of information and markets: Information technology networks, electronic commerce, and the battle for consumer surplus. *MIS Quarterly, 23*(4), 465-495.

Grover, V., & Saeed, K.A. (2004). Strategic orientation and performance of Internet-based businesses. *Information Systems Journal, 14,* 23-42.

Hayes, J., & Finnegan, P. (2005). Assessing the potential of e-business models: Towards a framework for assisting decision-makers. *European Journal of Operational Research, 160,* 365-379.

Kaplan, R. S., & Norton, D. P. (2004). *Strategy maps*. Boston: Harvard Business School Press.

Laudon, K. C., & Laudon, J. P. (2005). *Essentials of management information systems — managing the digital firm* (6th ed.). Upper Saddle River, NJ: Pearson Education.

Porter. M. E. (2001, March). Strategy and the Internet. *Harvard Business Review*, 63-78.

Ross, J. W., & Westerman, G. (2004). Preparing for utility computing: The role of IT architecture and relationship management. *IBM Systems Journal, 43*(1), 5-19.

Sambamurty, V., & Zmud, R. (2004, March). *Steps toward strategic agility: Guiding corporate transformations*. Presentations, Michigan State University and University of Oklahoma.

Sauer, C., & Willcocks, L. P. (2002, Spring). The evolution of the organizational architect. *MIT Sloan Management Review*, 41-49.

Turban, E., King, D., Lee, J., Warkentin, M., & Chung, H. M. (2002). *Electronic commerce: A managerial perspective.* Sydney, Australia: Pearson Educatin, Prentice Hall.

Weill, P., Subramani, M., & Broadbent, M. (2002, Fall). Building IT infrastructure for strategic agility. *MIT Sloan Management Review*, 57-65.

Weill, P., & Vitale, M. R. (2001). *Place to space, migrating to eBusiness models.* Boston: Harvard Business School Press.

Weill, P., & Vitale, M. R. (2002). What IT infrastructure capabilities are needed to implement e-business models? *MIS Quarterly Executive, 1*(1), 17-34.

Chapter VIII

The CIO Sourcing IT Services

Introduction

CEO compensation can influence outsourcing of information technology. Hall and Liedtka (2005) found a relationship between CEO self-interest and IT outsourcing decisions. Sourcing decisions such as IT outsourcing influences the position of the CIO and, hence, the CIO's potential to become the next CEO.

IT Sourcing Options

IT sourcing is concerned with defining, planning, and managing how an enterprise deploys internal and external resources and services to ensure the continuous fulfillment of its business objectives. A variety of sources have emerged. This variety is illustrated in Figure 8.1. Here, we find internal sourcing and external sourcing. Both can be managed either through organizational hierarchy or through market mechanism.

In general, organizations have three basic alternatives for acquiring technological know-how. They can: (1) develop the technology independently, (2) acquire another

Figure 8.1. Sourcing options

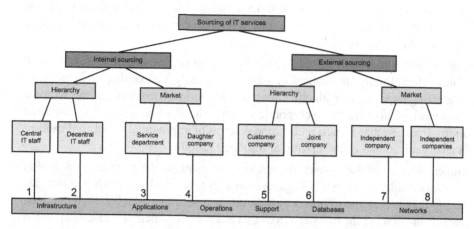

company that already has the technology, or (3) enter into a technology-sourcing arrangement. If a firm lacks the capabilities needed to develop a technology independently and other organizations already have the technology, management can consider external sourcing. There is a continuum of external sourcing methods based on the level of mutual commitment between the firm that has the technology (the source firm) and the firm that desires the know-how (the sourcing firm). These methods range from arms-length licensing contracts, through more tightly coupled co-development partnerships and joint ventures, to the outright acquisition of the source firm (Steensma & Corley, 2001).

Steensma and Corley (2001) focused on the two polar extremes in their study of technology sourcing: market contracting through licensing versus the use of firm hierarchy through acquisition. The polar cases are basic particles from which more elaborate arrangements are constructed. Hierarchy implies that the sourcing firm can hierarchically control the technology, personnel, and other assets of the IT function and apply it to its current needs at its discretion.

The Internal market as illustrated with numbers 3 and 4 in Figure 8.1 has a different sourcing logic. The concept of the internal market is not new. The concept was first perceived to have radical implications eliminating superior-subordinate relationships, organizing all activity in terms of self-responsible profit centers, determining compensation objectively, eliminating internal monopolies, allowing freedom of access to information, and establishing a corporate constitution (King & Malhotra, 2000).

These appear to be less radical in today's environment of matrix organizations, self-managed teams, and re-engineered business processes. However, the notion of internal markets is not as simple as first suggested. The internal market is a mechanism for unleashing market forces inside the firm. Firms selecting this alternative might be able to retain control of the function while achieving the objectives of cost savings and service-responsiveness that are often ascribed to an external vendor (King & Malhotra, 2000).

Today, the internal market within an organization is characterized by a setup in which internal units are enabled to act autonomously by exerting self-control in conducting transactions with other internal units and with external entities within a framework of an overarching corporate vision, values, and precepts. This notion of internal markets may be best understood in terms of its potential broad applicability in an organizational context (King & Malhotra, 2000).

Implementation of the internal market concept requires the creation of a market economy inside a firm. In this, organizational units buy and sell goods and services among themselves and to others outside the firm at prices established in the open market. In contrast, the transfer prices that are used for internal transactions often represent a simulation of a marketing-clearing mechanism (King & Malhotra, 2000).

In IT sourcing, the term strategic sourcing is often used. Strategic sourcing has the following characteristics (Else, 2002):

- Systematic, ongoing effort to align individual sources and the portfolio of sources with broad high-level corporate strategy.
- Choosing and managing a set of specific sources in ways that advances one or more strategic goals.
- Continuous business process—not a tactical procurement exercise—intended to dynamically map business requirements to service delivery options.
- Methodology to deploy technology strategy and the means by which a business strategy is optimized.
- Highly multisourced environments will be the norm.
- Enterprises must develop new roles, processes, and governance structures to effectively manage the sourcing spectrum.

The increasing complexity of sourcing options and combinations has led *Computerworld* (2005, p. 3) to stress qualifications needed by IT leaders:

Today's IT leaders operate in a vast sphere. They are multidimensional business executives, by turns global architects, employee boosters, and deal negotiators.

The purpose of IT sourcing can best be illustrated by sourcing principles developed for government agencies in the United States (Else, 2002, p. 35):

1. *Support agency missions, goals, and objectives.*

2. *Be consistent with human capital practices designed to attract, motivate, retain, and reward a high-performing federal workforce.*

3. *Recognize that inherently governmental and certain other functions should be performed by federal workers.*

4. *Create incentives and processes to foster high-performing, efficient, and effective organizations throughout the federal government.*

5. *Be based on a clear, transparent, and consistently applied process.*

6. *Avoid arbitrary full-time equivalent (FTE) or other arbitrary numerical goals.*

7. *Establish a process that, for activities that may be performed by either the public or the private sector, would permit public and private sources to participate in competitions for work currently performed in-house, work currently contracted to the private sector, and new work, consistent with these guiding principles.*

8. *Ensure that, when competitions are held, they are conducted as fairly, effectively, and efficiently as possible.*

9. *Ensure that competitions involve a process that considers both quality and cost factors.*

10. *Provide for accountability in connections with all sourcing decisions.*

Figure 8.2. IT function specialization as "IS Lite" (Adapted from Nielsen, 2004)

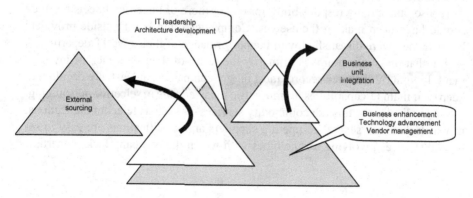

Nielsen (2004) tried to study IT sourcing by looking at the IS organization. As illustrated in Figure 8.2, the IS organization can be divided into different parts that may be delegated and integrated into other organizational arrangements.

IT Outsourcing Decisions

Information technology outsourcing is the practice of transferring responsibility to third-party vendors for the management of IT assets and staff, and for delivery of IT services such as data entry, data center operations, applications development, applications maintenance, and network management. Successful large-scale IT outsourcing can improve firm performance in several respects. By delegating complicated, time-consuming IT tasks to vendors, IT outsourcing customers can focus completely on those core competencies that create competitive advantage and thus firm value (Hall & Liedtka, 2005).

Given the potential headaches of managing IT, it is tempting to hand the job over to someone else. Indeed, outsourcing once appeared to be a simple solution to management frustrations, and senior management teams at many companies negotiated contracts with large service providers to run their entire IT functions. At a minimum, these providers were often able to provide IT capabilities for a lower cost and with fewer hassles than the companies had been able to themselves. But many of these outsourcing arrangements resulted in dissatisfaction, particularly as a company's business needs changed. Service providers, with their standard offerings and detailed contracts, provided IT capabilities that were not flexible enough to meet changing requirements, and they often seemed slow to respond to problems. Furthermore, a relationship with a supplier often required substantial investments of money and time, which entrenched that supplier in the company's strategic planning and business processes. The company then became particularly vulnerable if the supplier failed to meet its contractual obligations (Ross & Weill, 2002).

Problems arose because senior managers, in choosing to outsource the IT function, were also outsourcing responsibility for one or more of the crucial decisions they should have been making themselves. Companies often hired outside providers because they were dissatisfied with the performance of their own IT departments — but that dissatisfaction was primarily the result of their own lack of involvement. In light of this track record, most bigger companies, at least, are deciding to keep their main IT capabilities in-house. But many engage in selective outsourcing. Good candidates for this are commodity services — such as telecommunications, in which there are several competing suppliers and specifications are easy to set — and services involving technologies with which the company lacks expertise.

Unlike decisions to outsource the entire IT function, selective outsourcing decisions are usually best left to the IT unit — assuming that senior management has taken responsibility for overall strategy.

Beaumont and Costa (2002) studied information technology outsourcing in Australia. They found that close to 40% of Australian organizations outsource one or more IT applications. Large organizations tended to outsource more than small ones. The three most important reasons for outsourcing were access to skills, improved quality, and focus on core business. Four factors contributed to successful outsourcing: a tight contract, a partnership, a change process, and the IT manager's role changing from managing projects and operations to acquiring and managing the internal and external resources required to do the organization's IT work.

Successful IT outsourcing relationships enables participants to achieve organizational objectives and to build a competitive advantage that each organization could not easily attain by itself. Outsourcing success can be viewed as the level of fitness between the customer's requirements and the outsourcing outcomes. Outsourcing success can be measured in terms of both business and user perspectives. In a business perspective, outsourcing is motivated by the promise of strategic, economic, and technological benefits. The success of outsourcing, then, should be assessed in terms of attainment of these benefits. In a user perspective, outsourcing success is the level of quality of offered services. A decision to outsource on the basis of saving costs without analysis of the quality of services frequently leads to higher costs and lower user satisfaction. Therefore, it is imperative to conduct a proper analysis of the service quality before building a relationship with a service provider for a successful outsourcing arrangement (Lee & Kim, 1999).

The decision to outsource or insource enterprise-wide activities related to the acquisition, deployment, and management of IT represents one of the more complex choices facing a firm's managers. On the one hand, insourcing requires management to commit significant resources to a course of action, the effects of which may be costly to reverse, while forgoing numerous advantages associated with the marketplace. On the other hand, insourcing may be required for a firm to accumulate resources necessary to generate or maintain a competitive advantage.

The complexity of this decision is demonstrated in research conducted by Leiblein, Reuer, and Dalsace (2002). They examined the relationship between governance choice and technological performance. In contrast to popular arguments suggesting that insourcing or outsourcing will lead to superior technological performance, they found that governance decisions per se do not significantly influence technological performance directly. Rather, observed differences in the performance of transactions governed by different organizational forms are driven by factors underlying governance choice. While the increasing rapidity of technological change and the increasing dispersion of knowledge suggest an increased role for outsourcing in the economy, the relationship between governance choice and performance is dependent on the distribution of relevant capabilities and the degree to which performance is driven by autonomous or systemic innovation.

Empirical evidence suggests that carefully crafted outsourcing strategies increase the overall performance of the firm. Outsourcing is generally considered as a very powerful tool to cut costs and improve performance. Through outsourcing, firms can take advantage of the best outside vendors and restructure entrenched departments that are reluctant to change. Outsourcing can also help focus on the core business. Since building core competencies and serving customer needs are critical to firm success, anything that detracts from this focus may be considered for outsourcing (Barthélemy, 2003).

The decision to outsource is influenced by a number of factors. In this book, we will discuss factors such as production economies, transaction economies, technological uncertainty, functional complexity, transaction specific investments, supplier presence, slack resources, and criticality of IT. Many more factors will be presented.

Transformational Outsourcing

The traditional way of thinking in IT outsourcing is to move the current IT function out of the organization and let another organization handle it. There is no strategic thinking behind it, except the idea of solving a problem, saving some money, or improving a function by means of some undefined solutions. The new way of thinking is to make IT outsourcing part of a strategic transformation of the IT function, where new tasks and roles are implemented to replace old tasks and roles. A classic example of this new way of thinking was the transformation of the IT function at British Petroleum (BP) in the 1990s. The IT function went through a fundamental transformation consisting of the following changes (Cross, Earl, & Sampler, 1997):

- **From systems provider to infrastructure planner:** The mission of the IT function shifted from developing systems to overseeing technical integrity and pursuing value creation and cost reduction opportunities through information sharing.

- **From monopoly supplier to mixed sourcing:** In 1991, outsourcing of operations, telecommunications, systems development, and IT maintenance began, as BP recognized that it was not essential that these were carried out in-house. Some local sites already had experience in facilities management, and, as contracts came up for renewal, lessons were recorded and a worldwide outsourcing program implemented.

- **From business standards to industry standards:** IT managers have long been concerned about coordinating various types of computing and communication equipment. However, throughout most of the research on IT infrastructure, the focus has been directed at creating and managing the internal infrastructure. Therefore, BP spearheaded a unique initiative to help create an external software market by being one of the early advocates and founding members of the Petrotechnical Open Software Corporation, which was joined by a number of oil companies such as Elf, Mobil, Statoil, and Texaco.

- **From decentralized bias to centralized top sight:** The senior management team realized that the major benefit of centralized management of IT is not budget authority, but is in setting standards for infrastructure. While some IT resources still remain in the local businesses, it is the job of the top IT management team to provide the global perspective for infrastructure planning and cost control, which here is called top sight.

- **From systems analysts to business consultants:** A new skill set was defined for IT personnel. The new skill set has an equal balance between business, technical, and people skills. Such a radical change in the skill set of IT staff has been supported by a number of human resource initiatives such as skills testing, self-assessment, and personal development planning.

- **From craftsmen to project managers:** IT personnel no longer approach their job as craftsmen, viewing each job as a unique, customized process. Their task has switched to that of project managers, integrating and coordinating stakeholders involved in providing IT applications and operations.

- **From large function to lean teams:** Team orientation was stimulated in different ways. For example, staff was moved around the world to create global, not local, loyalties. A team building and team-working program was introduced stressing the use of multifunctional teams and diluting the functional focus.

The IT budget was reduced from $360 million in 1989 to $132 million in 1995 after this transformation. IT personnel were reduced from 1,400 persons to 150 persons in these six years. Hence, a large portion of the reduced IT budget went to external outsourcing vendors. As this pioneering case of IT outsourcing illustrates, outsourcing can be more than a tool for cutting costs and improving organizational focus. Increasingly, it is a means of acquiring new capabilities and bringing about fundamental strategic and structural change.

According to Linder (2004), the concept of transformational outsourcing is an emerging practice, where companies are looking outside for help for more fundamental reasons — to facilitate rapid organizational change, to launch new strategies, and to reshape company boundaries. In doing so, they are engaging in transformational outsourcing: partnering with another company to achieve a rapid, substantial, and sustainable improvement in enterprise-level performance.

Transformational outsourcing places the power to bring new capabilities to the organization squarely in the hands of executives who have and value those capabilities. In other words, the outsourcing partner provides a management team that is experienced in the capability that the organization seeking change needs. And those executives are empowered by the outsourcing process to implement the practices they bring with them.

Not all transformational outsourcing initiatives are alike. Linder (2004) identified four broad categories from her research on 20 companies that have attempted the practice: The four categories are start-ups (outsource to rapidly scale up a new business); pathway to growth (outsource to fix a key process that stands in the way of growth); change catalyst (outsource to signal broad change and focus on adding value); and radical renewal (outsource to improve core operating capabilities radically).

As executives get more experience with outsourcing, they are learning the tool's potential and beginning to wield it for more strategic purposes. Some will use it to shape and reshape their business models. Instead of massive, sweeping changes, many organizations will master the ability to use outsourcing to make continuous incremental improvements. But while the potential benefits are incontrovertible, the art of joining organizations with unique capabilities is extremely challenging and requires visionary leaders with strong hearts and a large capacity for hard work. By combining the tool's execution effectiveness with their own growing skills in partnering, leaders who display those characteristics will have a practical and realistic roadmap at their disposal for building strategic flexibility.

Transformational outsourcing is an emerging practice, but the track record of companies that have engaged in it is impressive. In a study of 20 companies, 17 of them have been in place long enough to show results. Of that group, 13 have achieved dramatic, organization-level impact. To the extent that other companies can replicate such success, transformational outsourcing may become a more effective way of improving performance than major internal change initiatives, mergers and acquisitions, or joint ventures (Linder, 2004).

The key issue is new capabilities. In undertaking an internal initiative, a company has concluded that it lacks an important set of skills — otherwise it would not be seeking transformation. But it often proves too time-consuming to develop the skills internally. In a mergers-and-acquisition scenario, the company acquires the capabilities it lacks, but cultural clashes often interfere with its ability to use them effectively. An acquiring company seldom, for example, puts executives from the acquired company in charge of its own organization in order to learn from them. Similar cultural impediments make it unlikely that a company will transform itself with the expertise it gains in a joint venture. But transformational outsourcing places the power to bring new capabilities to the organization squarely in the hands of executives who have and value those capabilities. The outsourcing partner provides a management team that is experienced in the capability that the organization seeking change needs. And those executives are empowered by the outsourcing process to implement the practices they bring with them.

Transformational outsourcing is concerned with bringing new capabilities to the organization through important sets of skills. These skills can be found in knowledge work, and knowledge management emerges as an important discipline in transformational outsourcing. Executives have to lead a transformational outsourcing initiative much differently from the way they would manage conventional outsourcing.

Dimensions of IT Outsourcing Strategy

IT outsourcing strategy can be defined as the logic underlying a firm's outsourcing decisions. This logic is visible in a firm's portfolio of IT outsourcing decisions. The logic may either have served to guide decisions regarding outsourcing of specific functions or may be revealed in the cumulative pattern visible in individual outsourcing decisions. Thus, strategy need not be a single decision that is consciously made, but rather the manifestation of multiple decisions (Lee, Miranda, & Kim, 2004).

Having defined strategy as such logic, we need to identify the decisions that are salient in constituting or reflecting an IT outsourcing strategy. Firms make decisions on the extent to which transactions will be vertically integrated (degree of integration), the extent to which they will relinquish control of transaction fulfillment (allocation of control), and the duration for which they will commit to a transaction decision (performance period). Lee et al. (2004) defined these decisions as dimensions of IT outsourcing strategy:

- **Degree of integration** has been the focus of much research on IT outsourcing. This focus stems from a recognition that the integration of the IS function is not an all-or-none activity. Outsourcing initiatives may be categorized as comprehensive, selective, and minimal outsourcing. Lacity and Willcocks (2000) found that firms predominantly engage in selective outsourcing, and that such selectivity yielded economies of scale and resulted in the expected cost savings more often than comprehensive or minimal levels of outsourcing. Therefore, Lee et al. (2004) suggested a hypothesis that selective outsourcing will be more successful than comprehensive or minimal outsourcing. However, in their empirical research, this hypothesis was not supported.

- **Allocation of control** in outsourcing relationships refers to the manner in which compensation or reward structures are set up and the manner in which authority is exercised in the relationship. One control structure is the buy-in contract (Lacity & Willcocks, 2000). This entails the hiring of hourly workers, thereby subjecting them to the day-to-day authority of the client. Here, the client firm retains rights of control because it owns the assets, including labor power, necessary for the completion of work. A second control structure is a fee-for-service contract, which stipulates detailed bases for compensation. Here, rights of control are implicitly allocated to the provider firm that owns resources necessary for work completion. Finally, partnerships rely on complementary resources and voluntary resource allocations so as to benefit the partnership. Authority tends to be internalized within the relationship. Rights of control are therefore shared by client and provider firms. Under ideal conditions, the integrative nature of a partnership orientation minimizes problems stemming from equivocal contracts or uncertainty. However, as the interests of the client and provider diverge, partnerships may prove to be problematic. Therefore, Lee et al. (2004) suggested a hypothesis that buy-in or fee-for-service controls will be more successful than partnerships. However, in their empirical research, this hypothesis was not supported.

- **Performance periods** have been studied in the past. Research indicates that short-term contracts yield cost savings more often than long-term contracts (Lacity & Willcocks, 2000). Short-term contracts motivate providers toward higher performance and allow clients to quickly recover from contractual mistakes. Furthermore, it is difficult for the client to completely anticipate long-term requirements, and client and provider interests are likely to diverge over time. Therefore, Lee et al. (2004) suggested a hypothesis that short-term outsourcing relationships will be more successful than medium- or long-term relationships. However, in their empirical research, the reversed hypothesis was supported, suggesting that medium- and long-term outsourcing relationships will be more successful than short-term relationships. It may not be surprising that their findings contradicted conventional wisdom with respect to performance period of outsourcing relationships. Longer-term contracts are often preferable because they enable initial setup costs to be distributed over a longer period of time. A long-term contract improves financial predictability and reduces the risk and uncertainties associated with important business functions. Time is a critical aspect in the development of relationships. While time introduces an element of risk in relationships, time also facilitates cooperation among self-interested parties and the development of trust. It enables voluntary sharing of resources, with anticipation of deferred compensation.

In their empirical study, Lee et al. (2004) defined outsourcing success in terms of three dimensions: strategic competence, cost efficiency, and technology catalysis. Strategic competence refers to a firm's efforts at redirecting the business and IT into core competencies, cost efficiency refers to improving the business' financial position, and technology catalysis refers to strengthening resources and flexibility in technology service to underpin business' strategic direction. Their research model is illustrated in Figure 8.3.

Figure 8.3. Research model to study dimensions of strategy and success (Adapted from Lee et al., 2004)

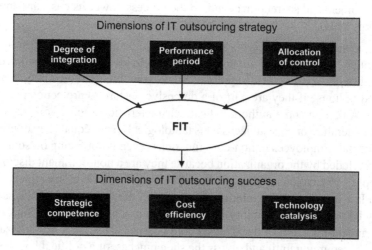

Sourcing Theories

In Chapter IV, general theories of the firm and value configurations of firms were introduced. Here, we return to more theories. We know that many companies choose IT outsourcing based on an analysis of core competencies. As we shall see, there are, however, many other theories that can be applied and that may provide both convergent and divergent answers to an outsourcing question. An example of divergent answer would be the theory of core competencies suggesting that non-core IT can be outsourced, while the resource-based theory suggests that non-core IT should be kept in-house if we have strategic IT-resources (valuable, non-imitable, non-substitutable, non-transferable, combinable, exploitable, and available).

Theories of the Firm

Theory of Core Competencies

Based on the notion of core competency, issues of sourcing should hinge on the degree of criticality of a specific component or business activity to an organization. An extreme case would be for a company to strip itself down to the essentials necessary to deliver to customers the greatest possible value from its core skills

— and outsource as much of the rest as possible. By limiting or shedding activities that provide no strategic advantage, a company can increase the value it delivers to both customers and shareholders and, in the process, lower its costs and investments (Ang, 1993).

Core competencies theory suggests activities should be performed either in-house or by suppliers. Activities that are not core competencies should be considered for outsourcing with best-in-world suppliers. Some non-core activities may have to be retained in-house if they are part of a defensive posture to protect competitive advantage. Although some authors indicate characteristics of core competencies, most of the literature on this subject seems tautological – core equals key or critical or fundamental. Employees in non-core functions (even if not facing outsourcing) may feel excluded by the organization because they are a non-dominant discipline. For example, information technology employees working on Web-based legal services in a law firm may feel excluded by lawyers in the firm. In the public sector, there may be particular uncertainty about what is core; and it has been suggested that government may aim to discover its core competencies via a residualization process — outsourcing until and unless the shoe pinches, or a political backlash is triggered (Hancox & Hackney, 2000).

An organization may view IT itself as a core competence. It seems that most successful companies have a good understanding of IT's potential. However, some organizations outsource IT even though they see it as core and delivering competitive advantage. This may be because IT can be considered core at the corporate level, but some of its aspects, at lower levels, might be commodities. Thus, the complexity of IT, and its (at least in part) core nature, may make the contracting out of IT a particularly challenging exercise. The ability to define IT requirements and to monitor their delivery by third parties may be some of the core IT competencies that any organization must have if it is to outsource IT successfully. It can even be argued that the very acts of specifying and managing supply contracts can themselves give competitive advantage (Hancox & Hackney, 2000).

Resource-Based Theory

The central tenet in resource-based theory is that unique organizational resources of both tangible and intangible nature are the real source of competitive advantage. With resource-based theory, organizations are viewed as a collection of resources that are heterogeneously distributed within and across industries. Accordingly, what makes the performance of an organization distinctive is the unique blend of the resources it possesses. A firm's resources include its physical assets, such as plant and location, as well as its competencies. The ability to leverage distinctive internal and external competencies relative to environmental situations ultimately affects the performance of the business (Peppard, Lambert, & Edwards, 2000).

The resource-based theory of the firm holds that, in order to generate sustainable competitive advantage, a resource must provide economic value and must be presently scarce, difficult to imitate, non-substitutable, and not readily obtainable in factor markets. This theory rests on two key points. First, resources are the determinants of firm performance; second, resources must be rare, valuable, difficult to imitate, and non-substitutable by other rare resources. When the latter occurs, a competitive advantage has been created (Priem & Butler, 2001).

Resources can simultaneously be characterized as valuable, rare, non-substitutable, and inimitable. To the extent that an organization's physical assets, infrastructure, and workforce satisfy these criteria, they qualify as resources. A firm's performance depends fundamentally on its ability to have a distinctive, sustainable competitive advantage, which derives from the possession of firm-specific resources (Priem & Butler, 2001).

Investments in IT represent a major approach to asset capitalization in organizations. IT may symbolize firm growth, advancement, and progress. Because investments in IT can promote social prominence and public prestige, managers are induced to utilize slack resources to internalize IS services. Inducements toward investments in in-house IS services are further reinforced by well-publicized case studies that demonstrate the competitive advantage and new business opportunities afforded by IT (Ang, 1993).

This reasoning suggests that managers may exhibit a penchant for building up internal IT resources such as IS employees, equipment, and computer capacity when organizations possess slack resources. In contrast, when slack resources are low, managers tend to conserve resources in response to the anxiety provoked by loss of financial resources. Anxiety is provoked because the loss of financial resources is often attributed to managerial incompetence and organizational ineffectiveness. As a result, leaders are more likely to be blamed and replaced when financial performance is poor. In response to the anxiety provoked by loss of financial resources, decision-makers have been observed to reduce costs through downsizing the company by selling off physical assets and laying off workers (Ang, 1993).

Theory of Firm Boundaries

There has been renewed debate on the determinants of firm boundaries and their implications for performance. According to Schilling and Steensma (2002), the widely accepted framework of transaction cost economics has come under scrutiny as a comprehensive theory for firm scale and scope. At the heart of this debate is whether the underlying mechanism determining firm boundaries is a fear of opportunism (as posited by transaction cost economics), a quest for sustainable advantage (as posed by resource-based view theorists and others), a desire for risk-reducing flexibility (as has recently gained increased attention in work on options), or a combination of factors. Although perspectives on firm boundaries such as transaction costs or the resource-based view are based on fundamentally different motivations for pursuing hierarchical control over market contracts, they rely on common resource or context attributes as antecedents.

Afuah (2003) found that the literature on vertical firm boundaries can be divided into two perspectives. In the first, researchers argue that firms decide to organize activities internally or through markets for efficiency reasons. In the second, researchers argue that firms decide to organize activities internally or through markets for strategic positioning reasons. Since the Internet's largest potential is in reducing costs, Afuah (2003) focused only on the first perspective to keep the arguments traceable. Thus, the decision to outsource or to develop an input internally depends on weighing external component production and transaction costs, on the one hand, and internal component production and transaction costs, on the other hand. If the former are greater than the latter, a firm is better off integrating vertically backward to produce the input internally.

Most studies of firm boundaries emphasize relationships between the division of labor and firms' boundaries. One of the oldest ideas in economics is that returns to specialization increase with market size. In our case of IT outsourcing, firms' boundaries are determined by the extent to which there are large markets for specialization. If there are large markets for IT services available from vendors, then a client company will tend to outsource more of its internal IT function.

Economic Theories

Transaction Cost Theory

In transaction cost analysis, outsourcing decisions are typically framed as determination of firm boundaries. In this perspective, vertical integration can be described as involving a variety of decisions concerning whether corporations, through their business units, should provide certain goods or services in-house or purchase them from outside instead. Therefore, the study of firm boundaries or vertical integration involves the study of outsourcing, describing which activities are conducted within a firm's hierarchy and which activities are conducted outside the hierarchy using market mechanisms or other forms of inter-organizational relationships (Ang, 1993).

Several studies have used the transaction cost perspective in their study of IT outsourcing (e.g., Ang & Straub, 1998; Grover, Teng, & Cheon, 1998; Langfield-Smith & Smith, 2003).

These studies generally support the thesis of transaction cost economics — whenever an activity is conducted under conditions of high uncertainty, or whenever an activity requires specific assets, transaction costs, the costs of writing, monitoring, and enforcing contracts, are likely to be high. When transaction costs are high, outsourcing is deemed to be relatively inefficient compared with internal, hierarchical administration. Therefore, the idea of achieving the economic goal of an efficient boundary in organization design is central to the arguments of transaction cost analysis (Ang, 1993).

Because production costs are objectively calculated by the accounting system, while transaction costs are assessed subjectively through indirect indicators, functional managers are likely to differ in the importance that they assign to reducing transaction costs. Consequently, the effect transaction costs have on a make-or-buy choice can partly reflect the influence exerted by the purchasing manager. Production cost differences seem more influential in sourcing decisions than transaction cost differences, and experience of the decision-maker is related to assessments of technological uncertainty. Profit center managers engage in influence activities that increase the costs of price renegotiations above the level that is observed in comparable external market transactions. Managers sometimes seem more reluctant to outsource when investments in specific assets are necessary; contrary to theory, managers sometimes consider previous internal investments in specific assets a reason to insource. In certain circumstances decision-makers systematically misestimate (or fail to consider) transaction costs (Anderson, Glenn, & Sedatole, 2000).

Neo-Classical Economic Theory

Neo-classical economic theory posits that firms outsource IT to attain cost advantages from assumed economies of scale and scope possessed by vendors (Ang & Straub, 1998). This theory is attained more empirical support in studies of outsourcing decisions than transaction cost economics. Neo-classical economic theory regards every business organization as a production function (Williamson, 1991), and where their motivation is driven by profit maximization. This means that companies offer products and services to the market where they have a cost or production advantage. They rely on the marketplace where they have disadvantages.

According to neo-classical economic theory, companies will justify their sourcing strategy based on evaluating possibilities for production cost savings. Thus, the question of whether or not to outsource is a question whether the marketplace can produce products and services at a lower price than internal production. In the context of IT outsourcing, a company will keep its IT-function internally if this has production cost advantages, and it will outsource when the marketplace can offer production cost savings.

However, defining outsourcing simply in terms of procurement activities does not capture the true strategic nature of the issues (Gilley & Rasheed, 2000). IT outsourcing is not only a purchasing decision — all firms purchase elements of their operations. This is done to achieve economic, technological, and strategic advantages. However, the economies of scale and scope argument would predict that outsourcing has little to offer to larger firms because they can generate economies of scale and scope internally by reproducing methods used by vendors. As documented by Levina and Ross (2003), there are other reasons for large firms to move into outsourcing.

In neo-classical economic theory, outsourcing may arise in two ways. First, outsourcing may arise through the substitution of external purchases for internal activities. In this way, it can be viewed as a discontinuation of internal production (whether it be production of goods or services) and an initiation of procurement from outside suppliers. To the extent this type of outsourcing reduces a firm's involvement in successive stages of production, substitution-based outsourcing may be viewed as vertical disintegration. This seems to be the most commonly understood type of outsourcing (Gilley & Rasheed, 2000).

Relational Theories

Contractual Theory

Luo (2002) examined how contract, cooperation, and performance are associated with one another. He argues that contract and cooperation are not substitutes but complements in relation to performance. Contracting and cooperation are two central issues in an IT outsourcing arrangement. A contract alone is insufficient to guide outsourcing evolution and performance. Since outsourcing involves repeated inter-organizational exchanges that become socially embedded over time, cooperation is an important safeguard mechanism mitigating external and internal hazards and overcoming adaptive limits of contracts. The simultaneous use of both contractual and cooperative mechanisms is particularly critical to outsourcing arrangements in an uncertain environment.

An outsourcing contract provides a legally bound, institutional framework in which each party's rights, duties, and responsibilities are codified and the goals, policies, and strategies underlying the arrangement are specified. Every outsourcing contract has the purpose of facilitating exchange and preventing opportunism. Appropriate contractual arrangements can attenuate the leeway for opportunism, prohibit moral hazards in a cooperative relationship, and protect each party's proprietary knowledge. A complete contract reduces the uncertainty faced by organizational decision-makers and the risks stemming from opportunism on the part of one or more contracting parties. It provides a safeguard against ex post performance problems by restraining each party's ability to pursue private goals at the expense of common benefits. An incomplete contract may bring about ambiguity, which creates a breeding ground for shirking responsibility and shifting blame, raises the likelihood of conflict, and hinders the ability to coordinate activities, utilize resources, and implement strategies (Luo, 2002).

Contractual completeness is not just term-specific (i.e., the extent to which all relevant terms and clauses are specified), nor should every outsourcing contract maintain the same level of completeness. Previous studies that view contractual completeness and term specificity as equivalent have created a controversy about the role of the contract. For instance, it has been suggested that incomplete contracts are optimal in situations where some elements of enforcement are unverifiable. Similarly, it has been argued that economic agents rarely write contracts that are complete because boundedly rational parties may not be able to distinguish certain contingencies. By contrast, others demonstrate that contractual completeness reduces role conflict and role ambiguity for outsourcing managers, which then enhances outsourcing performance. Furthermore, it has been suggested that term specificity protects a partner's strategic resources and reduces operational and financial uncertainties through controlling opportunism and spurring information flow within an outsourcing arrangement.

Agency Theory

Agency theory has broadened the risk-sharing literature to include the agency problem that occurs when cooperating parties have different goals and division of labor (Eisenhardt, 1985). The cooperating parties are engaged in an agency relationship defined as a contract under which one or more persons (the principal(s)) engage another person (agent) to perform some service on their behalf which involves delegating some decision-making authority to the agent (Jensen & Meckling, 1976). Agency theory describes the relationship between the two parties using the metaphor of a contract. In an IT outsourcing relationship this is a client-vendor relationship and an outsourcing contract.

The agency theory is applicable when describing client-vendor relationships in IT outsourcing arrangements. Typically, the client organization (principal) transfers property rights to the vendor organization (agent). In the context of IT, assets transferred might be infrastructure, systems and documentation, and employees. For a certain amount of money, the vendor organization provides services to the client organization. This implies a change in legal relationships, and IT services are carried out using a more formal transaction process. The status of personal relationships also changes, from that of a manager and a subordinate, to that of a client-manager and a vendor. According to agency theory, control mechanisms also change, from that of behavioral control, to that of outcome-based control.

The technological and business complexity of IT means that there may be major problems for the principal in choosing a suitable agent and in monitoring the agent's work. Only the agent knows how hard he or she is working, and that can be especially important in multilateral contracting where one agent acts for several principals. This is often the case in IT outsourcing because of the market dominance of one large firm. Given the difficulties of behavior-based contracts suggested by agency theory, it is reasonable to assume that the overwhelming majority of clients would insist on outcome-based contracts when acquiring IT products and services. Such a strategy can only succeed if the client can confidently specify current and future requirements. But accurate predictions by the client may not always be in the vendor's interests; since vendor account managers often are rewarded according to contract profitability, which is principally achieved through charging the client extra for anything which is not in the contract (Hancox & Hackney, 2000).

Partnership and Alliance Theory

Partnership, often referred to as an alliance, has frequently been noted as a major feature of IT outsourcing. Partnership can reduce the risk of inadequate contractual provision, which may be comforting for clients about to outsource a complex and high-cost activity such as IT. However, in the relationship between vendor and client, the latter may be over-dependent on the former and goals are not necessarily shared. A client may be more comfortable if it knows the vendor already. In partner selection, cultural compatibility is vital and shared values and objectives inform all stages of the partnership development process. This may make a successful relationship especially difficult if the putative partners are from fundamentally different domains and bring fundamentally different perspectives, as might well be argued is the case in a private sector — public sector arrangement. The difficulty may be compounded where, as in the UK government's compulsory competitive tendering policy, the outsourcing can be involuntary (Hancox & Hackney, 2000).

Hancox and Hackney (2000) found that few organizations claim to be in a strategic partnership with their IT suppliers. The contract is more likely to favor the vendor because he or she has greater experience in negotiation. Clients with loose contracts were more likely to regard outsourcing as a failure; yet, most respondents in a study used the vendor's standard contract as a basis for outsourcing agreement and most did not use external technical or legal advice. It was found that 80% of clients wished that they had more tightly defined contracts. Partly, the client's view of IT influences its relationship with the vendor, such that firms regarding IT as a core competence capability are more likely to look upon outsourcing as an alliance. Clients who view IT as a core also are more likely to be satisfied with the outsourcing arrangements because they negotiate from a more knowledgeable position (Hancox & Hackney, 2000).

Hancox and Hackney (2000) interviewed IT managers to find support for the partnership theory in IT outsourcing. Despite assurances found in vendors' marketing literature, most clients were skeptical about partnership. If partnership did exist, it was usually as a collection of some of the intangibles mentioned earlier, rather than as a formalized arrangement. Partnership was more likely to be claimed in the area of systems development, where vendors needed to have a greater understanding of the organization, than in outsourcing of operations and IT infrastructure support. There seemed to be no correlation between those organizations regarding IT as strategic and those regarding relationships with vendors as partnerships.

Relational Exchange Theory

Relational exchange theory is based on relational norms. According to this theory, the key to determining how efficiently contract governance is carried out lies in the relational norms between the transactors. For example, the degree to which transactors engage in joint planning or their extent of inter-firm information sharing are process elements that determine the costs associated with periodically renegotiating contracts. Those transactors who have established behavioral norms that can simplify and smooth the renegotiation process can reasonably expect to incur lower ex post bargaining costs than those who have not (Artz & Brush, 2000).

Artz and Brush (2000) examined supplier relationships that were governed by relational contracts and found support for the relational exchange theory. By altering the behavioral orientation of the alliance, relational norms lowered exchange costs.

In their measurement of relational norm, Artz and Brush (2000) included collaboration, continuity expectations, and communication strategies. Collaboration refers to the willingness of the client and vendor to work together to create a positive exchange relationship and improve alliance performance. Collaborative actions can act to enhance the client-vendor relationship as a whole and curtail opportunistic behaviors. For example, joint planning and forecasting can allow both the customer and the supplier to participate in determining each firm's roles and responsibilities and foster mutually beneficial expectations.

When one firm attempts to coerce another in order to gain a more favorable negotiation outcome, that firm is likely to be viewed by its alliance partner as exploitative rather than accommodative, and retaliatory behavior often results. In contrast, non-coercive strategies attempt to persuade rather than demand. Non-coercive communications center on beliefs about business issues and involve little direct pressure. Examples include simple requests or recommendations in which one party stresses the benefits the other party will receive by complying.

Stakeholder Theory

As far as we know, there is no comprehensive use of stakeholder theory in IT outsourcing research. Although Lacity and Willcocks (2000) have used the term identifying four distinct customer stakeholders and three distinct supplier stakeholders, their research has not gone further on this path. In an IT outsourcing relationship, a stakeholder theory approach will describe the relationship as a nexus of cooperative and competitive interests possessing intrinsic value.

The term stakeholder is a powerful one. To a significant degree this is due to its conceptual breath. The term means many different things to many different people and hence evokes praise and scorn from a wide variety of scholars and practitioners of myriad academic disciplines and backgrounds. Such breadth of interpretation, though one of stakeholder theory's greatest strengths, is also one of its most prominent theoretical liabilities as a topic of reasoned discourse. Much of the power of stakeholder theory is a direct result of the fact that, when used unreflectively, its managerial prescriptions and implications are merely limitless. When discussed in instrumental variation (i.e., that managers should attend to stakeholders as a means to achieving other organizational goals such as profit or shareholder wealth maximization), stakeholder theory stands virtually unopposed (Phillips, Freeman, & Wicks, 2003).

Stakeholder theory is a theory of organizational management and ethics. Indeed, all theories of strategic management have some moral content, though it is often implicit. Moral content in this case means that the subject matter of the theories are inherently moral topics (i.e., they are not amoral). Stakeholder theory is distinct because it addresses morals and values explicitly as a central feature of managing organizations. The ends of cooperative activity and the means of achieving these ends are critically examined in stakeholder theory in a way that they are not in many theories of strategic management (Phillips et al., 2003).

Social Exchange Theory

Typically, an IT outsourcing relationship will be a restricted social exchange. Social exchange theory can be traced to one of the oldest theories of social behavior — any interaction between individuals is an exchange of resources. The resources exchange may not be only tangible, such as goods or money, but also intangible, such as social amenities or friendship. The basic assumption of social exchange theory is that parties enter into and maintain relationships with the expectation that doing so will be rewarding (Lambe, Wittmann, & Spekman, 2001).

Social exchange theory postulates that exchange interactions involve economic and/or social outcomes. Over time, each party in the exchange relationship compares the social and economic outcomes from these interactions to those that are available from exchange alternatives, which determines their dependence on the exchange relationship. Positive economic and social outcomes over time increase the partners' trust of each other and commitment to maintaining the exchange relationship. Positive exchange interactions over time also produce relational exchange norms that govern the exchange partners' interactions (Lambe et al., 2001).

Implicit in these postulates, the four foundational premises of social exchange theory are: (1) exchange interactions result in economic and/or social outcomes; (2) these outcomes are compared over time to other exchange alternatives to determine dependence on the exchange relationship; (3) positive outcomes over time increase firms' trust of their trading partner(s) and their commitment to the exchange relationship; and (4) positive exchange interactions over time produce relational exchange norms that govern the exchange relationship (Lambe et al., 2001).

Commitment is a widely used construct in social exchange research. It has been defined as an exchange partner believing that an ongoing relationship with another is so important as to warrant maximum efforts at maintaining it; that is, the committed party believes the relationship is worth working on to ensure that it endures indefinitely (Lambe et al., 2001).

Comparison of Theories

We have introduced 11 theories concerned with outsourcing. In Figure 8.4, these theories are compared in terms of what they recommend for outsourcing. We find that some theories indicate possibilities for outsourcing (theory of core competencies, resource-based theory, transaction cost theory, neo-classical economic theory, and theory of firm boundaries), while others indicate limitations (contractual theory, partnership and alliance theory, relational exchange theory, social exchange theory, agency theory, and stakeholder theory).

Figure 8.5 lists a comparison of the theories when it comes to the next stage. The next stage is when outsourcing has occurred and both client and vendor want the outsourcing arrangement to be successful. What do the theories tell us? As is visible in Figure 8.5, the theories tell us a lot about what to do to be successful. Each theory provides recommendations for actions that will contribute to managing successful IT

Figure 8.4. Possibilities and limitations in IT outsourcing based on theories

Theory	What should be outsourced?
Theory of core competencies	All IT functions which are peripheral to the company's production of goods and services for the market.
Resource-based theory	All IT functions where the company does not have sufficient strategic resources to perform in a competitive way. Strategic resources are unique, valuable, difficult to imitate, exploitable, and difficult to substitute.
Transaction cost theory	All IT functions where benefits for the company are greater than the transaction costs. Benefits include increased revenues and reduced costs.
Contractual theory	Only IT functions where the company can expect and secure that vendor and customer will have the same contractual behavior. Common contract behavioral patterns include role integrity, reciprocity, implementation of planning, effectuation of consent, flexibility, contractual solidarity, reliance, restraint of power, proprietary of means, and harmonization with the social environment.
Neo-classical economic theory	All IT functions which an external vendor can operate at lower costs than the company.
Partnership and alliance theory	Only IT functions where the company can expect and secure a partnership and alliance with the vendor that imply interdependence between the partners based on trust, comfort, understanding, flexibility, co-operation, shared values, goals and problem-solving, interpersonal relations, and regular communication.
Relational exchange theory	Only IT functions where the company easily can develop and secure common norms with the vendor. Norms determine behavior in three main dimensions: flexibility, information exchange, and solidarity.
Social exchange theory	Only IT functions where each of the parties can follow their own self-interest when transacting with the other self-interested actor to accomplish individual goals that they cannot achieve alone and without causing hazards to the other party.
Agency theory	Only IT functions where the agent (vendor) and the principal (client) have common goals and the same degree of risk willingness and aversion.
Theory of firm boundaries	All IT functions that satisfy several of the other theories, mainly resource-based theory and transaction cost theory.
Stakeholder theory	Only IT functions where a balance can be achieved between stakeholders. Stakeholders relevant in IT outsourcing include business management, IT management, user management, and key IT personnel at the client, and business management, customer account management, and key service providers at the vendor.

Figure 8.5. Recommendations for managing successful IT outsourcing relationships based on theories

Theory	How to succeed in an outsourcing arrangement
Theory of core competencies	Capability to define IT needs and ability to manage IT services from the vendor represent the core competence within IT needed in the client organization to succeed in an IT outsourcing arrangement.
Resource-based theory	Capability to integrate and exploit strategic IT resources from the vendor together with own resources to produce competitive goods and services. An example of such a resource is the vendor's competence in an IT application area where the client has limited experience.
Transaction cost theory	Minimize transaction costs by reducing the need for lasting specific IT assets; increase transaction frequency; reduce complexity and uncertainty in IT tasks; improve performance measurements; and reduce dependence on other transactions.
Contractual theory	A complete IT contract based on information symmetry in a predictable environment with occurrence adoption that prevents opportunistic behavior in an efficient collaborative environment with balance of power between client and vendor, where the contract is a management instrument that grants decision rights and action duties.
Neo-classical economic theory	Capability to integrate and exploit IT services from the vendor together with own services to produce competitive goods and services. An example of such a service is the vendor's operation of the client's communication network.
Partnership and alliance theory	Develop experience with alliances, develop alliance managers, and develop the ability to identify potential partners.
Relational exchange theory	Develop and secure common norms that are relevant to both parties. Norms determine behavior and are mainly concerned with flexibility, information exchange, and solidarity. Norms shall secure integration in the relation, which takes place through involvement. Involvement occurs by coordination of activities, adoption of resources, and interaction between individuals. The degree of involvement in these three dimensions is called activity link, resource link, and actor link.
Social exchange theory	Enable social and economic outcomes in the exchange between client and vendor such that these outcomes outperform those obtainable in alternative exchanges. Positive economic and social outcomes over time increase the partners' trust of each other and commitment to maintaining the exchange relationship. Commitment is important, as it is an exchange partner's belief that an ongoing relationship with another is so important as to warrant maximum efforts at maintaining it.
Agency theory	It must be easy and inexpensive for the principal (client) to find out what the agent (vendor) is actually doing. In addition, both outcome-based and behavior-based incentives can be used to reduce and prevent opportunistic behavior.

Figure 8.5. continued

Theory of firm boundaries	The supply of IT services from the organization's environment should change firm boundaries between the firm that desires the competence (sourcing firm) and the firm having the technology (source firm) in a clear and unambiguous manner. This can be achieved in a strict and rigid division of labor between client and vendor.
Stakeholder theory	Create efficient and effective communication with and between stakeholders to secure continued support from all stakeholders, to balance their interests, and to make the IT outsourcing arrangement so that all stakeholders achieve their goals.

outsourcing relationships. From different theoretical perspectives, recommendations are made. Taken together, the list in Figure 8.5 represents critical success factors for an outsourcing arrangement.

References

Afuah, A. (2003). Redefining firm boundaries in the face of the Internet: Are firms really shrinking? *Academy of Management Review, 29*(1), 34-53.

Anderson, S. W., Glenn, D., & Sedatole, K. L. (2000). Sourcing parts of complex products: Evidence on transaction costs, high-powered incentives and ex-post opportunism. *Accounting, Organizations and Society, 25,* 723-749.

Ang, S. (1993). *The etiology of information systems outsourcing.* Doctoral dissertation PhD University of Minnesota.

Ang, S., & Straub, D. W. (1998). Production and transaction economics and IS outsourcing: A study of the U.S. banking industry. *MIS Quarterly, 22*(4), 535-552.

Artz, K. W., & Brush, T. H. (2000). Asset specificity, uncertainty and relational norms: An examination of coordination costs in collaborative strategic alliances. *Journal of Economic Behavior & Organization, 41,* 337-362.

Barthélemy, J. (2003). The seven deadly sins of outsourcing. *Academy of Management Executive, 17*(2), 87-100.

Beaumount, N., & Costa, C. (2002). Information technology outsourcing in Australia. *Information Resources Management Journal, 15*(3), 14-31.

Computerworld. (2005). Premier 100 IT leaders 2005 (January). Nortel Hires CEO (October). *Computerworld.* Retrieved from www.computerworld.com

Cross, J., Earl, M. J., & Sampler, J. L. (1997, December). Transformation of the IT function at British Petroleum. *MIS Quarterly,* 401-423.

Eisenhardt, K. M. (1985). Control: Organizational and economic approaches. *Management Science, 31*(2), 134-149.

Else, S. E. (2002). Strategic sourcing and federal government transformation. *Information Knowledge Systems Management, 3,* 31-52.

Gilley, M. K., & Rasheed, A. (2000). Making more by doing less: An analysis of outsourcing and its effects on firm performance. *Journal of Management, 26*(4), 763-790.

Grover, V., Teng, T. C., & Cheon, M. J. (1998). Towards a theoretically-based contingency model of information systems outsourcing. In L. P. Willcocks & M. C. Lacity (Eds.), *Strategic sourcing of information systems. Perspectives and practices* (pp. 79-101). London: John Wiley & Sons.

Hall, J. A., & Liedtka, S. L. (2005). Financial performance, CEO compensation, and large-scale information technology outsourcing decisions. *Journal of Management Information Systems, 22*(1), 193-221.

Hancox, M., & Hackney, R. (2000). IT outsourcing: Frameworks for conceptualizing practice and perception. *Information Systems Journal, 10*(3), 217-237.

Jensen, M. C., & Meckling, W. H. (1976). Theory of the firm: Managerial behavior, agency costs and ownership structures. *Journal of Financial Economics, 3*(4), 305-360.

King, W.R., & Malhotra, Y. (2000). Developing a framework for analyzing IS sourcing. *Information & Management, 37,* 323-334.

Lacity, M. C., & Willcocks, L. P. (2000). Relationships in IT outsourcing: A stakeholder perspective. In R. W. Zmud (Ed.), *Framing the domains of IT management: Projecting the future through the past* (pp. 355-384). Cincinnati, OH: Pinnaflex Educational Resources.

Lambe, C. J., Wittmann, C. M., & Spekman, R. E. (2001). Social exchange theory and research on business-to-business relational exchange. *Journal of Business-to-Business Marketing, 8*(3), 1-36.

Langfield-Smith, K., & Smith, D. (2003). Management control systems and trust in outsourcing relationships. *Management Accounting Research, 14,* 281-307.

Lee, J.-N., & Kim, Y.-G. (1999). Effect of partnership quality on IS outsourcing success: Conceptual framework and empirical validation. *Journal of Management Information Systems, 15*(4), 29-61.

Lee, J. N., Miranda, S. M., & Kim, Y. G. (2004). IT outsourcing strategies: Universalistic, contingency, and configurational explanations of success. *Information Systems Research, 15*(2), 110-131.

Leiblein, M. J., Reuer, J. J., & Dalsace, F. (2002). Do make or buy decisions matter? The influence of organizational governance on technological performance. *Strategic Management Journal, 23*, 817-833.

Levina, N., & Ross, J. W. (2003). From the vendor's perspective: Exploring the value proposition in information technology outsourcing. *MIS Quarterly, 27*(3), 331-364.

Linder, J. C. (2004, Winter). Transformational outsourcing. *MIT Sloan Management Review*, 52-58.

Luo, Y. (2002). Contract, cooperation, and performance in international joint ventures. *Strategic Management Journal, 23*, 903-911.

Nielsen, K. B. (2004, October). *Reality of IS lite — and more.* EXP Client presentation, Gartner Group. Retrieved from www.gartner.com

Peppard, J., Lambert, R., & Edwards, C. (2000). Whose job is it anyway? Organizational information competencies for value creation. *Information Systems Journal, 10*, 291-322.

Phillips, R., Freeman, R. E., & Wicks, A.C. (2003). What stakeholder theory is not. *Business Ethics Quarterly, 13*(4), 479-502.

Priem, R. L., & Butler, J. E. (2001). Is the resource-based view a useful perspective for strategic management research? *Academy of Management Review, 26*(1), 22-40.

Ross, J. W., & Weill, P. (2002, November). Six IT decisions your IT people shouldn't make. *Harvard Business Review*, 84-91.

Schilling, M. A., & Steensma, H. K. (2002). Disentangling the theories of firm boundaries: A path model and empirical test. *Organization Science, 13*(4), 387-401.

Steensma, H. K., & Corley, K. G. (2001). Organizational context as moderator of theories on firm boundaries for technology sourcing. *Academy of Management Journal, 44*(2), 271-291.

Williamson, O. E. (1991). Comparative economic organization: The analysis of discrete structural alternatives. *Administrative Science Quarterly, 36*, 269-296.

Chapter IX

The CIO Enabling
IT Governance

Introduction

It is important for the CIO to play a key role in developing IT governance arrangements to increase his or her chances for becoming the next CEO. While corporate
governance allocates decision rights in the overall company affecting the CEO
position, IT governance allocates decisions rights in all IT-related dimensions affecting the CIO position.

In many organizations, information technology has become crucial in the support, the
sustainability, and the growth of the business. This pervasive use of technology has
created a critical dependency on IT that calls for a specific focus on IT governance.
IT governance consists of the leadership and organizational structures and processes
that ensure that the organization's IT sustains and extends the organization's strategy
and objectives (Grembergen, Haes, & Guldentops, 2004).

IT governance matters because it influences the benefits received from IT investments. Through a combination of practices (such as redesigning business processes
and well-designed governance mechanisms) and appropriately matched IT investments, top-performing enterprises generate superior returns on their IT investments
(Weill, 2004).

What is IT Governance?

*IT governance can be defined as specifying decision rights and account-
ability framework to encourage desirable behavior in the use of IT.* (Weill
& Ross, 2004)

This is the definition we will use here.

Other definitions are: (1) IT governance is the structures and processes that ensure that
IT supports the organization's mission. The purpose is to align IT with the enterprise,
maximize the benefits of IT, use IT resources responsibly, and manage IT risks; (2) A
structure of relationships and processes to direct and control the enterprise in order
to achieve the enterprise's goals by adding value while balancing risk versus return
over IT and its processes; (3) IT governance is the responsibility of the board of
directors and executive management. It is an integral part of enterprise governance
and consists of the leadership and organizational structures, and processes that
ensure that the organization's IT sustains and extends the organization's strategies
and objectives; and (4) IT governance is the system by which an organization's IT
portfolio is directed and controlled. IT governance describes (a) the distribution
of decision-making rights and responsibilities among different stakeholders in the
organization, and (b) the rules and procedures for making and monitoring decisions
on strategic IT concerns (Peterson, 2004).

An extensive definition was presented by the IT Governance Institute (2004) as follows. It is a board or senior management responsibility in relation to IT to ensure
that:

- IT is aligned with the business strategy, or in other words, IT delivers the functionality and services in line with the organization's needs, so the organization
  can do what it wants to do.

- IT and new technologies enable the organization to do new things that were
  never possible before.

- IT-related services and functionality are delivered at the maximum economi-
  cal value or in the most efficient manner. In other words, resources are used
  responsibly.

- All risks related to IT are known and managed, and IT resources are se-
  cured.

A distinction has to be made between IT management as discussed previously in this
book and IT government that we introduce here. IT management is focused on the

Figure 9.1. Distinction between IT management and IT governance

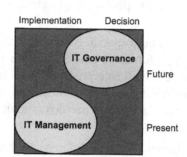

internal effective supply of IT services and products and the management of present IT operations (Grembergen et al., 2004). In turn, IT governance is much broader and concentrates on performing and transforming IT to meet present and future demands of the business (internal focus) and the business' customers (external focus).

The difference between IT management and IT governance is illustrated in Figure 9.1. While IT management is concerned with implementing IT services at the present, IT governance is concerned with making decisions for the future.

Whereas the domain of IT management focuses on the efficient and effective supply of IT services and products, and the management of IT operations, IT governance faces the dual demand of (1) contributing to present business operations and performance, and (2) transforming and positioning IT for meeting future business challenges. This does not undermine the importance or complexity of IT management, but goes to indicate that IT governance is both internally and externally oriented, spanning both present and future time frames. One of the key challenges in IT governance is therefore how to simultaneously perform and transform IT in order to meet the present and future demands of the business and the business' customers in a satisfying manner (Peterson, 2004).

IT governance is concerned with decision rights. In a survey by Gartner (2005) on how IT spending is controlled, it was found that 62% of IT spending was centrally controlled by the IT organization in the United States. Thirty-five percent was blended controlled by IT and business units or functions, while 3% was directly controlled by business units or function.

IT governance encourages desirable behavior in the use of IT. A desirable behavior is one that is consistent with the organization's mission, strategy, values, norms, and culture, such as behavior promoting entrepreneurship, sharing and reuse, or relentless cost reduction. IT governance is not about what specific decisions are made. That is management. Rather, governance is about systematically determining who makes each type of decision (a decision right), who has input to a decision (an input right), and how these people (or groups) are held accountable for their role (Weill, 2004).

Good IT governance draws on corporate governance principles to manage and use IT to achieve corporate performance goals. Effective IT governance encourages and leverages the ingenuity of all enterprise personnel in using IT, while ensuring compliance with the enterprise's overall vision and principles. As a result, good IT governance can achieve a management paradox: simultaneously empowering and controlling (Weill, 2004).

All enterprises have IT governance. The difference is that enterprises with effective governance have actively designed a set of IT governance mechanisms (e.g., committees, budgeting processes, approvals, IT organizational structure, chargeback, etc.) that encourage behaviors consistent with the organization's mission, strategy, values, norms, and culture. In these enterprises, when the "desirable behaviors" change, IT governance also changes (Weill, 2004).

IT governance cannot be considered in isolation because it links to the governance of other key enterprise assets (such as financial, human, intellectual property, etc.). Governance of the key assets, in turn, links to corporate governance and desirable behaviors (Weill, 2004).

In the models of *corporate governance,* one can organize the variety of variables and concepts used to describe the complexity of corporate governance mechanisms into two main categories: capital-related and labor-related. The capital-related aspects contain, among others, variables like ownership structure, corporate voting, the identity of owners, and the role of institutional owners. The labor-related aspects refer mainly to the stakeholding position of labor in corporate governance. Here, one could mention employee involvement schemes, participatory management, co-determination, and so forth (Cernat, 2004).

Corporate Governance

Before we dive into IT outsourcing governance, we must look at the broader issue of corporate governance in enterprises. Corporate governance is concerned with governing key assets, such as (Weill & Ross, 2004):

- **Human assets:** People, skills, career paths, training, reporting, mentoring, competencies, and so on.

- **Financial assets:** Cash, investments, liabilities, cash flow, receivables and so on.

- **Physical assets:** Buildings, plant, equipment, maintenance, security, utilization, and so on.

- **IP assets:** Intellectual property (IP), including product, services, and process know-how formally patented, copyrighted, or embedded in the enterprises' people and systems.

- **Information and IT assets:** Digitized data, information, and knowledge about customers, processes performance, finances, information systems, and so on.

- **Relationship assets:** Relationships within the enterprise as well as relationships, brand, and reputation with customers, suppliers, business units, regulators, competitors, channel partners, and so on.

As we can see from this list, IT outsourcing governance includes not only information and IT assets. IT outsourcing governance is concerned with several of these assets, sometimes even all of these assets. In this perspective, IT outsourcing governance may be as comprehensive in scope as corporate governance.

In governing IT outsourcing, we can learn from good financial and corporate governance. For example, the chief financial officer (CFO) does not sign every check or authorize every payment. Instead, he or she sets up financial governance specifying who can make the decisions and how. The CFO then oversees the enterprise's portfolio of investments and manages the required cash flow and risk exposure. The CFO tracks a series of financial metrics to manage the enterprise's financial assets, intervening only if there are problems or unforeseen opportunities. Similar principles apply to who can commit the enterprise to a contract or a partnership. Exactly the same approach should be applied to IT governance (Weill & Ross, 2004).

The dichotomy market or hierarchy has exercised a dominant influence on the study of forms of governance and their operation for some time. However, in the past two decades, there have been large numbers of investigations of intermediate forms of governance. Subsequently, it has been recognized that the behavior that occurs within exchanges is not necessarily determined by the forms of governance used, and this points to a need to understand behavior within a variety of exchanges (Blois, 2002).

Contracts in Governance

Blois (2002) defines governance as the institutional framework in which contracts are initiated, monitored, adapted, and terminated. An exchange occurs between two organizations when resources are transferred from one party to the other in return for resources controlled by the other party.

The organization of inter-firm exchanges has become of critical importance in today's business environment. Many scholars have criticized the inadequacies of legal contracts as mechanisms for governing exchange, especially in the face of uncertainty and dependence. Other scholars argue that it is not the contracts per se but the social contexts in which they are embedded that determine their effectiveness. Cannon, Achrol, and Gundlach (2000) investigated the performance implications of governance structures involving contractual agreements and relational social norms, individually and in combination (plural form) under varying conditions and forms of transactional uncertainty and relationship-specific adaptation. Hypotheses were developed and tested on a sample of buyer-seller relationships. The results provide support for the plural form thesis — increasing the relational content of a governance structure containing contractual agreements enhanced performance when transactional uncertainty was high, but not when it was low.

Cannon et al. (2000) applied the term legal bonds to refer to the extent to which detailed and binding contractual agreements were used to specify the roles and obligations of the parties. To the extent contracts were characterized in this way, they were less flexible and therefore more constrained in their adaptive properties. Highly detailed contracts were also less likely to possess the kinds of general safeguards that are more effective in thwarting self-interest-seeking behavior under circumstances of ambiguity.

Various perspectives on the nature of contracts as a mechanism of governance may be found in the literature. According to the original transaction cost framework (Williamson, 1979), formal contingent claims contracts (i.e., classical contracts) are inefficient mechanisms of governance in the face of uncertainty because organizations are bounded in their rationality and find it impossible to contemplate all possible future contingencies. For exchanges involving high levels of idiosyncratic investments and characterized by uncertainty, internal organization or hierarchy is predicted to be a more efficient form of governance than the market (Cannon et al., 2000).

However, neo-classical contract law argues that contracts can provide useful governance in exchange relationships even in the face of uncertainty and risk. This tradition of contract law is marked by doctrine and rules that attempt to overcome the difficulties posed by the classical tradition's emphasis on discreteness and presentation of exchange. The new doctrines enable parties to respond to unforeseen contingencies by making adjustments to ongoing exchange and ensuring continuity in their relationships. For example, concepts such as "good faith" and "reasonable commercial standards of fair dealing in the trade" are recognized under the Uniform Commercial Code (UCC) of 1978 in the United States as general provisions for contracting behavior that also help to ensure continuity in exchange relationships.

Similarly, "gap filler" provisions of the UCC rely on "prior dealings" between parties and "customary practices" across an industry or trading area for completing contract terms intentionally left open or omitted, thus allowing for adjustments to contingencies (Cannon et al., 2000).

However, neo-classical contracts are not indefinitely elastic (Williamson, 1991). Many scholars remain skeptical of how effective even the most carefully crafted contracts can be. It is argued that the scope for drafting rules in contracts to address changing or ambiguous conditions, or the ability to rely on general legal safeguards for controlling commercial conduct, is limited by both practicality and the law itself.

Drawing on these views, Cannon et al. (2000) argue that when a transaction involves relationship-specific adaptations and is (1) subject to dynamic forces and future contingencies that cannot be foreseen or (2) involves ambiguous circumstances where tasks are ill-defined and prone to exploitation, the difficulty of writing, monitoring, and enforcing contracts is increased, and their overall governance effectiveness weakened. In each case, efforts to govern the relationship on the basis of detailed and formal contracts — without the benefit of some additional apparatus — are not likely to enhance performance.

Social or relational norms are defined generally as shared expectations regarding behavior. The norms reflect expectations about attitudes and behaviors parties have in working cooperatively together to achieve mutual and individual goals. The spirit of such sentiments is captured by many overlapping types of relational contracting norms. These can be reduced to a core set of five (Cannon et al., 2000):

- **Flexibility:** The attitude among parties that an agreement is but a starting point to be modified as the market, the exchange relationship, and the fortunes of the parties evolve.

- **Solidarity:** The extent to which parties believe that success comes from working cooperatively together versus competing against one another. It dictates that parties stand by one another in the face of adversity and the ups and downs of marketplace competition.

- **Mutuality:** The attitude that each party's success is a function of everyone's success and that one cannot prosper at the expense of one's partner. It expresses the sentiment of joint responsibility.

- **Harmonization of conflict:** The extent to which a spirit of mutual accommodation toward cooperative ends exists.

- **Restraint in the use of power:** Forbearance from taking advantage of one's bargaining position in an exchange. It reflects the view that the use of power not only exacerbates conflict over time but also undermines mutuality and solidarity, opening the door to opportunism.

Together, these cooperative norms define relational properties that are important in affecting adaptations to dynamic market conditions and safeguarding the continuity of exchanges subject to task ambiguity (Cannon et al., 2000).

Norms represent important social and organizational vehicles of control in exchange where goals are ill-defined or involve open-ended performance. They provide a general frame of reference, order, and standards against which to guide and assess appropriate behavior in uncertain and ambiguous situations. In such situations, contracts are often incomplete, and legal remedies can undermine relationship continuity. In contrast, norms motivate performance through focusing attention on the shared values of the partners to safeguard and rely on peer pressure and social sanctions to mitigate the risk of shirking and opportunistic expropriation. Because they involve expectations rather than rigid requirements of behavior, they create a cooperative as opposed to a confrontational environment for negotiating adaptations, thus promoting continuity in exchange (Cannon et al., 2000).

The plural form thesis contends that exchange is best understood as embedded in a complex matrix of economic, social, and political structures and that the governance of exchange relations more often relies on combinations of market, social, or authority-based mechanisms than on any one category exclusively. While the plural-form thesis is that the various mechanisms in fact work together to reinforce or complement one another in some way, little attention has focused on exactly how these mechanisms actually complement one another (Cannon et al., 2000).

Academic literature and business practice are directing increased attention to the importance of creating value in buyer-supplier relationships. One method for creating value is to reduce costs in commercial exchange. Cannon and Homburg (2001) developed a model that explains how supplier behaviors and the management of suppliers affect a customer firm's direct product, acquisition, and operations costs. The model proposes that these costs mediate the relationship between buyer-supplier relationship behaviors and the customer firm's intentions to expand future purchases from the supplier, as illustrated in Figure 9.2.

Cannon and Homburg (2001) empirically tested all relationships in their model in Figure 9.2. Their findings provide support for the expectation that more complex operational issues at times may require the richer interaction provided in face-to-face communications but at other times may benefit from simpler written exchanges. As expected, the more standardized issues typical of product acquisition benefit from more efficient written/electronic communication.

In contrast, open information sharing by suppliers was not found to be related to a customer firm's costs. The lack of support for these hypotheses may be caused by buying firms' failure to use the information received from suppliers effectively. For example, customer firms may suffer from information overload and be unable to process and act on such information effectively.

Figure 9.2. Model explaining how supplier effect customer costs (Adapted from Cannon & Homburg, 2001)

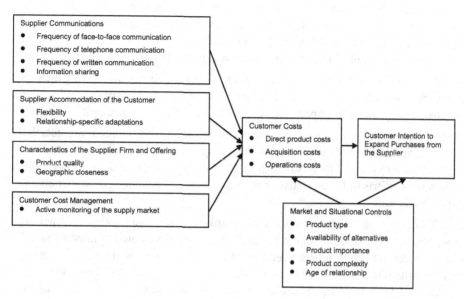

Further hypotheses in Figure 9.2 predict the effects supplier accommodation would have on customer costs. The empirical results support the prediction that greater supplier flexibility results in lower acquisition and operations costs. Contrary to the researchers' predictions, higher levels of relationships-specific adaptation did not lead to lower acquisition or operations costs. This may be because many of these adaptations are targeted at enhancing value through increasing the benefits a customer receives, not through cost reduction.

Whereas Cannon and Homburg (2001) developed a hypothesis that higher direct product costs would be associated with greater supplier adaptation, the result was statistically significant in the opposite direction. Several factors may explain this unanticipated finding. First, relationship-specific adaptations may evolve into regular business practices with all customers, which may subsequently lower the cost of accommodation. Second, buying organizations may effectively bargain away the premium prices a supplier must initially charge for customized products. Finally, at a more general level, buyers may compensate suppliers through long-term commitments and/or promises of higher sales volume. Typically, such agreements also involve lower prices over time.

As predicted in the model in Figure 9.2, geographic proximity of the supplier's facilities helped lower acquisition costs. The expected effects of quality in lowering the customer's acquisition costs and operations costs were found, but Cannon and Homburg (2001) were surprised to find that higher-quality products had lower direct product costs. Possible explanations for the unexpected finding for the product quality-direct product costs relationship can be drawn from the quality literature. It may be that quality operates as an order qualifier and high quality is necessary just to be considered as a supplier but does not allow a supplier to charge higher prices.

Another hypothesis in Figure 9.2 predicts the effects of actively monitoring the supply market on each cost. More active monitoring of the supply market was found to be associated with higher operations costs but not with higher acquisition costs.

A final hypothesis in Figure 9.2 was supported in the empirical data. It predicts that lowering the customer firm's direct product, acquisition, and operations costs leads the customer to expand its business with the supplier. These findings suggest that a supplier's efforts to lower a customer firm's costs can have long-term benefits to suppliers as well.

As IT outsourcing becomes more commonplace, new organizational forms are emerging to facilitate these relationships. Chase Bank has created "shared services" units that compete with outside vendors to furnish services to the bank's own operating units. Delta Airlines has established a "business partners" unit to oversee its relations with vendors. Microsoft outsources almost everything — from the manufacturing of its computer software to the distribution of its software products, thereby focusing the organization on its primary area of competitive advantage: the writing of software code. Still other firms are creating "strategic services" divisions in which activities formerly decentralized into autonomous business units are now being recentralized for outside contracting. As these various approaches suggest, the best ways to structure outsourcing remain the subject of ongoing management debate and media coverage (Useem & Harder, 2000).

As companies devise new forms of organization to ensure that outsourcing works as intended, those responsible require a new blend of talents. Rather than issuing orders, managers must concentrate on negotiating results, replacing a skill for sending work downward with a talent for arranging work outward. Thus, the outsourcing of services necessitates lateral leadership, according to Useem and Harder (2000).

Useem and Harder (2000) reached this conclusion about leadership capabilities required for outsourcing through interviews conducted with several companies. What emerged from the interviews and a broader survey was a picture of a more demanding leadership environment, even as day-to-day management tasks are streamlined by outsourcing. They found that four individual capabilities encompass much of what is required of managers as outsourcing becomes commonplace:

- **Strategic thinking:** Within the outsourcing framework, managers must understand whether and how to outsource in ways that improve competitive advantage.

- **Deal making:** Outsource process managers must broker deals in two directions simultaneously — securing the right services from external providers and ensuring their use by internal managers.

- **Partnership governing:** After identifying areas suitable for outsourcing through strategic assessment and upon clinching a deal, effectively overseeing the relationship is essential.

- **Managing change:** Forcefully spearheading change is critical because companies are certain to encounter employee resistance.

These four capabilities emerged repeatedly when Useem and Harder (2000) were discussing the essential skills of those responsible for outsourcing decisions, contracting, and oversight. None of these qualities taken singly were found to be unique to outsourcing, but their combination is critical to leading laterally.

Governance and Management Roles

Managers undertake activities to achieve the objectives of the organization. In the context of IT management, the relevance of six management roles has been identified — leader, resource allocator, spokesman, entrepreneur, liaison, and monitor.

The six roles are again illustrated in Figure 9.3. Leader and resource allocator are roles internal to the IT function. Spokesman and entrepreneur are roles internal to the organization. Monitor and liaison are roles external to the organization.

In terms of decision-making for IT governance, two management roles are visible. First, the resource allocator role is mainly concerned with decisions. The manager must decide how to allocate human, financial, and information resources to the activities of the IT function. Second, the entrepreneur role is mainly concerned with decisions. The manager identifies the users' needs and management expectations and makes decisions concerning solutions that change business situations. Hence, IT governance affects the two CIO leadership roles of resource allocator and entrepreneur.

Why is IT Governance Important?

IT governance matters because it influences the benefits received from IT investments. Through a combination of practices (such as redesigned business processes and well-designed governance mechanisms) and appropriately matched IT invest-

Figure 9.3. Management roles for the CIO

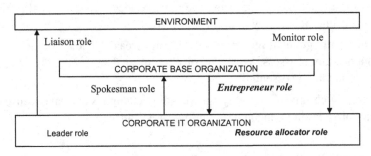

ments, top-performing enterprises generate superior returns on their IT investments (Weill, 2004).

Weill and Ross (2004, p. 22) list the following reasons why IT governance is important:

- **Good IT governance pays off:** Among the for-profit firms we studied, the ones pursuing a specific strategy (for example, customer intimacy or operational excellence) with above-average IT governance performance had superior profits as measured by a three-year industry adjusted return on assets.

- **IT is expensive:** The average enterprise's IT investment is now greater than 4.2% of annual revenues and still rising. This investment results in IT exceeding 50% of the annual total capital investment of many enterprises. As IT has become more important and pervasive, senior management teams are increasingly challenged to manage and control IT to ensure that value is created. To address this issue, many enterprises are creating or refining IT governance structures to better focus IT spending on strategic priorities.

- **IT is pervasive:** In many enterprises, centrally managed IT is no longer possible or desirable. There was a time when requests for IT spending came only from the IT group. Now, IT spending originates all over the enterprise. Some estimates suggest that only 20% of IT spending is visible in the IT budget. The rest of the spending occurs in business process budgets, product development budgets, and every other type of budget. Well-designed IT governance arrangements distribute IT decision-making to those responsible for outcomes.

- **New information technologies bombard enterprises with new business opportunities:** Foresight is more likely if an enterprise has formalized governance processes for harmonizing desirable behaviors and IT principles.

- **IT governance is critical to organizational learning about IT value:** Effective governance creates mechanisms through which enterprises can debate potential value and formalize their learning. Governance also facilitates learning by formalizing exception processes. Enterprises often learn through exceptions — where a different approach from standard practice is used for good reasons. Effective governance makes learning via exceptions explicit and shares any new practices across the enterprise if appropriate.

- **IT value depends on more than good technology:** In recent years, there have been spectacular failures of large IT investments — major enterprise resource planning (ERP) systems initiatives that were never completed, e-business initiatives that were ill-conceived or poorly executed, and data-mining experiments that generated plenty of data but few valuable leads. Successful firms not only make better IT decisions, they also have better IT decision-making processes. Specifically, successful firms involve the right people in the process. Having the right people involved in IT decision-making yields both more strategic applications and greater buy-in.

- **Senior management has limited bandwidth:** Senior management does not have the bandwidth to consider all the requests for IT investments that occur in a large enterprise, let alone get involved in many other IT-related decisions. If senior managers attempt to make too many decisions, they become a bottleneck. But decisions throughout the enterprise should be consistent with the direction in which senior management is taking the organization. Carefully designed IT governance provides a clear, transparent IT decision-making process that leads to consistent behavior linked back to the senior management vision while empowering everyone's creativity.

- **Leading enterprises govern IT differently:** Top-performing firms balancing multiple performance goals had governance models that blended centralized and decentralized decision-making. All top performers' governance had one aspect in common. Their governance made transparent the tensions around IT decisions such as standardization versus innovation.

The Outsourcing Governance Model

IT outsourcing governance can be defined as specifying the decision rights and accountability framework to encourage desirable behavior in the IT outsourcing arrangement, where resources are transferred from one party to the other in return for resources controlled by the other party. Governance is not about making specific decisions — management does that — but rather determines who systematically makes and contributes to those decisions. Governance reflects broader principles, while focusing on the management of the outsourcing relationship to achieve performance goals for both client and vendor. Governance is the institutional framework in which contracts are monitored, adapted, and renewed. Effective outsourcing governance encourages and leverages the ingenuity of the vendor's and client's people in IT usage and ensures compliance with both enterprises' overall vision and values (Gottschalk & Solli-Sæther, 2006).

Our governance model is illustrated in Figure 9.4. It consists of five elements (contracts, principles, resources, activities, and managers), two main links (terms-exchanges link between contracts and resources, and norms-relationships link between principles and activities), and four local links (roles between contracts and principles, capabilities between principles and resources, efficiencies between resources and activities, and outcomes between activities and contracts).

Contracts provide a legally bound, institutional framework in which each party's rights, duties, and responsibilities are codified and the goals, policies, and strategies underlying the arrangement are specified. *Principles* define decision rights concerning general IT principles, IT infrastructure, IT architecture, business application needs, and IT investments. *Resources* define decision rights concerning human assets, financial assets, physical assets, IP assets, information and IT assets, and relationship assets. *Activities* define decision rights concerning transactions, projects, problem-solving, and reporting. *Managers* are classified into stakeholder groups of client business management, client IT management, vendor business management, and vendor account management.

Exchanges of resources occur through transactions based on contracts. *Terms* for use of resources are defined in contracts. *Norms* create expectations of behavior and imply a certain action and are shared by the actors. Norms are based on principles and occur in activities. Norms are concerned with flexibility, solidarity, mutuality, harmonization, and power. *Relationships* frame activities based on principles and norms.

Roles are defined by contracts and carried out when making decisions about principles. Management roles include spokesperson, entrepreneur, personnel leader, resource allocator, monitor, and liaison roles. *Capabilities* enable the use of resources based on principles. *Efficiencies* are determined by the use of resources in activities. *Outcomes* occur in activities that are performance results from contracts.

Figure 9.5 illustrates how managers and principles are related through decision rights. *General principles* are high-level statements about how IT is used in the business. *IT infrastructure* are strategies for the base foundation of budgeted-for IT capability (technical and human), shared throughout the firm as reliable services, and centrally coordinated such as network, help desk, and shared data. *IT architecture* is an integrated set of technical choices to guide the organization in satisfying business needs. The architecture is a set of policies and rules that govern the use of IT and plot a migration path to the way business will be done (includes data, technology, and applications). *Business application needs* are concerned with business applica-

Figure 9.4. Governance model for outsourcing relationships

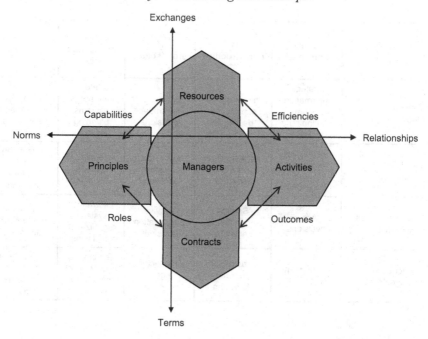

tions to be acquired and built. *IT investment* and prioritization are decisions about how much and where to invest in IT, including project approvals and justification techniques (Weill & Ross, 2004).

Figure 9.6 illustrates how managers and resources are related through decision rights. *Human assets* are people, skills, career paths, training, reporting, mentoring, competencies, and so on. *Financial assets* are cash, investments, liabilities, cash flow, receivables, and so on. *Physical assets* are buildings, plant, equipment, maintenance, security, utilization, and so on. *IP assets* are intellectual property (IP), including product, services, and process know-how formally patented, copyrighted, or embedded in the enterprises' people and systems. *Information and IT assets* are digitized data, information, and knowledge about customers, processes performance, finances, information systems, and so on. *Relationship assets* are relationships within the enterprises as well as relationships between client and vendor at all levels (Weill & Ross, 2004).

IT outsourcing governance consists of five elements as illustrated in Figure 9.4. Four of these elements are really dimensions of governance, while the remaining element is management, which integrates the four dimensions of governance. In

Figure 9.5. The governance model defines decision rights concerning principles

Principles / Stakeholders	General principles	IT infrastructure	IT architecture	Business application needs	IT investments
Client business management	Strategic information systems planning decisions	Infrastructure capabilities decisions	Architecture performance decisions	Strategic information systems planning decisions	Financial investments decisions
Client IT management	Technology business alignment decisions	Infrastructure functions decisions	Architecture structure decisions	Information systems decisions	Investment analysis contents decisions
Vendor business management	Service-level decisions	Service organization decisions	Service organization decisions	Information systems organization decisions	Financial investments decisions
Vendor account management	Technology decisions	Infrastructure integration decisions	Architecture integration decisions	Technology decisions for information systems	Investment analysis contents decisions

Figure 9.7, the four dimensions of governance are illustrated along the time dimension, defined as the formation stage (vision, evaluation, negotiation), the operation stage (transition, improvement), and the outcome stage (performance, results, goals, objectives).

In the formation stage, contracts are concerned with transactions in the outsourcing arrangement. Later, as relationships and norms develop between vendor and client, contracts will be renegotiated, shifting focus from transactions to relationships and partnerships. While the first contracts will be transactional contracts, later contracts will be relational contracts. Contract work is characterized by progressive contractual work, where focus slowly shifts from transactions to relationships as contract outcomes start to materialize.

It is important to design effective IT outsourcing governance. We defined governance as specifying the decision rights and accountability framework to encourage desirable behavior in an IT outsourcing relationship. Governance performance must then be how well the governance arrangements encourage desirable behaviors and ultimately how well both firms achieve their desired performance goals as vendor and client.

There are many IT outsourcing theories (Gottschalk & Solli-Sæther, 2006). Each theory implies suggestions for managing successful IT outsourcing relationships. As a total set of suggestions and ideas from all theories, these guidelines represent

Figure 9.6. The governance model defines decision rights concerning resources

Resources / Stakeholders	Human assets	Financial assets	Physical assets	IP assets	Information and IT assets	Relationship assets
Client business management	Knowledge management decisions	User investment decisions	Tangible assets policy	Intangible assets policy	Strategic information systems planning decisions	Information sharing policy
Client IT management	Internal IT personnel decisions	User tehnology investment decision	Tangible assets management	Intangible assets management	Technology business alignment decision	Project sharing policy
Vendor business management	Knowledge management decisions	Vendor investment decisions	Tangible assets governance	Intangible assets governance	Service- level decisions	Competence sharing policy
Vendor account management	Internal IT personnel decisions	Vendor technology investment decisions	Tangible assets governance	Intangible assets governance	Technology decisions	Knowledge transfer policy

Figure 9.7. Stages of growth in IT outsourcing

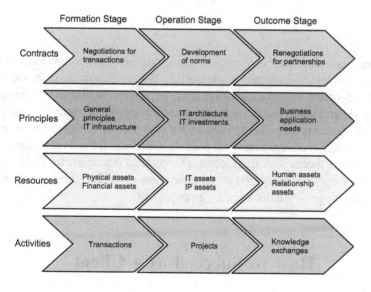

Figure 9.8. Managing successful IT outsourcing relationships through the governance model based on IT outsourcing theories

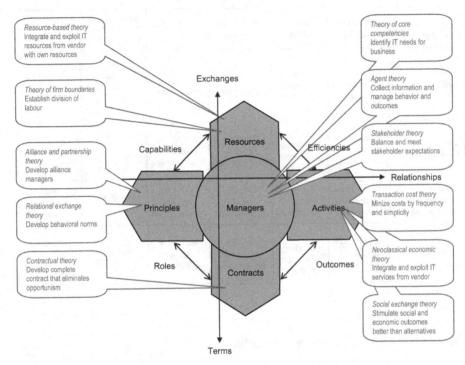

critical success factors after outsourcing. The guidelines can be implemented in the governance model as illustrated in Figure 9.8. We see that resource-based theory and the theory of firm boundaries both provide guidelines for resource management. Alliance and partnership theory and relational exchange theory both provide guidelines for principles management. Transaction cost theory, neo-classical economic theory, and social exchange theory all provide guidelines for activity management, while contractual theory provide guidelines for contract management. Theory of core competencies, agency theory, and stakeholder theory provide guidelines directly to managers in charge of the outsourcing arrangement.

How to Succeed as a Client

Based on outsourcing theories and practice, we are able to list the following key success factors for a sourcing firm as listed in Figure 9.9.

Figure 9.9. Key success factors for the client in managing successful IT outsourcing relationships based on theories

Theory	How to succeed as a client company in an outsourcing arrangement
Theory of core competencies	We have to define our IT needs and manage IT services from the vendor.
Resource-based theory	We have to integrate and exploit strategic IT resources from the vendor together with our own resources to produce competitive goods and services.
Transaction cost theory	We have to minimize transaction costs by reducing the need for lasting specific IT assets; increase transaction frequency; reduce complexity and uncertainty in IT tasks; improve performance measurements; and reduce dependence on other transactions.
Contractual theory	We must have a complete IT contract based on information symmetry in a predictable environment with occurrence adoption that prevents opportunistic behavior in an efficient collaborative environment with balance of power between client and vendor, where the contract is a management instrument that grants decision rights and action duties.
Neo-classical economic theory	We have to integrate and exploit IT services from the vendor together with our own services to produce competitive goods and services.
Partnership and alliance theory	We have to develop experience with alliances, develop alliance managers, and develop the ability to identify potential vendors.
Relational exchange theory	We have to develop and secure common norms that are relevant to both parties.
Social exchange theory	We have to enable social and economic outcomes in the exchange between the vendor and us such that these outcomes outperform those obtainable in alternative exchanges.
Agency theory	We have to make it easy and inexpensive for us to find out what the vendor is actually doing. In addition, both outcome-based and behavior-based incentives can be used to reduce and prevent opportunistic vendor behavior.
Theory of firm boundaries	We have to implement a strict and rigid division of labor between the vendor and us.
Stakeholder theory	We must create efficient and effective communication with and between stakeholders to secure continued support from all stakeholders, to balance their interests, and to make the IT outsourcing arrangement so that all stakeholders achieve their goals.

Figure 9.10. Key success factors for the vendor in managing successful IT outsourcing relationships based on theories

Theory	How to succeed as a vendor company in an outsourcing arrangement
Theory of core competencies	We have to provide complementary core competencies, such as personnel, methodologies, and services to the client.
Resource-based theory	We have to enable the client to integrate and exploit strategic IT resources from us together with the clients' own resources to produce competitive goods and services.
Transaction cost theory	We have to minimize transaction costs by reducing the need for lasting specific IT assets; increase transaction frequency; reduce complexity and uncertainty in IT tasks; improve performance measurements; and reduce dependence on other transactions.
Contractual theory	We must have a complete IT contract based on information symmetry in a predictable environment with occurrence adoption that prevents opportunistic behavior in an efficient collaborative environment with balance of power between client and vendor, where the contract is a management instrument that grants decision rights and action duties.
Neo-classical economic theory	We have to enable the client to integrate and exploit IT services from us together with own services to produce competitive goods and services.
Partnership and alliance theory	We have to develop experience with alliances, develop alliance managers, and develop the ability to identify potential clients.
Relational exchange theory	We have to develop and secure common norms that are relevant to both parties.
Social exchange theory	We have to enable social and economic outcomes in the exchange between the client and us such that these outcomes outperform those obtainable in alternative exchanges.
Agency theory	It must be easy and inexpensive for the principal (client) to find out what the agent (vendor) is actually doing. In addition, both outcome-based and behavior-based incentives can be used to reduce and prevent opportunistic behavior.
Theory of firm boundaries	We have to implement a strict and rigid division of labor between the client and us.
Stakeholder theory	We have to create efficient and effective communication with and between stakeholders to secure continued support from all stakeholders, to balance their interests, and to make the IT outsourcing arrangement so that all stakeholders achieve their goals.

How to Succeed as a Vendor

Based on outsourcing theories and practice, we are able to list the following key success factors for a source firm as listed in Figure 9.10.

CIO Leadership and IT Governance

Monnoyer and Willmott (2005) are skeptical of IT governance. They argue that something has gone very wrong with the structures, processes, and policies that govern how a business makes IT decisions and who within the organization makes them. They find that IT governance arrangements have become a substitute for real leadership. Companies are relying on tightly scripted meetings, analyses, and decision frameworks to unite CIOs and business executives around a common vision for IT. But committee meetings and processes are poor stand-ins for executives who can forge a clear agreement among their peers about IT investment choices and drive the senior-level conversations needed to make tough trade-offs.

Monnoyer and Willmott (2005) find that in companies with strong IT leaders, governance constitutes a much more flexible set of managerial activities, involves fewer people and fewer meetings, and is typically tailored to fit the IT leader's style, much as executive committee activities often reflect a CEO's leadership approach.

References

Blois, K. (2002). Business to business exchanges: A rich descriptive apparatus derived from MacNeil's and Menger's analysis. *Journal of Management Studies, 39*(4), 523-551.

Cannon, J. P., Achrol, R. S., & Gundlach, G. T. (2000). Contracts, norms, and plural form governance. *Journal of the Academy of Marketing Science, 28*(2), 180-194.

Cannon, J. P., & Homburg, C. (2001). Buyer-supplier relationships and customer firm costs. *Journal of Marketing, 65,* 29-43.

Cernat, L. (2004). The emerging European corporate governance model: Anglo-Saxon, continental, or still the century of diversity? *Journal of European Public Policy, 11*(1), 147-166.

Gartner. (2005). The changing role of the CIO. The state of the CIO around the world. CIO 100 2005: The bold 100. State of the CIO 2004: The CEO view. *Gartner Group Insight.* Retrieved from www.gartner.com

Gottschalk, P., & Solli-Sæther, H. (2006). *Managing successful IT outsourcing relationships.* Hershey, PA: Idea Group Publishing.

Grembergen, W. V., Haes, S. D., & Guldentops, E. (2004). Structures, processes and relational mechanisms for IT governance. In W. V. Grembergen (Eds.), *Strategies for information technology governance* (pp. 1-36). Hershey, PA: Idea Group Publishing.

IT Governance Institute. (2004). IT Governance Global Status Report. *IT Governance Institute,* Rolling Meadows, IL. Retrieved from www.itgi.org

Monnoyer, E., & Willmott, P. (2005, August). What IT leaders do. *McKinsey Quarterly,* Web exclusive, 5 pages. Retrieved from www.mckinseyquarterly

Peterson, R. R. (2004). Integration strategies and tactics for information technology governance. In W. V. Grenbergen (Eds.), *Strategies for information technology governance* (pp. 37-80). Hershey, PA: Idea Group Publishing.

Useem, M., & Harder, J. (2000, Winter). Leading laterally in company outsourcing. *Sloan Management Review,* 25-36.

Weill, P. (2004). *Don't just lead, govern: How top-performing firms govern IT.* Research Article, Center for Information Systems Research, CISR WP No. 341, Sloan School of Management, Massachusetts Institute of Technology (MIT).

Weill, P., & Ross, J. W. (2004). *IT governance.* Boston: Harvard Business School Press.

Williamson, O. E. (1979). Transaction-cost economics: The governance of contractual relations. *The Journal of Law and Economics, 22,* 233-261.

Williamson, O. E. (1991). Comparative economic organization: The analysis of discrete structural alternatives. *Administrative Science Quarterly, 36,* 269-296.

Chapter X

The CIO as Chief Knowledge Officer

Introduction

The centrality of knowledge in organizations is reflected in the emergence of the knowledge-based view as an important theoretical stance in contemporary organizational research. Theoretical proposals indicate that advantages for a firm arise from cooperative social contexts that are conducive to the creation, coordination, transfer, and integration of knowledge distributed among its employees, departments, and cooperating agencies.

In some organizations there is the position of a knowledge manager — often called chief knowledge officer (CKO). While the CIO is in charge of systems for electronic data and electronic information, the CKO is in charge of systems for knowledge management. Since knowledge is information combined with reflection, interpretation, and context, the CIO might expand his or her power base by occupying or combining the CKO position as well.

Knowledge Management

Knowledge is a complex concept and a number of factors determine the nature of knowledge creation, management, valuation, and sharing. Organizational knowledge is created through cycles of combination, internalization, socialization, and externalization that transform knowledge between tacit and explicit modes.

Knowledge management is of particular relevance to information systems because the functionalities of information technologies play a critical role in shaping organizational efforts for knowledge creation, acquisition, integration, valuation, and use. Information systems have been central to organizational efforts to enable work processes, flows of information, and sources of knowledge to be integrated and for synergies from such combinations to be realized.

The focus of the deployment of knowledge management systems in organizations has been on developing searchable document repositories to support the digital capture, storage, retrieval, and distribution of an organization's explicitly documented knowledge. Knowledge management systems also encompass other technology-based initiatives such as the creation of databases of experts, the development of decision aids and expert systems, and the hardwiring of social networks to aid access to resources of non-collocated individuals (Sambamurthy & Subramani, 2005).

Information systems developers have evolved several frameworks to articulate themes related to knowledge management. There is a diversity of organizational processes through which information systems affect the management of intangible assets in and between organizations. Furthermore, technical and social processes interact in complementarities to shape knowledge management efforts. For example, although information technologies foster electronic communities of practice, there are social dynamics through which such communities become effective forums for knowledge dissemination, integration, and use.

Sambamurthy and Subramani (2005) presented three types of organizational problems where knowledge management systems can make a difference:

- **The problem of knowledge coordination:** Individuals or groups face knowledge coordination problems when the knowledge needed to diagnose and solve a problem or make an appropriate decision exists (or is believed to exist), but knowledge about its existence or location is not available to the individual or group. Knowledge coordination problems require a search for expertise and are aided by an understanding of patterns of knowledge distribution – of who knows what and who can be asked for help. Research suggests that personal, social, or organizational networks facilitate awareness about knowing entities and their possession of knowledge. Similarly, information technologies can facilitate the efficient and effective nurturing of communities of practice through which distributed knowledge can be coordinated.

- **The problem of knowledge transfer:** This problem is often faced by individuals or groups once an appropriate source of knowledge is located (generally after solving knowledge coordination problems). In particular, knowledge is found to be sticky and contextualized as a result of which it might not be easily transferable. Further, the absorptive capacity of the individuals, units, or organizations seeking knowledge might either enable or inhibit their ability to make sense of the transferred knowledge.

- **The problem of knowledge reuse:** This is a problem of motivation and reward related to the reuse of knowledge. This occurs when individuals or groups may prefer to devise a unique solution to a problem, rather than reuse the standard knowledge available in repositories. Often, recognizing individuals for knowledge contributions (such as rewarding contributions to the organizational document repository or rewarding individuals for being helpful in sharing their expertise) appears to create disincentives to reuse of the knowledge, particularly when reuse involves explicitly acknowledging the inputs or assistance received.

Advances in information technologies and the growth of a knowledge-based service economy are transforming the basis of technological innovation and organizational performance. This transformation requires taking a broader, institutional and political view of information technology and knowledge management. To succeed, organizations need to focus on building their distinctive competencies (Van de Ven, 2005).

The development of information technologies during the past few years has enabled many organizations to improve both the understanding and the dissemination of information. The development of powerful databases allows information to be organized in a manner that improves access to it, increases speed of retrieval, and expands searching flexibility. Furthermore, the Internet now provides a vehicle for sharing of information across geographical distance that encourages collaboration between people and organizations (Hauck & Chen, 2005).

Knowledge is an important organizational resource. Unlike other inert organizational resources, the application of existing knowledge has the potential to generate new knowledge. Not only can knowledge be replenished in use, it can also be combined and recombined to generate new knowledge. Once created, knowledge can be articulated, shared, stored, and recontextualized to yield options for the future. For all of these reasons, knowledge has the potential to be applied across time and space to yield increasing returns (Garud & Kumaraswamy, 2005).

The strategic management of organizational knowledge is a key factor that can help organizations to sustain competitive advantage in volatile environments. Organizations are turning to knowledge management initiatives and technologies to leverage their knowledge resources. Knowledge management can be defined as a systemic and organizationally specified process for acquiring, organizing, and communicating knowledge of employees so that other employees may make use of it to be more effective and productive in their work (Kankanhalli, Tan, & Wei, 2005).

Knowledge management is also important in inter-organizational relationships. Inter-organizational relationships have been recognized to provide two distinct potential benefits: short-term operational efficiency and longer-term new knowledge creation. For example, the need for continual value innovation is driving supply chains to evolve from a pure transactional focus to leveraging inter-organizational partnerships for sharing information and, ultimately, market knowledge creation. Supply chain partners are engaging in interlinked processes that enable rich (broad-ranging, high quality, and privileged) information sharing, and building information technology infrastructures that allow them to process information obtained from their partners to create new knowledge (Malhotra, Gosain, & El Sawy, 2005).

The Chief Knowledge Officer

One action for knowledge management is to establish support functions dedicated to knowledge management in the organization. The person leading this function is typically called knowledge manager or chief knowledge officer (CKO). A CKO is responsible for knowledge-based innovations in the firm. While the chief information officer (CIO) is concerned with applications of information technology in the firm, the CKO is only interested in information technology to the extent that it enables knowledge-based innovations in the firm. In addition to the CKO, we find knowledge engineers, librarians, project managers, and database experts in knowledge management support functions.

The CKO role is an important one for both operational and symbolic reasons, according to Grover and Davenport (2001). Operationally, CKOs perform a variety of key roles, including serving as the chief designer of the knowledge architecture, the top of the reporting relationship for knowledge professionals, the head technologist for knowledge technologies, and the primary procurement officer for external knowledge content. Symbolically, the presence of a CKO serves as an important indicator that a firm views knowledge and its management as critical to its success. If the CKO is a member of the senior executive team, it becomes obvious to employees that knowledge is a critical business resource on the level of labor and capital.

Davenport and Prusak (2000) suggest the following main tasks for a CKO:

- Advocate or "evangelize" for knowledge and learning from it. Particularly given the important role for knowledge in the strategies and processes of many firms today, long-term changes are necessary in organizational cultures and individual behaviors relative to knowledge. These changes will require sustained and powerful advocacy.

- Design, implement, and oversee a firm's knowledge infrastructure, including its libraries, knowledge bases, human and computer knowledge networks, research centers, and knowledge-oriented organizational structure.

- Manage relationships with external providers of information and knowledge (e.g., academic partners or database companies) and negotiate contracts with them. This is already a major expense item for many companies, and efficient and effective management of it is important.

- Provide critical input to the process of knowledge creation and use around the firm (e.g., new product development, market research, and business strategy development) and facilitate efforts to improve such processes if necessary.

- Design and implement a firm's knowledge codification approaches. Such approaches specify key categories of information or knowledge that the organization would address, and entail mapping both the current knowledge inventory and future knowledge models.

- Measure and manage the value of knowledge, either by conventional financial analysis or by anecdote management. If the organization has no sense of the value of knowledge and its management, the function will not last long.

- Manage the organization's professional knowledge managers, giving them the sense of community, establishing professional standards, and managing their careers. These workers may be reporting in a matrix between the CKO and managers of the domains where the company focuses knowledge management efforts (e.g.,, a particular market, product set, or type of customer).

- Lead the development of knowledge strategy, focusing the firm's resources on the type of knowledge it needs to manage most, and the knowledge processes with the largest gaps between need and current capability.

Leadership Requirements

In many large organizations, and some small ones, this new corporate executive is emerging — the chief knowledge officer. Companies are creating the position to initiate, drive, and coordinate knowledge management programs. Earl and Scott (1999) studied 20 CKOs in North America and Europe both to understand their roles and to gain insight on evolving knowledge management practice. Most of the CKOs studied agreed on three points:

1.   Knowledge today is a necessary and sustainable source of competitive advantage. In an era characterized by rapid change and uncertainty, it is claimed that successful companies are those that consistently create new knowledge, disseminate it through the organization, and embody it in technologies, products, and services. Several sectors, such as the financial services, consulting, and software industries, depend on knowledge as their principal way to create value. Thus, knowledge is displacing capital, natural resources, and labor as the basic economic resource.

2.   There is general recognition that companies are not good at managing knowledge. They may undervalue the creation and capture of knowledge, they may lose or give away what they possess, they may deter or inhibit knowledge sharing, and they may under-invest in both using and reusing the knowledge they have. Above all, perhaps, they may not know what they know. This may be true of explicit or articulated knowledge: that which can be expressed in words and numbers and can be easily communicated and shared in hard form, as scientific formulas, codified procedures, or universal principles. It is probably true of tacit or unarticulated knowledge: that which is more personal, experiential, context specific, and hard to formalize; is difficult to communicate or share with others; and is generally in the heads of individuals and teams.

3.   Recognizing the potential of knowledge in value creation and the failure to fully exploit it, some corporations have embarked on knowledge management programs. These are explicit attempts to manage knowledge as a resource, in particular:

   •   Designing and installing techniques and processes to create, protect, and use known knowledge.

   •   Designing and creating environments and activities to discover and release knowledge that is not known.

   •   Articulating the purpose and nature of managing knowledge as a resource and embodying it in other initiatives and programs.

According to Earl and Scott (1999), these three activities need not be solely, or even mainly, intra-organizational. There is usually potential for improving knowledge capabilities, both within and between units of an organization. But external or inter-organizational possibilities may be at least as attractive and ultimately more important. These include, for example, mutual sharing of knowledge with partners, allies, intermediaries, suppliers, and customers. Equally, protecting external leakage of some knowledge can be a vital concern to companies that have focused on intellectual capital formation.

Earl and Scott (1999) found that current movements such as intellectual asset (or capital) management and organizational intelligence are closely related to knowledge management. Together with other related themes such as organizational learning and information management, they may be conceptualized or practiced differently from the emerging praxis of knowledge management or, in some cases, they may be much the same. Consequently, there are some corporate executives leading such initiatives who will feel that they are, in effect, CKOs. However, they have different titles, such as director of intellectual capital or vice president of organizational learning (Earl & Scott, 1999, p. 30):

> The much commoner and well-established role of chief information officer, or CIO, although sometimes thought to be similar to that of CKO, is quite different. CIOs have distinct responsibilities — IT strategy, IT operations, and managing the IT function — and so far have not formally taken on the full range of knowledge management activities. Where a CKO exists, there is also likely to be a CIO, but the corollary is not true.

> Those 'chief knowledge officers' we studied are senior corporate executives with 'knowledge' in their titles. In other words, we could assume that they had been appointed specifically to orchestrate a knowledge management program. They are all first incumbents in the role, most having been in office less than two years. We studied them using semi-structured face-to-face interviews plus a personality assessment questionnaire. Subsequently, we conducted two workshops with some of the participants to compare our results with their collective experiences.

> Although, not surprisingly, we found differences in what CKOs did in their particular organizations, we found a remarkable similarity in their personal profiles and in their experiences to date. 'Chief knowledge officer' is an unusual and arresting title; as one participant said: 'I have the honor of having the most pretentious title in the corporation.' Our study suggests that CKOs are also unusual and arresting people.

Earl and Scott (1999) found that the role of the CKO is so immature that there is no job specification. Different corporations are likely to have different expectations of it. So CKOs have had first to work out an agenda for themselves, and they commonly refer to the rapid learning involved. This is mainly because their mission or mandate is not clear. "Everybody here, me included, is on a vertical learning curve about knowledge management," admitted one CKO. Almost invariably, CKOs are appointed by the CEO; one CEO said, "At the time, appointing a CKO was much more through intuition and instinct than through analysis or strategic logic" (Earl & Scott, 1999, p. 31).

The CKOs studied thus had to discover and develop the CEO's implicit vision of how knowledge management would make a difference. On the one hand, the CEOs were thinking boldly; on the other hand, they were not thinking in detail. Their goals, however, were fairly clear, usually concerned with correcting one or more of these perceived corporate deficiencies:

- Inattention to the explicit or formal management of knowledge in ongoing operations.
- Failure to leverage the hidden value of corporate knowledge in business development.
- Inability to learn from past failures and successes in strategic decision-making.
- Not creating value or "making money" from knowledge embedded in products or held by employees.

So the primary task of a first-generation CKO is to articulate a knowledge management program. This is a twofold task that involves evangelizing the nature and value potential of knowledge and selling not only the concept of knowledge management but also how to sell it to both corporate and line or local management. In particular, CKOs have found they need to engage senior executives one on one to understand possible individual or local knowledge gaps or opportunities and to initiate customized knowledge management projects. As one CKO explained to Earl and Scott (1999, p. 32):

"Unless I can persuade people that knowledge management is not just for the benefit of other people, I haven't got much hope of persuading them to buy into it. They have to believe there's something in it for them and that I care about that as much as they do. Otherwise it just comes across as the latest form of cynical manipulation."

Therefore, CKOs spend a lot of time walking around the organization. In particular, they interact with four types of managers (Earl & Scott, 1999):

- They look for those who are excited about a particular knowledge management idea or project and thus have identified where improvement is possible and are likely to want to try something new. These are their **knowledge champions**.

- They also seek to identify from the senior executive cadre those who are enthused by knowledge management, identify with the concept, and make public statements about it. These are potential **knowledge sponsors** who will invest in and support knowledge management projects.

- Surprisingly, several CKOs studied also spent time identifying executives who are hostile to knowledge management and/or the appointment of a CKO. They sense that in a new and as yet ill-defined corporate initiative, especially one with the CEO's personal support, there will be doubters and reactionaries who must be converted to the cause or avoided for now. These are the **knowledge skeptics**.

- Finally, the CKO, once he or she has initiated a project of any substance, will need allies in implementation, typically, IS executives and HR professionals. These are the **knowledge partners**. Rarely did these partners come from outside the organization. For example, CKOs are skeptical about how management consultants can help, feeling they are lower down the learning curve than themselves. One interviewee complained, "The consultants who have woken up to knowledge management as an opportunity and are peddling expertise in this field actually know less about it than we do." In a similar vein, CKOs have soon concluded there is little to be learned from conferences and external contacts, as they discover that knowledge extraction is more common than knowledge sharing.

Earl and Scott (1999) found that a common word in the CKO's vocabulary is "design." CKOs are designers of knowledge directories, knowledge-based systems, knowledge-intensive business and management processes, knowledge exchange events, knowledge-sharing physical spaces, and knowledge protection policies. Mostly, their design is conceptual. In other words, they work on an idea with a champion and contribute design suggestions and inject thinking from emerging knowledge management practice, as a consultant or systems analyst would. They then enlist the help of relevant partners.

Applehans, Globe, and Laugero (1999) defined the CKO as part of the knowledge architecture. The knowledge architecture identifies the scope of the investment that will be made in managing knowledge. More than a technical solution, it encompasses three components: people, content, and technology. A knowledge architecture brings these components together into a powerful working relationship. In this architecture, the CKO or the chief learning officer (CLO) is the change agent who markets the importance of knowledge inside the company and enables a global audience to take advantage of it. The CKO ensures that the knowledge architecture is funded, designed, built, and administered.

Should companies really appoint a CKO to the job of managing knowledge? According to Foote, Matson, and Rudd (2001), the answer depends on whether the CEO and senior management are prepared to make the position succeed. The limits of the CKO's potential contribution are set by what the CEO and senior management have done before the position was created. A candidate should hesitate before accepting an offer from an organization whose top managers do not see the point of managing knowledge and whose employees do not have a thirst for acquiring it.

Managing Knowledge

Foote et al. (2001) found that most top managers recognize the value of managing knowledge. In a 1998 survey of North American senior executives, 77% rated "improving the development, sharing, and use of knowledge throughout the business" as very or extremely important. Thanks to the groundwork laid by pioneering knowledge managers, CKOs can now create substantial value. First employed in the early 1990s to foster the flow of knowledge throughout increasingly complex organizations, they functioned rather like plumbers, routing bits of information through different pipes to the right people. They then built better pipes, such as company-wide e-mail networks and corporate intranets, and still later, redesigned work and communications processes to promote collaboration.

Foote et al. (2001) suggest that today, in organizations that already have these technical and social networks, CKOs can take a more strategic perspective, scanning the enterprise to discover how they might improve processes and customer relationship management as well as promote employee learning. Other senior managers might be able to see how knowledge can be better used in their particular units or functions, but the CKO can stand back and manage interventions that cross formal business boundaries, thus helping the enterprise as a whole. In organizations where cross-business and cross-functional interventions are not likely to happen unless someone from the top team takes express responsibility for them, appointing a CKO would seem to be a good idea.

What can be done to ensure that the CKO unlocks a company's latent potential? To find out, Foote et al. (2001) asked CKOs at various companies for their views about the make-or-break factors. Although the CKOs had different experiences, all concurred that success depends on two things: first, on the ability of senior management to agree about what it hopes to gain from managing knowledge explicitly and from creating a performance culture (which raises the staff's demand for knowledge); and, second, on how well the CKO develops and executes a knowledge management agenda.

The value that senior managers hope to create from managing knowledge generally lies at one of three levels (Foote et al., 2001, p. 3):

At the lowest level, the managers aim to help their organization become better at what it already does. International Computers Limited (ICL), the UK information technology service provider, found that several of its business groups wanted to improve the speed and quality of their services to customers. Elizabeth Lank, ICL's program director for mobilizing knowledge, decided that these groups would benefit if the company shared three kinds of information: about projects already completed, skills already developed, and customer concerns the business groups were working to address.

She therefore organized databases to capture that knowledge and created networks permitting those who needed it to communicate with those who had it. Lank appointed the sales and marketing director, for example, to 'own' the third piece of knowledge and to work out exactly what had to be shared and how, with a focus on enabling conversations rather than compiling documents. The speed and quality of service to customers subsequently improved: there were fewer cases in which three parts of the organization competed for the same business or customer information couldn't be found quickly.

At the second level, knowledge can be used to underpin new forms of commercial activity, such as customer-focused teams and cross-unit coordination. Wunderman Cato Johnson, the relationship-management arm of the advertising agency Young & Rubicam, provides an example. In 1996 it was shifting from a service-line business to one organized around key clients throughout the world. Nicholas Rudd, who was then CKO, promoted the transition to 'seamless' worldwide service by improving customer relations and pursuing new business. This approach put a premium on knowledge that supported two new forms of behavior: sharing lessons learned from experience and focusing business-development efforts on network success. At this level, knowledge management goes beyond the 'basic hygiene' of improving current processes to supporting new ones.

Knowledge management can go even further by generating an entirely new value proposition for customers. A business might, for instance, decide to offer previously 'internal' knowledge as part of its product. The World Bank, to cite one case, used to provide primarily financial resources to developing countries. Now it also offers direct access to huge reserves of knowledge about what forms of economic development do and don't work. This approach not only benefits clients but also strengthens the *commitment of the bank's shareholders, which see the effectiveness of their capital enhanced. Steve Denning, the bank's former director of knowledge management, observed that 'internal knowledge sharing improves our efficiency, but sharing it externally has a much larger impact, improving our quality of service and reaching a much wider group of clients.'*

If a company wishes only to improve its current processes, bringing in the appropriate experts (rather than hiring a CKO) may suffice to achieve the necessary social and technical objectives –creating new teams or new electronic forums, for example. If aspirations run higher, the chief executive officer may need an informed CKO to pinpoint the most valuable links between knowledge and the business and to plan how best to exploit them.

For knowledge to create value, people must want knowledge and know how to use it. Companies that are good at using their knowledge to boost performance (Goldman Sachs, say, or Hewlett-Packard) stretch employees to perform. This approach obliges them to reach out and pull in better knowledge from every part of the organization and, for that matter, from outside in. It is no accident that Jack Welch spent his first years as CEO of GE — before he started advocating 'boundaryless' knowledge sharing and collaboration — driving up performance demands. In the absence of a performance culture, people will feel swamped by information for which they see no need.

Top performers such as Goldman Sachs and GE have been evolving a performance culture over decades; companies that haven't done so must compress that development into a few years. This can be done. During the early 1990s, British Petroleum, for example, was able to transform itself from a centralized organization run by large, functional departments into a collection of focused, high-performance units with extensive mechanisms for sharing knowledge across them.

If the preconditions can be fulfilled, success hangs on the ability of the CKO to identify, launch, operate, and evaluate knowledge-related change initiatives that are worthwhile in themselves and can be replicated in various sectors of the organization. Although the tasks sound fairly straightforward, the CKO must succeed in winning support from the wider organization in order to execute any of them. The truth is that CKOs stand or fall by their power to influence.

The knowledge management agenda is implemented through a cadre of managers who understand knowledge and its uses in various aspects of the business, the motivational and attitudinal factors necessary to get people to create, share, and use knowledge effectively, and the ways to use technology to enhance knowledge activities. On a daily basis, knowledge managers perform a broad collection of tasks, including (Grover & Davenport, 2001):

- Facilitation of knowledge sharing networks and communities of practice
- Creation, editing, and pruning of "knowledge objects" in a repository
- Building and maintaining technology-based knowledge applications
- Incorporating knowledge-oriented job descriptions, motivational approaches, and evaluation and reward systems into the human resource management processes of the organization
- Redesigning knowledge work processes and incorporating knowledge tasks and activities into them

To develop and execute a knowledge management agenda, the CKO should develop skills in intrapreneurship. *Intrapreneurship* (entrepreneurship within existing organizations) has been of interest to scholars and practitioners for the past two decades. Intrapreneurship is viewed as being beneficial for revitalization and performance of corporations. According to Antoncic and Hisrich (2001, p. 496), the concept has four distinct dimensions:

> *First, the new-business-venturing dimension refers to pursuing and entering new businesses related to the firm's current products or markets. Second, the innovativeness dimension refers to the creation of new products, services, and technologies. Third, the self-renewal dimension emphasizes the strategy reformulation, reorganization, and organizational change. Finally, the proactiveness dimension reflects top management orientation in pursuing enhanced competitiveness and includes initiative and risk-taking, and competitive aggressiveness, and boldness. While differing somewhat in their emphasis, activities and orientations, the four dimensions pertain to the same concept of intrapreneurship because they are factors of Schumpeterian innovation, the building block of entrepreneurship. The pursuit of creative or new solutions to challenges confronting the firm, including the development or enhancement of old and new products and services, markets, administrative techniques, and technologies for performing organizational functions (e.g., production, marketing, sales, and distribution), as well as changes in strategy, organizing, and dealings with competitors are innovations in the broadest sense.*

Knowledge management will never be the sole responsibility of a CKO. Line managers have responsibilities as well. Hansen and Oetinger (2001) argue that there is a need for T-shaped managers. They call the approach *T-shaped management*: (Hansen & Oetinger, 2001, p. 108):

> *We call the approach T-shaped management. It relies on a new kind of executive, one who breaks out of the traditional corporate hierarchy to share knowledge freely across the organization (the horizontal part of the 'T') while remaining fiercely committed to individual business unit performance (the vertical part).*

IS/IT in Knowledge Management

As we trace the evolution of computing technologies in business, we can observe their changing level of organizational impact. The first level of impact was at the point work got done and transactions (e.g., orders, deposits, reservations) took place. The inflexible, centralized mainframe allowed for little more than massive number crunching, commonly known as electronic *data* processing. Organizations became data heavy at the bottom and data management systems were used to keep the data in check. Later, the management *information* systems were used to aggregate data into useful information reports, often prescheduled, for the control level of the organization — people who were making sure that organizational resources like personnel, money, and physical goods were being deployed efficiently. As information technology (IT) and information systems (IS) started to facilitate data and information overflow, and corporate attention became a scarce resource, the concept of *knowledge* emerged as a particularly high-value form of information (Grover & Davenport, 2001).

Information technology can play an important role in successful knowledge management initiatives. However, the concept of coding and transmitting knowledge in organizations is not new: Training and employee development programs, organizational policies, routines, procedures, reports, and manuals have served this function for many years. What is new and exciting in the knowledge management area is the potential for using modern information technology (e.g., the Internet, intranets, extranets, browsers, data warehouses, data filters, software agents, expert systems) to support knowledge creation, sharing, and exchange in an organization and between organizations. Modern information technology can collect, systematize, structure, store, combine, distribute, and present information of value to knowledge workers (Nahapiet & Ghoshal, 1998).

According to Davenport and Prusak (2000), more and more companies have instituted knowledge repositories, supporting such diverse types of knowledge as best practices, lessons learned, product development knowledge, customer knowledge, human resource management knowledge, and methods-based knowledge. Groupware and intranet-based technologies have become standard knowledge infrastructures. The new set of professional job titles – the knowledge manager, the chief knowledge officer (CKO), the knowledge coordinator, and the knowledge-network facilitator — affirms the widespread legitimacy that knowledge management has earned in the corporate world.

The low cost of computers and networks has created a potential infrastructure for knowledge sharing and opened up important knowledge management opportunities. The computational power as such has little relevance to knowledge work, but the communication and storage capabilities of networked computers make it an important enabler of effective knowledge work. Through e-mail, groupware, the Internet, and intranets, computers and networks can point to people with knowledge and connect people who need to share knowledge independent of time and place.

For example, electronic networks of practice are computer-mediated discussion forums focused on problems of practice that enable individuals to exchange advice and ideas with others based on common interests. Electronic networks make it possible to share information quickly, globally, and with large numbers of individuals. Electronic networks that focus on knowledge exchange frequently emerge in fields where the pace of technological change requires access to knowledge unavailable within any single organization (Wasko & Faraj, 2005).

In the knowledge-based view of the firm, knowledge is the foundation of a firm's competitive advantage and, ultimately, the primary driver of a firm's value. Inherently, however, knowledge resides within individuals and, more specifically, in the employees who create, recognize, archive, access, and apply knowledge in carrying out their tasks. Consequently, the movement of knowledge across individual and organizational boundaries, into and from repositories, and into organizational routines and practices is ultimately dependent on employees' knowledge sharing behaviors (Bock, Zmud, & Kim, 2005).

According to Grover and Davenport (2001), most knowledge management projects in organizations involve the use of information technology. Such projects fall into relatively few categories and types, each of which has a key objective. Although it is possible, and even desirable, to combine multiple objectives in a single project, this was not normally observed in a study of 31 knowledge management projects in 1997 (Davenport & Prusak, 1998). Since that time, it is possible that projects have matured and have taken on more ambitious collections of objectives.

Regardless of definition of knowledge as the highest value of content in a continuum starting at data, encompassing information, and ending at knowledge, knowledge managers often take a highly inclusive approach to the content with which they deal. In practice, what companies actually manage under the banner of knowledge management is a mix of knowledge, information, and unrefined data — in short, whatever anyone finds that is useful and easy to store in an electronic repository. In the case of data and information, however, there are often attempts to add more value and create knowledge. This transformation might involve the addition of insight, experience, context, interpretation, or the myriad of other activities in which human brains specialize (Grover & Davenport, 2001).

Identifying, nurturing, and harvesting knowledge is a principal concern in the information society and the knowledge age. Effective use of knowledge-facilitating tools and techniques is critical, and a number of computational tools have been developed. While numerous techniques are available, it remains difficult to analyze or compare the specific tools. In part, this is because knowledge management is a young discipline. The arena is evolving rapidly as more people enter the fray and encounter new problems (Housel & Bell, 2001).

In addition, new technologies support applications that were impossible before. Moreover, the multidisciplinary character of knowledge management combines several disciplines, including business and management, computer science, cybernetics, and philosophy. Each of these fields may lay claim to the study of knowledge management, and the field is frequently defined so broadly that anything can be incorporated. Finally, it is difficult to make sense of the many tools available. It is not difficult to perform a search to produce a list of more than 100 software providers. Each of the software packages employ unique visions and aims to capture its share of the market (Housel & Bell, 2001).

Ward and Peppard (2002) find that there are two dominant and contrasting views of IS/IT in knowledge management: the engineering perspective and the social process perspective. The engineering perspective views knowledge management as a technology process. Many organizations have taken this approach in managing knowledge, believing that it is concerned with managing pieces of intellectual capital. Driving this view is the view that knowledge can be codified and stored; in essence that knowledge is explicit knowledge and therefore is little more than information.

The alternative view is that knowledge is a social process. As such, it asserts that knowledge resides in people's heads and that it is tacit. It cannot be easily codified and only revealed through its application. As tacit knowledge cannot be directly transferred from person to person, its acquisition occurs only through practice. Consequently, its transfer between people is slow, costly, and uncertain. Technology, within this perspective, can only support the context of knowledge work. It has been argued that IT-based systems used to support knowledge management can only be of benefit if used to support the development and communication of human meaning. One reason for the failure of IT in some knowledge management initiatives is that the designers of the knowledge management systems fail to understand the situation and work practices of the users and the complex human processes involved in work.

While technology can be used with knowledge management initiatives, Ward and Peppard (2002) argue that it should never be the first step. Knowledge management is to them primarily a human and process issue. Once these two aspects have been addressed, then the created processes are usually very amenable to being supported and enhanced by the use of technology.

What then is knowledge management technology? According to Davenport and Prusak (2000), the concept of knowledge management technology is not only broad but also a bit slippery to define. Some infrastructure technology that we do not ordinarily think of in this category can be useful in facilitating knowledge management. Examples are videoconferencing and the telephone. Neither of these technologies capture or distribute structured knowledge, but they are quite effective at enabling people to transfer tacit knowledge.

Our focus here, however, is on technology that captures, stores, and distributes structured knowledge for use by people. The goal of these technologies is to take knowledge that exists in human heads and partly in paper documents, and make it widely available throughout an organization. Similarly, Alavi and Leidner (2001) argue that information systems designed to support knowledge in organizations may not appear radically different from other forms of IT support, but will be geared toward enabling users to assign meaning to information and to capture some of their knowledge in information. Therefore, the concept of knowledge management technology in this book is less concerned with any degree of technology sophistication and more concerned with the usefulness in performing knowledge work in organizations and between organizations.

Moffett and McAdam (2003) illustrate the variety of knowledge management technology tools by distinguishing between collaborative tools, content management, and business intelligence. Collaborative tools include groupware technology, meeting support systems, knowledge directories, and intranets/extranets. Content management includes the Internet, agents and filters, electronic publishing systems, document management systems, and office automation systems. Business intelligence includes data warehousing, decision support systems, knowledge-based systems, and workflow systems.

Knowledge Management Processes

Alavi and Leidner (2001) have developed a systematic framework that will be used to analyze and discuss the potential role of information technology in knowledge management. According to this framework, organizations consist of four sets of socially enacted knowledge processes: (1) creation (also referred to as construction), (2) storage and retrieval, (3) transfer, and (4) application. The knowledge-based view of the firm represents both the cognitive and social nature of organizational knowledge and its embodiment in the individual's cognition and practices as well as the collective (i.e., organizational) practices and culture. These processes do not represent a monolithic set of activities, but rather a set of activities that is interconnected and intertwined.

Knowledge Creation

Organizational knowledge creation involves developing new content or replacing existing content within the organization's tacit and explicit knowledge. Through social and collaborative processes as well as individual's cognitive processes (e.g., reflection), knowledge is created. The model developed by Nonaka, Toyama, and Konno (2000) involving SECI, ba (a physical or virtual place) and knowledge assets, views organizational knowledge creation as involving a continual interplay between the tacit and explicit dimensions of knowledge. Furthermore, the model represents a growing spiral flow as knowledge moves through individual, group, and organizational levels. Four modes of knowledge creation have been identified: socialization, externalization, internalization, and combination.

Nonaka et al. (2000) suggest that the essential question of knowledge creation is establishing an organization's ba, defined as a commonplace or space for creating knowledge. Four types of ba corresponding to the four modes of knowledge creation are identified: (1) originating ba, (2) interacting ba, (3) cyber ba, and (4) exercising ba. Originating ba entails the socialization mode of knowledge creation and is the ba from which the organizational knowledge creation process begins. Originating ba is a common place in which individuals share experiences primarily through face-to-face interactions and by being at the same place at the same time. Interacting ba is associated with the externalization mode of knowledge creation and refers to a space where tacit knowledge is converted to explicit knowledge and shared among individuals through the process of dialogue and collaboration. Cyber ba refers to a virtual space of interaction and corresponds to the combination mode of knowledge creation. Finally, exercising ba involves the conversion of explicit to tacit knowledge through the internalization process. Thus, exercising ba involves the conversion of explicit to tacit knowledge through the internalization process.

Understanding the characteristics of various ba and the relationship with the modes of knowledge creation is important to enhancing organizational knowledge creation. For example, the use of IT capabilities in cyber ba is advocated to enhance the efficiency of the combination mode of knowledge creation. Data warehousing and data mining, document management systems, software agents, and intranets may be of great value in cyber ba. Considering the flexibility of modern IT, other forms of organizational ba and the corresponding modes of knowledge creation can be enhanced through the use of various forms of information systems. For example, information systems designed for support or collaboration, coordination, and communication processes, as a component of the interacting ba, can facilitate teamwork and thereby increase an individual's contact with other individuals.

Electronic mail and group support systems have the potential of increasing the number of weak ties in organizations. In turn, this can accelerate the growth of knowledge creation. Intranets enable exposure to greater amounts of online organizational information, both horizontally and vertically, than may previously have been the case. As the level of information exposure increases, the internalization mode of knowledge creation, wherein individuals make observations and interpretations of information that result in new individual tacit knowledge, may increase. In this role, an intranet can support individual learning (conversion of explicit knowledge to personal tacit knowledge) through provision of capabilities such as computer simulation (to support learning-by-doing) and smart software tutors.

Computer-mediated communication may increase the quality of knowledge creation by enabling a forum for constructing and sharing beliefs, for confirming consensual interpretation, and for allowing expression of new ideas. By providing an extended field of interaction among organizational members for sharing ideas and perspectives, and for establishing dialog, information systems may enable individuals to arrive at new insights and/or more accurate interpretations than if left to decipher information on their own.

Although most information repositories serve a single function, it is increasingly common for companies to construct an internal "portal" so that employees can access multiple different repositories and sources from one screen. It is also possible and increasingly popular for repositories to contain not only information, but also pointers to experts within the organization on key knowledge topics. It is also feasible to combine stored information with lists of the individuals who contributed the knowledge and could provide more detail or background on it (Grover & Davenport, 2001).

According to Grover and Davenport (2001), firms increasingly view attempts to transform raw data into usable knowledge as part of their knowledge management initiatives. These approaches typically involve isolating data in a separate "warehouse" for easier access and the use of statistical analysis or data mining and visualization tools. Since their goal is to create data-derived knowledge, they are increasingly addressed as a part of knowledge management. Some vendors have already begun to introduce e-commerce tools. They serve to customize the menu of available knowledge to individual customers, allowing sampling of information before buying and carrying out sales transactions for knowledge purchases. Online legal services are typical examples where clients can sample legal information before buying lawyer's time.

For knowledge creation, there is currently idea-generation software emerging. Idea-generation software is designed to help stimulate a single user or a group to produce new ideas, options, and choices. The user does all the work, but the software encourages and pushes, something like a personal trainer. Although idea-generation software is relatively new, there are several packages on the market. IdeaFisher, for example, has an associative lexicon of the English language that cross-references words and phrases. These associative links, based on analogies and metaphors, make it easy for the user to be fed words related to a given theme. Some software packages use questions to prompt the user toward new, unexplored patterns of thought. This helps users to break out of cyclical thinking patterns and conquer mental blocks.

Knowledge Storage and Retrieval

According to Alavi and Leidner (2001), empirical studies have shown that while organizations create knowledge and learn, they also forget (i.e., do not remember or lose track of the acquired knowledge). Thus, the storage, organization, and retrieval of organizational knowledge, also referred to as organizational memory, constitute an important aspect of effective organizational knowledge management. Organizational memory includes knowledge residing in various component forms, including written documentation, structured information stored in electronic databases, codified human knowledge stored in expert systems, documented organizational procedures and processes, and tacit knowledge acquired by individuals and networks of individuals.

Advanced computer storage technology and sophisticated retrieval techniques, such as query languages, multimedia databases, and database management systems, can be effective tools in enhancing organizational memory. These tools increase the speed at which organizational memory can be accessed.

Groupware enables organizations to create intra-organizational memory in the form of both structured and unstructured information and to share this memory across time and space. IT can play an important role in the enhancement and expansion of both semantic and episodic organizational memory. Semantic memory refers to general, explicit, and articulated knowledge, whereas episodic memory refers to context-specific and situated knowledge. Document management technology allows knowledge of an organization's past, often dispersed among a variety of retention facilities, to be effectively stored and made accessible. Drawing on these technologies, most consulting firms have created semantic memories by developing vast repositories of knowledge about customers, projects, competition, and the industries they serve.

Grover and Davenport (2001) found that in western organizations, by far the most common objective of knowledge management projects involves some sort of knowledge repository. The objective of this type of project is to capture knowledge for later and broader access by others within the same organization. Common repository technologies include Lotus Notes, Web-based intranets, and Microsoft's Exchange, supplemented by search engines, document management tools, and other tools that allow editing and access. The repositories typically contain a specific type of information to represent knowledge for a particular business function or process, such as:

- "Best practices" information within a quality or business process management function
- Information for sales purposes involving products, markets, and customers
- Lessons learned in projects or product development efforts
- Information around implementation of information systems
- Competitive intelligence for strategy and planning functions
- "Learning histories" or records of experience with a new corporate direction or approach

The mechanical generation of databases, Web sites, and systems that process data are good and have the potential to take us to a higher plane in the organization, help us understand workflows better, and help us deal with organizational pathologies and problems. The data-to-information transition often involves a low-level mechanical process that is well within the domain of contemporary information technologies, though humans are helpful in this transition as well. This information could exist in different forms throughout the organization and could even form the basis of competitive advantage or information products. For example, provision of information to customers about their order or shipment status is something that companies like Baxter and FedEx have been doing for years. But unlike knowledge, mechanically supplied information cannot be the source of sustained competitive advantage, particularly when the architectures on which it is based are becoming more open and omnipresent.

IT in knowledge management can be used to store various kinds of information. For example, information about processes, procedures, forecasts, cases, and patents in the form of working documents, descriptions, and reports can be stored in knowledge management systems. TietoEnator, a Scandinavian consulting firm, has a knowledge base where they store methods, techniques, notes, concepts, best practices, presentations, components, references, guidelines, quality instructions, process descriptions, routines, strategies, and CVs for all consultants in the firm (Halvorsen & Nguyen, 1999).

Knowledge retrieval can find support in content management and information extraction technology, which represents a group of techniques for managing and extracting information from documents, ultimately delivering a semantic meaning for decision-makers or learners alike. This type of computer application is targeted at capturing and extracting the content of free-text documents. Several tasks fall within the scope of content management and information extraction (Wang, Hjelmervik, & Bremdal, 2001):

- **Abstracting and summarizing:** This task aims at delivering shorter, informative representations of larger (sets of) documents.

- **Visualization:** Documents can often be visualized according to the concepts and relationships that play a role. Visualization can be either in an introspective manner, or using some reference model/view of a specific topic.

- **Comparison and search:** This task finds semantically similar pieces of information.

- **Indexing and classification:** This considers (partial) texts, usually according to certain categories.

- **Translation:** Context-driven translation of texts from one language into another. Language translation has proven to be highly context specific, even among closely related languages. Some kind of semantic representation of meaning is needed in order to be able to make good translations.

- **Question formulation and query answering:** This is a task in human-computer interaction systems.

- **Extraction of information:** This refers to the generation of additional information that is not explicit in the original text. This information can be more or less elaborate.

A group of computational techniques are available to alleviate the burden of these tasks. They include fuzzy technology, neural networks, and expert systems. On a more application-oriented level, there are several approaches that apply one or more of the general techniques. The field is currently very dynamic, and new advances are made continuously. One novel approach is the CORPORUM system to be presented in the section on expert systems.

Knowledge Transfer

Knowledge transfer can be defined as the communication of knowledge from a source so that it is learned and applied by a recipient (Ko, Kirsch, & King, 2005). Knowledge transfer occurs at various levels in an organization: transfer of knowledge between individuals, from individuals to explicit sources, from individuals to groups, between groups, across groups, and from the group to the organization. Considering the distributed nature of organizational cognition, an important process of knowledge management in organizational settings is the transfer of knowledge to locations where it is needed and can be used. However, this is not a simple process in that organizations often do not know what they know and have weak systems for locating and retrieving knowledge that resides in them. Communication processes and information flows drive knowledge transfer in organizations.

Depending on the completeness or incompleteness of the sender's and the receiver's information sets, there are four representative types of information structure in knowledge transfer: symmetric complete information, sender-advantage asymmetric information, symmetric incomplete information, and receiver-advantage asymmetric information. Because of asymmetry and incompleteness, parties seeking knowledge may not be able to identify qualified knowledge providers, and the appropriate experts may fail to be motivated to engage in knowledge transfer (Lin, Geng, & Whinston, 2005).

Knowledge transfer channels can be informal or formal, personal or impersonal. IT can support all four forms of knowledge transfer, but has mostly been applied to informal, impersonal means (e.g., discussion databases) and formal, impersonal means (e.g., corporate directories). An innovative use of technology for transfer is the use of intelligent agent software to develop interest profiles of organizational members in order to determine which members might be interested recipients of point-to-point electronic messages exchanged among other members. Employing video technologies can also enhance transfer.

IT can increase knowledge transfer by extending the individual's reach beyond the formal communication lines. The search for knowledge sources is usually limited to immediate coworkers in regular and routine contact with the individual. However, individuals are unlikely to encounter new knowledge through their close-knit work networks because individuals in the same clique tend to possess similar information. Moreover, individuals are often unaware of what their cohorts are doing. Thus, expanding the individual's network to more extended, although perhaps weaker, connection is central to the knowledge diffusion process because such networks expose individuals to more new ideas.

Computer networks and electronic bulletin boards and discussion groups create a forum that facilitates contact between the person seeking knowledge and those who may have access to the knowledge. Corporate directories may enable individuals to rapidly locate the individual who has the knowledge that might help them solve a current problem. For example, the primary content of such a system can be a set of expert profiles containing information about the backgrounds, skills, and expertise of individuals who are knowledgeable on various topics. Often such metadata (knowledge about where knowledge resides) proves to be as important as the original knowledge itself. Providing taxonomies or organizational knowledge maps enables individuals to rapidly locate either the knowledge or the individual who has the needed knowledge, more rapidly than would be possible without such IT-based support.

The term IT for information technology is used in this book. Some use ICT for information and communication technology to stress the importance of communications in knowledge management. Communication is important in knowledge management because technology provides support for both intra-organizational as well as inter-organizational knowledge networks. Knowledge networks need technology in the form of technical infrastructure, communication networks, and a set of information services. Knowledge networks enable knowledge workers to share information from various sources.

Traditional information systems have been of importance to vertical integration for a long time. Both customers and suppliers have been linked to the company through information systems. Only recently has horizontal integration occurred. Knowledge workers in similar businesses cooperate to find optimal solutions for customers. IT has become an important vertical and horizontal inter-organizational coordination mechanism. This is not only because of the availability of broadband and standardized protocols. It is also caused by falling prices for communication services and by software program's ability to coordinate functions between firms.

One way to reduce problems stemming from paper workflow is to employ document-imaging systems. Document imaging systems are systems that convert paper documents and images into digital form so they can be stored and accessed by a computer. Once the document has been stored electronically, it can be immediately retrieved and shared with others. An imaging system requires indexes that allow users to identify and retrieve a document when needed (Laudon & Laudon, 2005).

Knowledge Application

An important aspect of the knowledge-based view of the firm is that the source of competitive advantage resides in the application of the knowledge rather than in the knowledge itself. Information technology can support knowledge application by embedding knowledge into organizational routines. Procedures that are culture-bound can be embedded into IT so that the systems themselves become examples of organizational norms. An example according to Alavi and Leidner (2001) is Mrs. Field's use of systems designed to assist in every decision from hiring personnel to when to put free samples of cookies out on the table. The system transmits the norms and beliefs held by the head of the company to organizational members.

Technology enforced knowledge application raises a concern that knowledge will continue to be applied after its real usefulness has declined. While the institutionalization of best practices by embedding them into IT might facilitate efficient handling of routine, linear, and predictable situations during stable or incrementally changing environments, when change is radical and discontinuous, there is a persistent need for continual renewal of the basic premises underlying the practices archived in the knowledge repositories. This underscores the need for organizational members to remain attuned to contextual factors and explicitly consider the specific circumstances of the current environment.

Although there are challenges with applying existing knowledge, IT can have a positive influence on knowledge application. IT can enhance knowledge integration and application by facilitating the capture, updating, and accessibility of organizational directives. For example, many organizations are enhancing the ease of access and maintenance of their directives (repair manuals, policies, and standards) by making them available on corporate intranets. This increases the speed at which changes can be applied. Also, organizational units can follow a faster learning curve by accessing the knowledge of other units having gone through similar experiences. Moreover, by increasing the size of individuals' internal social networks and by increasing the amount of organizational memory available, information technologies allow for organizational knowledge to be applied across time and space.

IT can also enhance the speed of knowledge integration and application by codifying and automating organizational routines. Workflow automation systems are examples of IT applications that reduce the need for communication and coordination and enable more efficient use of organizational routines through timely and automatic routing of work-related documents, information, rules, and activities. Rule-based expert systems are another means of capturing and enforcing well specified organizational procedures.

To summarize, Alavi and Leidner (2001) has developed a framework to understand IS/IT in knowledge management processes through the knowledge-based view of the firm. One important implication of this framework is that each of the four knowledge processes of creation, storage and retrieval, transfer, and application can be facilitated by IT:

- **Knowledge creation:** Examples of supporting information technologies are data mining and learning tools, which enable combining new sources of knowledge and just in time learning.

- **Knowledge storage and retrieval:** Examples of supporting information technologies are electronic bulletin boards, knowledge repositories, and databases, which provide support of individual and organizational memory as well as inter-group knowledge access.

- **Knowledge transfer:** Examples of supporting information technologies are electronic bulletin boards, discussion forums, and knowledge directories, which enable more extensive internal network, more available communication channels, and faster access to knowledge sources.

- **Knowledge application:** Examples of supporting information technologies are expert systems and workflow systems, which enable knowledge application in many locations and more rapid application of new knowledge through workflow automation.

Knowledge Management Systems

There is no single information system that is able to cover all knowledge management needs in a firm. This is evident from the widespread potential of IT in knowledge management processes. Rather, knowledge management systems (KMS) refer to a class of information systems applied to managing organizational knowledge. These systems are IT applications to support and enhance the organizational processes of knowledge creation, storage and retrieval, transfer, and application.

Despite widespread belief that information technology enables knowledge management and knowledge management improves firm performance, researchers have only recently found empirical evidence of these relationships. For example, Tanriverdi (2005) used data from 250 Fortune 1000 firms to provide empirical support for these relationships.

Knowledge management systems are becoming ubiquitous in today's organizations. Knowledge management systems facilitate the efficient and effective sharing of an organization's intellectual resources. To ensure effective usage, a knowledge management system must be designed such that knowledge workers can readily find high-quality content without feeling overwhelmed (Poston & Speier, 2005).

Requirements from Knowledge Management

The critical role of information technology and information systems lies in the ability to support communication, collaboration, and those searching for knowledge, and the ability to enable collaborative learning (Ryu, Kim, Chaudhury, & Rao, 2005). We have already touched on important implications for information systems:

1.   **Interaction between information and knowledge:** Information becomes knowledge when it is combined with experience, interpretation, and reflection. Knowledge becomes information when assigned an explicit representation. Sometimes information exists before knowledge, sometimes knowledge exists before information. One important implication of this two-way direction between knowledge and information is that information systems designed to support knowledge in organizations may not appear radically different from

other forms of IT support, but will be geared toward enabling users to assign meaning to information and to capture some of their knowledge in information (Alavi & Leidner, 2001).

2. **Interaction between tacit and explicit knowledge:** Tacit and explicit knowledge depend on each other, and they influence each other. The linkage of tacit and explicit knowledge suggests that only individuals with a requisite level of shared knowledge are able to exchange knowledge. They suggest the existence of a shared knowledge space that is required in order for Individual A to understand Individual B's knowledge. The knowledge space is the underlying overlap in knowledge base of A and B. This overlap is typically tacit knowledge. It may be argued that the greater the shared knowledge space, the less the context needed for individuals to share knowledge within the group and, hence, the higher the value of explicit knowledge. IT is both dependent on the shared knowledge space and an important part of the shared knowledge space. IT is dependent on the shared knowledge space because knowledge workers need to have a common understanding of available information in information systems in the organization. If common understanding is missing, then knowledge workers are unable to make use of information. IT is an important part of the shared knowledge space because information systems make common information available to all knowledge workers in the organization. One important implication of this two-way relationship between knowledge space and information systems is that a minimum knowledge space has to be present, while IT can contribute to growth in the knowledge space (Alavi & Leidner, 2001).

3. **Knowledge management strategy:** Efficiency-driven businesses may apply the stock strategy where databases and information systems are important. Effectiveness-driven businesses may apply the flow strategy where information networks are important. Expert-driven businesses may apply the growth strategy where networks of experts, work processes, and learning environments are important (Hansen, Nohria, & Tierny, 1999).

4. **Combination in SECI process:** The SECI process consists of four knowledge conversion modes. These modes are not equally suited for IT support. Socialization is the process of converting new tacit knowledge to tacit knowledge. This takes place in the human brain. Externalization is the process of converting tacit knowledge to explicit knowledge. The successful conversion of tacit knowledge into explicit knowledge depends on the sequential use of metaphors, analogy, and model. Combination is the process of converting explicit knowledge into more complex and systematic sets of explicit knowledge. Explicit knowledge is collected from inside and outside the organization and then combined, edited, and processed to form new knowledge. The new explicit knowledge is then disseminated among the members of the organization. According to Nonaka et al. (2000), creative use of computerized communication networks and large-

scale databases can facilitate this mode of knowledge conversion. When the financial controller collects information from all parts of the organization and puts it together to show the financial health of the organization, that report is new knowledge in the sense that it synthesizes explicit knowledge from many different sources in one context. Finally, internalization in the SECI process converts explicit knowledge into tacit knowledge. Through internalization, explicit knowledge created is shared throughout an organization and converted into tacit knowledge by individuals.

5. **Explicit transfer of common knowledge:** If management decides to focus on common knowledge as defined by Dixon (2000), knowledge management should focus on the sharing of common knowledge. Common knowledge is shared in the organization using five mechanisms: serial transfer, explicit transfer, tacit transfer, strategic transfer, and expert transfer. Management has to emphasize all five mechanisms for successful sharing and creation of common knowledge. For serial transfer, management has to stimulate meetings and contacts between group members. For explicit transfer, management has to stimulate documentation of work by the previous group. For tacit transfer, management has to stimulate contacts between the two groups. For strategic transfer, management has to identify strategic knowledge and knowledge gaps. For expert transfer, management has to create networks where experts can transfer their knowledge. These five mechanisms are not equally suited for IT support. Explicit transfer seems very well suited for IT support as the knowledge from the other group is transferred explicitly as explicit knowledge in words and numbers and shared in the form of data, scientific formulae, specifications, manuals, and the like. Expert transfer also seems suited for IT support when generic knowledge is transferred from one individual to another person to enable the person to solve new problems with new methods.

6. **Link knowledge to its uses:** One of the mistakes in knowledge management presented by Fahey and Prusak (1998) was disentangling knowledge from its uses. A major manifestation of this error is that knowledge management initiatives become ends in themselves. For example, data warehousing can easily degenerate into technological challenges. The relevance of a data warehouse for decisions and actions gets lost in the turmoil spawned by debates about appropriate data structures.

7. **Treat knowledge as an intellectual asset in the economic school:** If management decides to follow the economic school of knowledge management, then intellectual capital accounting should be part of the knowledge management system. The knowledge management system should support knowledge markets where knowledge buyers, knowledge sellers, and knowledge brokers can use the system.

8. **Treat knowledge as a mutual resource in the organizational school:** The potential contribution of IT is linked to the combination of intranets and groupware to connect members and pool their knowledge, both explicit and tacit.

9. **Treat knowledge as a strategy in the strategy school:** The potential contribution of IT is manifold once knowledge as a strategy is the impetus behind knowledge management initiatives. One can expect quite an eclectic mix of networks, systems, tools, and knowledge repositories.

10. **Value configuration determines knowledge needs in primary activities:** Knowledge needs can be structured according to primary and secondary activities in the value configuration. Depending on the firm being a value chain, a value shop, or a value network, the knowledge management system must support more efficient production in the value chain, adding value to the knowledge work in the value shop, and more value by use of IT infrastructure in the value network.

11. **Incentive alignment:** The first dimension of information systems design is concerned with software engineering (error-free software, documentation, portability, modularity & architecture, development cost, maintenance cost, speed, and robustness). The second dimension is concerned with technology acceptance (user friendliness, user acceptance, perceived ease-of-use, perceived usefulness, cognitive fit, and task-technology fit). The third dimension that is particularly important to knowledge management systems is concerned with incentive alignment. Incentive alignment includes incentives influencing user behavior and the user's interaction with the system, deterrence of use for personal gain, use consistent with organizational goals, and robustness against information misrepresentation (Ba, Stallaert, & Whinston, 2001).

Expert Systems

Expert systems can be seen as extreme knowledge management systems on a continuum representing the extent to which a system possesses reasoning capabilities. Expert systems are designed to be used by decision-makers who do not possess expertise in the problem domain. The human expert's representation of the task domain provides the template for expert system design. The knowledge base and heuristic rules, which are used to systematically search a problem space, reflect the decision processes of the expert. A viable expert system is expected to perform this search as effectively and efficiently as a human expert. An expert system incorporates the reasoning capabilities of a domain expert and applies them in arriving at a decision. The system user needs little domain-specific knowledge in order for a decision or judgment to be made. The user's main decision is whether to accept the system's result (Dillard & Yuthas, 2001).

Decisions or judgments made by an expert system can be an intermediate component in a larger decision context. For example, an audit expert system may provide a judgment as to the adequacy of loan loss reserves that an auditor would use as input for making an audit opinion decision. The fact that the output supports or provides input for another decision does not make the system any less an expert system, according to Dillard and Yuthas (2001). The distinguishing feature of an expert system lies in its ability to arrive at a non-algorithmic solution using processes consistent with those of a domain expert.

Curtis and Cobham (2002) define an expert system as a computerized system that performs the role of an expert or carries out a task that requires expertise. In order to understand what an expert system is, it is worth paying attention to the role of an expert and the nature of expertise. It is then important to ascertain what types of expert and expertise there are in business and what benefits will accrue to an organization when it develops an expert system.

For example, a doctor having a knowledge of diseases arrives at a diagnosis of an illness by reasoning from information given by the patient's symptoms and then prescribes medication on the basis of known characteristics of available drugs together with the patient's history. The lawyer advises the client on the likely outcome of litigation based on the facts of the particular case, an expert understanding of the law, and knowledge of the way the courts work and interpret this law in practice. The accountant looks at various characteristics of a company's performance and makes a judgment as to the likely state of health of that company.

All of these tasks involve some of the features for which computers traditionally have been noted – performing text and numeric processing quickly and efficiently — but they also involve one more ability: reasoning. Reasoning is the movement from details of a particular case and knowledge of the general subject area surrounding that case to the derivation of conclusions. Expert systems incorporate this reasoning by applying general rules in an information base to aspects of a particular case under consideration (Curtis & Cobham, 2002).

Expert systems are computer systems designed to make expert-level decisions within complex domains. The business applications of this advanced information technology has been varied and broad reaching, directed toward making operational, management, and strategic decisions.

Audit expert systems are such systems applied in the auditing environment within the public accounting domain. Major public accounting firms have been quite active in developing such systems, and some argue that these tools and technologies will be increasingly important for survival as the firms strive to enhance their competitive position and to reduce their legal and business risk.

Dillard and Yuthas (2001) find that the implementation and use of these powerful systems raise a variety of significant ethical questions. As public accounting firms continue to devote substantial resources to the development of audit expert systems, dealing with the ethical risks and potential consequences to stakeholders takes on increasing significance. For example, when responsible behavior of an auditor is transferred to an audit expert system, then the system is incapable of being held accountable for the consequences of decisions. Rather, the developers of the system, the operators of the system, and the auditors of the system (who certified it was accurate and stable to use) can all be held accountable for errors and omissions made by the software package. Attorneys will seek to obtain damages from all humans and organizations who believed the system was as good as, or better than, human judgment.

Expert systems can be used in all knowledge management processes described earlier. For knowledge retrieval, content management and information extraction technology represent a useful group of techniques. An example of an expert system for knowledge retrieval is the CORPORUM system. There are three essential aspects of this system (Wang et al., 2001).

First, the system interprets text in the sense that it builds ontologies. Ontologies describe concepts and relationships between them. Ontologies can be seen as the building blocks of knowledge. The system captures ontologies that reflect world concepts as the user of the system sees and expresses them. The ontology produced constitutes a model of a person's interest or concern. Second, the interest model is applied as a knowledge base in order to determine contextual and thematic correspondence with documents available in the system. Finally, the interest model and the text interpretation process drive an information search and extraction process that characterizes hits in terms of both relevance and content. This new information can be stored in a database for future reference.

The CORPORUM software consists of a linguistic component, taking care of tasks such as lexical analysis and analysis at the syntactical level. At the semantic level, the software performs word sense disambiguation by describing the context in which a particular word is being used. This is naturally closely related to knowledge representation issues. The system is able to augment meaning structures with concepts that are invented from the text. The core of the system is also able to extract information most pertinent to a specific text for summary creation, extract the so-called core concept area from a text, and represent results according to ranking which is based on specified interest for a specific contextual theme set by the user. In addition, the system generates explanations, which will allow the user to make an informed guess about which documents to look at and which to ignore. The system can point to exactly those parts of targeted documents that are most pertinent to a specific user's interest (Wang et al., 2001).

Like all software, CORPORUM is continuously improved and revised. The content management support (CMS) was introduced in 2005 (www.cognit.no). It is based on technology that applies linguistics to characterize and index document content. The ontology-based approach focuses on semantics rather than shallow text patterns. The software can be applied for intelligent search and indexing, structure content in portals, annotate documents according to content, summarize and compress information, and extract names and relations from text.

Another software in 2005, CORPORUM Best Practice, enables organizations to structure their business and work processes and improve value creation. It is a software tool and associated methodology to build organization-wide Best Practice. In operation, the Web part of the system is a work portal. It embraces an ontology-based set of templates that helps to publish work-related documentation. Company resources like checklists, control plans, MS Word templates, images, and e-learning material that is relevant for any process or activity described can be linked in where it is useful and intuitive (www.cognit.no).

A final software to be mentioned is CORPORUM Intranet Search & Navigation (SLATEWeb), which is indexing and categorizing corporate information sources. Featuring language detection and find-related concept search, this tool lets companies find documents that would otherwise be hard to find. Categories are available to dynamically classify documents into a taxonomy or group structure (www.cognit. no).

Analysis and design necessary for building an expert system differ from a traditional data processing or information system. There are three major points of distinction that prevent expert systems development being subsumed under general frameworks of systems development (Curtis & Cobham, 2002):

1. **The subject matter is knowledge and reasoning as contrasted with data and processing:** Knowledge has both form and content, which need investigation. Form is connected with the mode of representation chosen — for instance, rules, semantic networks, or logic. Content needs careful attention as once the form is selected it is still a difficult task to translate the knowledge into the chosen representation form.

2. **Expert systems are expert/expertise-orientated whereas information systems are decision/function/organization directed:** The expert system encapsulates the abilities of an expert or expertise and the aim is to provide a computerized replica of these facilities.

3. **Obtaining information for expert systems design presents different problems from those in traditional information systems design:** Many expert systems rely, partly at least, on incorporating expertise obtained from an expert. Few rely solely on the representation of textbook or rulebook knowledge. It

is difficult generally to elicit this knowledge from an expert. In contrast, in designing an information system, the analyst relies heavily on existing documentation as a guide to the amount, type, and content of formal information being passed around the system. In the development of an expert system, the experts are regarded as repositories of knowledge.

Expert systems and traditional information systems have many significant differences. While processing in a traditional information system is primarily algorithmic, processing in an expert system includes symbolic conceptualizations. Input must be complete in a traditional system, while input can be incomplete in an expert system. Search approach in a traditional system is frequently based on algorithms, while search approach in an expert system is frequently based on heuristics. Explanations are usually not provided in a traditional system. Data and information is the focus of a traditional system, while knowledge is the focus of an expert system.

Expert systems can deliver the right information to the right person at the right time if it is known in advance what the right information is, who the right person to use or apply that information would be, and what would be the right time when that specific information would be needed. Detection of non-routine and unstructured change in business environment will, however, depend upon sense-making capabilities of knowledge workers for correcting the computational logic of the business and the data it processes (Malhotra, 2002).

The KMT Stage Model

Stages of knowledge management technology is a relative concept concerned with IT's ability to process information for knowledge work. IT at later stages is more useful to knowledge work than IT at earlier stages. The relative concept implies that IT is more directly involved in knowledge work at higher stages and that IT is able to support more advanced knowledge work at higher stages.

The knowledge management technology (KMT) stage model consists of four stages. The first stage is general IT support for knowledge workers. This includes word processing, spreadsheets, and e-mail. The second stage is information about knowledge sources. An information system stores information about who knows what within the firm and outside the firm. The system does not store what they actually know. A typical example is the company intranet. The third stage is information representing knowledge. The system stores what knowledge workers know in terms of information. A typical example is a database. The fourth and final stage is information processing. An information system uses information to evaluate situations. A typical example here is an expert system.

Figure 10.1. The knowledge management technology stage model

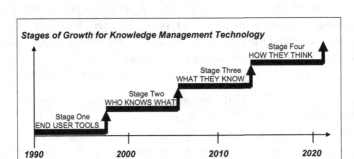

The contingent approach to firm performance implies that Stage 1 may be right for one firm, while Stage 4 may be right for another firm. Some firms will evolve over time from Stage 1 to higher stages as indicated in Figure 10.1. The time axis ranging from 1990 to 2020 in Figure 10.1 suggests that it takes time for an individual firm and a whole industry to move through all stages.

Stages of IT support in knowledge management are useful for identifying the current situation as well as planning for future applications in the firm. Each stage is described in the following (Gottschalk, 2005):

1.   **Tools for end users** are made available to knowledge workers. In the simplest stage, this means a capable networked PC on every desk or in every briefcase, with standardized personal productivity tools (word processing, presentation software) so that documents can be exchanged easily throughout a company. More complex and functional desktop infrastructures can also be the basis for the same types of knowledge support. Stage 1 is recognized by widespread dissemination and use of end-user tools among knowledge workers in the company. For example, in this stage, lawyers in a law firm will use word processing, spreadsheets, legal databases, presentation software, and scheduling programs.

     Stage 1 can be labeled **end-user-tools** or **people-to-technology** as information technology provides knowledge workers with tools that improve personal efficiency.

2.   **Information about who knows what** is made available to all people in the firm and to selected outside partners. Search engines should enable work with a thesaurus, since the terminology in which expertise is sought may not always match the terms the expert uses to classify that expertise.

According to Alavi and Leidner (2001), the creation of corporate directories, also referred to as the mapping of internal expertise, is a common application of knowledge management technology. Because much knowledge in an organization remains uncodified, mapping the internal expertise is a potentially useful application of technology to enable easy identification of knowledgeable persons.

Here we find the cartographic school of knowledge management (Earl, 2001), which is concerned with mapping organizational knowledge. It aims to record and disclose who in the organization knows what by building knowledge directories. Often called yellow pages, the principal idea is to make sure knowledgeable people in the organization are accessible to others for advice, consultation, or knowledge exchange. Knowledge-oriented directories are not so much repositories of knowledge-based information as gateways to knowledge, and the knowledge is as likely to be tacit as explicit.

Information about who knows what is sometimes called metadata, representing knowledge about where the knowledge resides. Providing taxonomies or organizational knowledge maps enables individuals to rapidly locate the individual who has the needed knowledge, more rapidly than would be possible without such IT-based support.

One starting approach in Stage 2 is to store curriculum vitae (CV) for each knowledge worker in the firm. Areas of expertise, projects completed, and clients helped may over time expand the CV. For example, a lawyer in a law firm works on cases for clients using different information sources that can be registered on yellow pages in terms of an intranet.

At Stage 2, firms apply the personalization strategy in knowledge management. According to Hansen et al. (1999), the personalization strategy implies that knowledge is tied to the person who developed it and is shared mainly through direct person-to-person contact. This strategy focuses on dialogue between individuals: Knowledge is transferred mainly in personal e-mail, meetings, and one-on-one conversations.

The creation of a knowledge network is an important part of Stage 2. Unless specialists can communicate easily with each other across platform types, expertise will deteriorate. People have to be brought together both virtually and face-to-face to exchange and build their collective knowledge in each of the specialty areas. The knowledge management effort is focused on bringing the experts together so that important knowledge can be shared and amplified, rather than on mapping expertise or benchmarking which occurs in Stage 3.

Electronic networks of practice are computer-mediated discussion forums focused on problems of practice that enable individuals to exchange advice and ideas with others based on common interests. Electronic networks have been found to support organizational knowledge flows between geographically dispersed coworkers and distributed research and development efforts. These networks also assist cooperative open-source software development and open congregation on the Internet for individuals interested in a specific practice. Electronic networks make it possible to share information quickly, globally, and with large numbers of individuals (Wasko & Faraj, 2005).

The knowledge network is built on modern communication technology. Advances in portable computers such as palmtops and laptops, in conjunction with wireless network technologies, has engendered mobile computing. In the mobile computing environment, users carrying portable computers are permitted to access the shared computing resources on the network through wireless channel regardless of their physical locations.

According to Earl (2001), knowledge directories represent more of a belief in personalized knowledge of individuals than the codified knowledge of knowledge bases and may demonstrate organizational preferences for human, not technology-mediated, communication and exchange. The knowledge philosophy of firms that settle in Stage 2 can be seen as one of people connectivity. Consequently, the principal contribution from IT is to connect people via intranets and to help them locate knowledge sources and providers using directories accessed by the intranet. Extranets and the Internet may connect knowledge workers to external knowledge sources and providers.

Communication competence is important at Stage 2. Communication competence is the ability to demonstrate skills in the appropriate communication behavior to effectively achieve one's goals. Communication between individuals requires both the decoding and encoding of messages (Ko et al., 2005). Lin et al. (2005) found that knowledge transfer depends on the completeness or incompleteness of the sender's and the receiver's information sets.

The dramatic reduction in electronic communication costs and ease of computer-to-computer linkages has resulted in opportunities to create new channel structures, fueling interest in inter-organizational systems. Inter-organizational systems are planned and managed ventures to develop and use IT-based information exchange systems to support collaboration and strategic alliances between otherwise independent actors. These systems allow for the exchange of information between partners for the purpose of coordination, communication, and cooperation (Malhotra et al., 2005).

Stage 2 can be labeled who-knows-what or people-to-people as knowledge workers use information technology to find other knowledge workers.

3. **Information from knowledge workers** is stored and made available to everyone in the firm and to designated external partners. Data-mining techniques can be applied here to find relevant information and combine information in data warehouses. On a broader basis, search engines are Web browsers and server software that operate with a thesaurus, since the terminology in which

expertise is sought may not always match the terms used by the expert to classify that expertise.

One starting approach in Stage 3 is to store project reports, notes, recommendations, and letters from each knowledge worker in the firm. Over time, this material will grow fast, making it necessary for a librarian or a chief knowledge officer (CKO) to organize it. In a law firm, all client cases will be classified and stored in databases using software such as Lotus Notes.

An essential contribution that IT can make is the provision of shared databases across tasks, levels, entities, and geographies to all knowledge workers throughout a process (Earl, 2001). For example, Infosys Technologies — a $1 billion company with over 23,000 employees and globally distributed operations — created a central knowledge portal called KShop. The content of KShop was organized into different content types, for instance, case studies, reusable artifacts, and downloadable software. Every knowledge asset under a content type was associated with one or more nodes (representing areas of discourse) in a knowledge hierarchy or taxonomy (Garud & Kumaraswamy, 2005).

According to Alavi and Leidner (2001), one survey found that 74% of respondents believed that their organization's best knowledge was inaccessible and 68% thought that mistakes were reproduced several times. Such a perception of failure to apply existing knowledge is an incentive for mapping, codifying, and storing information derived from internal expertise.

However, sifting though the myriad of content available through knowledge management systems can be challenging, and knowledge workers may be overwhelmed when trying to find the content most relevant for completing a new task. To address this problem, system designers often include rating schemes and credibility indicators to improve users' search and evaluation of knowledge management system content (Poston & Speier, 2005).

According to Alavi and Leidner (2001), one of the most common applications is internal benchmarking with the aim of transferring internal best practices. To be successful, best practices have to be coded, stored, and shared among knowledge workers.

In addition to (1) best practices knowledge within a quality or business process management function, other common applications include (2) knowledge for sales purposes involving products, markets, and customers, (3) lessons learned in projects or product development efforts, (4) knowledge around implementation of information systems, (5) competitive intelligence for strategy and planning functions, and (6) learning histories or records of experience with a new corporate direction or approach (Grover & Davenport, 2001).

In Stage 3, access both to knowledge (expertise, experience, and learning) and to information (intelligence, feedback, and data analyses) is provided by systems and intranets to operatives, staff, and executives. The supply and distribution of knowledge and information are not restricted. Whereas we might say in Stage 1, "give knowledge workers the tools to do the job," we now add, "give knowledge workers the knowledge and information to do the job." According to Earl (2001), this is another way of saying that the philosophy is enhancing the firm's capabilities with knowledge flows.

Although most knowledge repositories serve a single function, Grover and Davenport (2001) found that it is increasingly common for companies to construct an internal portal so that employees can access multiple different repositories and sources from one screen. It is also possible and increasingly popular for repositories to contain information as well as pointers to experts within the organization on key knowledge topics. Often called knowledge yellow pages, these systems facilitate contact and knowledge transfer between knowledgeable people and those who seek their knowledge. Stored, codified knowledge is combined with lists of individuals who contributed the knowledge and could provide more detail or background on it.

An enterprise information portal is viewed as a knowledge community. Enterprise information portals are of multiple forms, ranging from Internet-based data management tools that bring visibility to previously dormant data so that their users can compare, analyze, and share enterprise information to a knowledge portal, which enables its users to obtain specialized knowledge that is related to their specific tasks (Ryu et al., 2005).

Individuals' knowledge does not transform easily into organizational knowledge even with the implementation of knowledge repositories. According to Bock et al. (2005), individuals tend to hoard knowledge for various reasons. Some empirical studies have shown that the greater the anticipated reciprocal relationships are, the more favorable the attitude toward knowledge sharing will be. Other studies have shown that individuals who believed they will be terminated once their personal knowledge has been extracted from them and embedded in software will refuse to cooperate in sharing their knowledge. Understanding this rational is often critical to developing and loading a knowledge management system.

Electronic knowledge repositories are electronic stores of content acquired about all subjects for which the organization has decided to maintain knowledge. Such repositories can comprise multiple knowledge bases as well as the mechanisms for acquisition, control, and publication of the knowledge. The process of knowledge sharing through electronic knowledge repositories involves people contributing knowledge to populate repositories (e.g., customer and supplier knowledge, industry best practices, and product expertise) and people seeking knowledge from repositories for use (Kankanhalli et al., 2005).

In Stage 3, firms apply the codification strategy in knowledge management. According to Hansen et al. (1999), the codification strategy centers on information technology: Knowledge is carefully codified and stored in knowledge databases and can be accessed and used by anyone. With a codification strategy, knowledge is extracted from the person who developed it, is made independent from the person, and stored in form of interview guides, work schedules, benchmark data, and so forth; then, searched, retrieved, and used by many employees.

According to Grover and Davenport (2001), firms increasingly view attempts to transform raw data into usable knowledge as part of their knowledge management initiatives. These approaches typically involve isolating data in a separate warehouse for easier access and the use of statistical analysis or data-mining and visualization tools. Since their goal is to create data-derived knowledge, they are increasingly addressed as part of knowledge management in Stage 3.

Stage 3 can be labeled *what-they-know* or *people-to-docs* as information technology provides knowledge workers with access to information that is typically stored in documents. Examples of documents are contracts and agreements, reports, manuals and handbooks, business forms, letters, memos, articles, drawings, blueprints, photographs, e-mail and voicemail messages, video clips, script and visuals from presentations, policy statements, computer printouts, and transcripts from meetings.

Sprague (1995) argues that concepts and ideas contained in documents are far more valuable and important to organizations than facts traditionally organized into data records. A document can be described as a unit of recorded information structured for human consumption. It is recorded and stored, so a speech or conversation for which no transcript is prepared is not a document. A document is a snapshot of some set of information that can incorporate many complex information types, exist in multiple places across a network, depend on other documents for information, change as subordinate documents are updated, and be accessed and modified by many people simultaneously.

4. **Information systems solving knowledge problems** are made available to knowledge workers and solution seekers. Artificial intelligence is applied in these systems. For example, neural networks are statistically oriented tools that excel at using data to classify cases into one category or another. Another example is expert systems that can enable the knowledge of one or a few experts to be used by a much broader group of workers requiring the knowledge.

According to Alavi and Leidner (2001), an insurance company was faced with the commoditization of its market and declining profits. The company found that applying the best decision-making expertise via a new underwriting process, supported by a knowledge management system based on best practices, enabled it to move into profitable niche markets and, hence, to increase income.

According to Grover and Davenport (2001), artificial intelligence is applied in rule-based systems, and, more commonly, case-based systems are used to capture and provide access to resolutions of customer service problems, legal knowledge, new product development knowledge, and many other types of knowledge.

Biodiversity is a data-intense science, drawing as it does on data from a large number of disciplines in order to build up a coherent picture of the extent and trajectory of life on earth. Bowker (2000) argues that as sets of heterogeneous databases are made to converge, there is a layering of values into the emergent infrastructure. This layering process is relatively irreversible, and it operates simultaneously at a very concrete level (fields in a database) and at a very abstract one (the coding of the relationship between the disciplines and the production of a general ontology).

Knowledge is explicated and formalized during the knowledge codification phase that took place in Stage 3. Codification of tacit knowledge is facilitated by mechanisms that formalize and embed it in documents, software, and systems. However, the higher the tacit elements of the knowledge, the more difficult it is to codify. Codification of complex knowledge frequently relies on information technology. Expert systems, decision support systems, document management systems, search engines, and relational database tools represent some of the technological solutions developed to support this phase of knowledge management. Consequently, advanced codification of knowledge emerges in Stage 4, rather than in Stage 3, because expert systems and other artificial intelligence systems have to be applied to be successful.

Stage 4 can be labeled how-they-think or people-to-systems where the system is intended to help solve a knowledge problem.

Stage 1 is a technology-centric stage, while Stage 2 is a people-oriented stage. Stage 3 is a technology-driven stage, while Stage 4 is a process-centric stage. A people-oriented perspective draws from the work of Nonaka et al. (2000). Essential to this perspective of knowledge sharing and knowledge creation is that people create knowledge and that new knowledge or the increasing of the extant knowledge base occurs as a result of human cognitive activities and the effecting of specific knowledge transformations (Wasko & Faraj, 2005). A technology-driven perspective to knowledge management at Stage 3 is often centered on the computerized technique of data mining and the many mathematical and statistical methods available to transform data into information and then meaningful knowledge (e.g., Poston & Speier, 2005). A process-centric approach tries to combine the essentials of both the people-centric and the technology-centric and technology-driven perspectives in the earlier stages. It emphasizes the dynamic and ongoing nature of the process, where artificial intelligence might help people understand how to proceed in their tasks. Process-centered knowledge generation is concerned with extraction of critical and germane knowledge in a decision-making perspective (Bendoly, 2003).

KMT Model for the Police CIO

Knowledge management as a field of study is concerned with simplifying and improving the process of sharing, distributing, creating, capturing, and understanding knowledge. Hence, knowledge management has direct relevance to policing, So much so that Europol has a Knowledge Management Centre (KMC) at The Hague in the Netherlands. Europol regularly updates its databases at KMC to ensure it keeps abreast of new developments in technology, science, or other specialized fields in order to provide optimal law enforcement. As any other CIO in knowledge-intensive organizations, the CIO in law enforcement must work actively and aggressively to implement knowledge management technology.

Figure 10.2 Officer-to-technology systems at Stage 1 of the knowledge management technology stage model

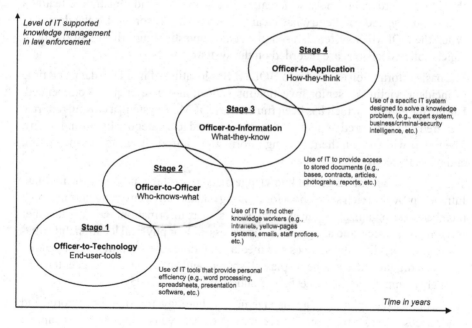

It is argued that knowledge is the most important resource in police investigations, and several police researchers make the case that successful investigation depends on knowledge availability (e.g., Chen et al., 2002). Furthermore, Chen et al. (2002) also point out that knowledge management in the knowledge-intensive and time-critical work of police investigations presents a real challenge to investigation managers.

Part of the reason for this challenge that knowledge management presents to police investigations has to do with the level of IT support required in organizations as knowledge management becomes more sophisticated. In this regard, Figure 10.2 depicts the KMT stage model that conceptualizes on a continuum the stages involved in the growth of knowledge management systems and their relationship to the level of information technology support required.

The transformation that has occurred in report writing and recordkeeping is related to the new changes in computer technology. Every police activity or crime incident demands a report on some kind of form. The majority of police patrol reports written before 1975 were handwritten.

Today, officers can write reports on small notebook computers located in the front seat of the patrol unit; discs are handed in at the end of the shift for hard copy needs. Cursor keys and spell-check functions in these report programs are useful timesaving features (Thibault, 1998).

An example of an officer-to-technology system is the Major Incident Policy Document in the UK (Home Office, 2005). This document is maintained whenever a Major Incident Room using HOLMES system is in operation. Decisions, which should be recorded, are those which affect the practical or administrative features of the enquiry, and each entry has clearly to show the reasoning for the decision. When the HOLMES system is used, the senior investigating officer (SIO) directs which policy decisions are recorded on the system.

The basic information entered into HOLMES is location of incident, data, and time of incident, victim(s), senior investigating officer, and date enquiry commenced. During the enquiry, which has been run on the HOLMES system, a closing report is prepared and registered as another document linked to a category of closing report. The report will contain the following information: introduction, scene, the victim, and miscellaneous.

The typical system at Stage 2 of knowledge management technology is the intranet. Intranets provide a rich set of tools for creating collaborative environments in which members of an organization can exchange ideas, share information, and work together on common projects and assignments regardless of their physical location. Information from many different sources and media, including text, graphics, video, audio, and even digital slides can be displayed, shared, and accessed across an enterprise through a simple common interface (Laudon & Laudon, 2005).

At the third stage of knowledge management technology, information is stored and made accessible as a resource. The resource perspective is important. An example of police work using stored information at Stage 3 is eyewitness reports stored in databases.

Strategy has traditionally focused on products and services to gain competitive advantage. Recent work in the area of strategic management and economic theory has begun to focus on the internal side of the equation — the organization's resources and capabilities. This new perspective is referred to as the resource-based theory of the firm as described earlier in this book.

The resource-based theory has been adopted in police organizations because of rising costs, limited resources, and growing service demands. Murphy (2004) documents the police adoption of neo-liberal business models and values in order to facilitate rationalization of police governance, organization, management, and services. His analysis concludes that limited, rationalized, and modern police services require a new strategic formulation of the police role to address public interest and the rapidly expanding policing and security demands of late-modern Canadian society. He argues that without institutional capacity for generation, accumulation, communication, and implementation of knowledge resources, a skeptical and challenging market-society may well be unsympathetic to the expensive and expansive needs of public policing.

Widespread use of computers and networks in both business and personal life has created new forms of documentary evidence used in courts of law. Much of the evidence today for stock frauds, embezzlements, theft of company trade secrets, computer crimes, and many civil cases is in digital form. In the past, documentary evidence used to prove crimes was on paper. In addition to information from printed or typewritten pages, legal cases today will increasingly rely on evidence represented as computer data stored on computer disks as well as e-mail, instant messages, and e-commerce over the Internet.

A new field called computer forensics has sprung up to deal specifically with computer-based evidence. Computer-forensics is the scientific collection, examination, authentication, preservation, and analysis of data held on or retrieved from computer storage media in such a way that the information can be used as evidence in a court of law. It deals with the following problems (Laudon & Laudon, 2005):

- Recovering data from computers while preserving evidential integrity
- Securely storing and handling recovered electronic data
- Finding significant information in a large volume of electronic data
- Presenting the information to a court of law

Computer evidence can reside on computer storage media in the form of computer files and as ambient data, which are not visible to the average user. Data that a computer user may have deleted on computer storage media may be recoverable through various techniques. Computer forensics experts try to recover such "hidden" data for presentation as evidence.

At Stage 3 of the knowledge management technology model we find both structured and semi-structured systems. A structured system has the content of explicit, codified knowledge that exists in formal documents. Here, we find online corporate libraries based on organization documents. Semi-structured information is all the digital information in an organization that does not exist in a formal document or a formal report that was written by a designated author. It has been estimated that at least 80% of an organization's work content is unstructured — information in folders, messages, memos, proposals, e-mails, graphics, electronic slide presentations, and even videos created in different formats and stored in many locations.

Two examples of knowledge management systems at Stage 3 in law enforcement are COPLINK and geo-demographics. COPLINK has a relational database system for crime-specific cases such as gang-related incidents, and serious crimes such as homicide, aggravated assault, and sexual crimes. Deliberately targeting these criminal areas allows a manageable amount of information to be entered into a database (Chen et al., 2002). Geo-demographic profiles of the characteristics of individuals and small areas are central to efficient and effective deployment of law enforcement resources. Geo-computation is based on geographical information systems (Ashby & Longley, 2005).

Information systems solving knowledge problems are made available to knowledge workers and knowledge seekers at Stage 4. Artificial intelligence is applied in these systems. Expert systems, decision support systems, document management systems, intelligent search engines, and relational database tools represent some of the technologies and techniques developed to support Stage 4.

Officer-to-application systems will only be successful if they are built on a thorough understanding of law enforcement. Therefore, Gottschalk (2007) concentrated on presenting two important knowledge application tasks in police investigations: profiling and cross+check. Offender profiling and cross+check in police investigations are examples of law enforcement work that can benefit from technologies such as artificial intelligence, knowledge-based systems, and case-based reasoning systems (Becerra-Fernandez et al., 2004).

Artificial intelligence (AI) is an area of computer science that endeavors to build machines exhibiting human-like cognitive capabilities. Most modern AI systems are founded on the realization that intelligence is tightly intertwined with knowledge. Knowledge is associated with the symbols we manipulate.

Knowledge-based systems deal with solving problems by exercising knowledge. The most important parts of these systems are the knowledge base and the inference engine. The former holds the domain-specific knowledge whereas the latter contains the functions to exercise the knowledge in the knowledge base. Knowledge can be represented as either rules or frames. Rules are a natural choice for representing conditional knowledge, which is in the form of if-when statements. Inference engines supply the motive power to the knowledge. There are several ways to exercise knowledge, depending on the nature of the knowledge. For example, backward-chaining systems work backward from the conclusions to the inputs. These systems attempt to validate the conclusions by finding evidence to support them. In law enforcement, this is an important system feature, as evidence determines whether a person is charged or not for a crime.

Case-based reasoning systems are a different way to represent knowledge through explicit historical cases. This approach differs from the rule-based approach because the knowledge is not complied and interpreted by an expert. Instead, the experiences that possibly shaped the expert's knowledge are directly used to make decisions. Learning is an important issue in case-based reasoning, because with the mere addition of new cases to the library, the system learns. In law enforcement, police officers are looking for similar cases to learn how they were handled in the past, making case-based reasoning systems an attractive application in policing.

Use of expert systems in law enforcement includes systems that attempt to aid in information retrieval by drawing upon human heuristics or rules and procedures to investigate tasks. The AICAMS project is a knowledge-based system for identifying suspects. AICAMS also includes a component to fulfill the needs for a simple but effective facial identification procedure based on a library of facial components. The system provides a capability for assembling an infinite number of possible facial composites by varying the position and size of the components. AICAMS also provides a geo-mapping component by incorporating a map-based user interface (Chen et al., 2002).

References

Alavi, M., & Leidner, D. E. (2001). Knowledge management and knowledge management systems: Conceptual foundations and research issues. *MIS Quarterly*, *25*(1), 107-136.

Antoncic, B., & Hisrich, R. D. (2001). Intrapreneurship: Construct refinement and cross-cultural validation. *Journal of Business Venturing, 16*, 495-527.

Applehans, W., Globe, A., & Laugero, G. (1999). *Managing knowledge: A practical Web-based approach*. USA: Addison-Wesley.

Ba, S., Stallaert, J., & Whinston, A. B. (2001). Research commentary: Introducing a third dimension in information systems design — the case of incentive alignment. *Information Systems Research, 12*(3), 225-239.

Becerra-Fernandez, I., Gonzalez, A., & Sabherwal, R. (2004). *Knowledge management: Challenges, solutions, and technologies.* Upper Saddle River, NJ: Prentice Hall.

Bendoly, E. (2003). Theory and support for process frameworks of knowledge discovery and data mining from ERP systems. *Information & Management, 40,* 639-647.

Bock, G. W., Zmud, R. W., & Kim, Y. G. (2005). Behavioral intention formation in knowledge sharing: Examining the roles of extrinsic motivators, social-psychological forces, and organizational climate. *MIS Quarterly, 29*(1), 87-111.

Bowker, G. C. (2000). Biodiversity datadiversity. *Social Studies of Science, 30*(5), 643-683.

Chen, H., Schroeder, J., Hauck, R. V., Ridgeway, L., Atabakhsh, H., Gupta, H., Boarman, C., Rasmussen, K., & Clements, A. W. (2002). COPLINK connect: Information and knowledge management for law enforcement. *Decision Support Systems, 34,* 271-285.

Curtis, G., & Cobham, D. (2002). *Business information systems: Analysis, design and practice.* Prentice Hall.

Davenport, T. H., & Prusak, L. (2000). *Working knowledge.* Boston: Harvard Business School Press.

Dillard, J. F., & Yuthas, K. (2001). Responsibility ethic for audit expert systems. *Journal of Business Ethics, 30,* 337-359.

Dixon, N. M. (2000). *Common knowledge.* Boston: Harvard Business School Press.

Earl, M. J. (2001). Knowledge management strategies: Toward a taxonomy. *Journal of Management Information Systems, 18*(1), 215-233.

Earl, M. J., & Scott, I. A. (1999, Winter). What is a chief knowledge officer? *Sloan Management Review,* 29-38.

Fahey, L., & Prusak, L. (1998). The eleven deadliest sins of knowledge management. *California Management Review, 40*(3), 265-276.

Foote, N. W., Matson, E., & Rudd, N. (2001). Managing the knowledge manager. *The McKinsey Quarterly, 3.* Retrieved from www.mckinseyquarterly.com

Garud, R., & Kumaraswamy, A. (2005). Vicious and virtuous circles in the management of knowledge: The case of Infosys Technologies. *MIS Quarterly, 29*(1), 9-33.

Gottschalk, P. (2005). *Strategic knowledge management technology.* Hershey, PA: Idea Group Publishing.

Gottschalk, P. (2007). *Knowledge management systems in law enforcement: Technologies and techniques.* Hershey, PA: Idea Group Publishing.

Grover, V., & Davenport, T. H. (2001). General perspectives on knowledge management: Fostering a research agenda. *Journal of Management Information Systems, 18*(1), 5-21.

Halvorsen, K., & Nguyen, M. (1999, June 17-19). A successful software knowledge base. *Proceedings of the Eleventh International Conference on Software Engineering and Knowledge Engineering.* Germany: Kaiserslautern.

Hansen, M. T., Nohria, N., & Tierny, T. (1999, March-April). What's your strategy for managing knowledge? *Harvard Business Review,* 106-116.

Hansen, M. T., & Oetinger, B. (2001, March). Introducing t-shaped managers, knowledge management's next generation. *Harvard Business Review,* 107-116.

Hauck, R. V., & Chen H. (2005). *COPLINK: A case of intelligent analysis and knowledge management.* Draft conference paper, University of Arizona.

Home Office. (2005). *Guidance on statutory performance indicators for policing 205/2006,* Police Standards Unit, Home Office of the UK Government. Retrieved from www.policereform.gov.uk

Housel, T., & Bell, A. H. (2001). *Measuring and managing knowledge.* New York: McGraw-Hill Irwin.

Kankanhalli, A., Tan, B. C. Y., & Wei, K. K. (2005). Contributing knowledge to electronic knowledge repositories: An empirical investigation. *MIS Quarterly, 29*(1), 113-143.

Ko, D. G., Kirsch, L. J., & King, W. R. (2005). Antecedents of knowledge transfer from consultants to clients in enterprise system implementations. *MIS Quarterly, 29*(1), 59-85.

Laudon, K. C., & Laudon, J. P. (2005). *Essentials of management information systems — managing the digital firm* (6th ed.). Upper Saddle River, NJ: Pearson Education.

Lin, L., Geng, X., & Whinston, A. B. (2005). A sender-receiver framework for knowledge transfer. *MIS Quarterly, 29*(2), 197-219.

Malhotra, A. (2002). Why knowledge management systems fail? Enablers and constraints of knowledge management in human enterprises. In C. W. Holsapple (Ed.), *Handbook of knowledge management I: Knowledge Matters* (pp. 577-599). Heidelberg, Germany: Springer Verlag.

Malhotra, A., Gosain, S., & El Sawy, O. A. (2005). Absorptive capacity configurations in supply chains: Gearing for partner-enabled market knowledge creation. *MIS Quarterly, 29*(1), 145-187.

Moffett, S., & McAdam, R. (2003). Contributing and enabling technologies for knowledge management. *International Journal of Information Technology and Management, 2*(1/2), 31-49.

Murphy, C. (2004). The rationalization of Canadian public policing: A study of the impact and implications of resource limits and market strategies. *The Canadian Review of Policing Research*, ISSN: 1710-6915.

Nahapiet, J., & Ghoshal, S. (1998). Social capital, intellectual capital, and the organizational advantage. *Academy of Management Review, 23*(2), 242-266.

Nonaka, I., Toyama, R., & Konno, N. (2000). SECI, Ba and leadership: A unified model of dynamic knowledge creation. *Long Range Planning, 33*(1), 5-34.

Poston, R. S., & Speier, C. (2005). Effective use of knowledge management systems: A process model of content ratings and credibility indicators. *MIS Quarterly, 29*(2), 221-244.

Ryu, C., Kim, Y. J., Chaudhury, A., & Rao, H. R. (2005). Knowledge acquisition via three learning processes in enterprise information portals: Learning-by-investment, learning-by-doing, and learning-from-others. *MIS Quarterly, 29*(2), 245-278.

Sambamurthy, V., & Subramani, M. (2005). Special issue on information technologies and knowledge management. *MIS Quarterly, 29*(1), 1-7; *29*(2), 193-195.

Sprague, R. H. (1995, March). Electronic document management: Challenges and opportunities for information systems managers. *MIS Quarterly*, 29-49.

Tanriverdi, H. (2005). Information technology relatedness, knowledge management capability, and performance of multibusiness firms. *MIS Quarterly, 29*(2), 311-334.

Thibault, E. A., Lynch, L. M., & McBride, R. B. (1998). *Proactive police management* (4th ed.). Upper Saddle River, NJ: Prentice Hall.

Van de Ven, A. H. (2005). Running in packs to develop knowledge-intensive technologies. *MIS Quarterly, 29*(2), 365-378.

Wang, K., Hjelmervik, O. R., & Bremdal, B. (2001). *Introduction to knowledge management*. Trondheim, Norway: Tapir Academic Press.

Ward, J., & Peppard, J. (2002). *Strategic planning for information systems*. UK: Wiley.

Wasko, M. M., & Faraj, S. (2005). Why should I share? Examining social capital and knowledge contribution in electronic networks of practice. *MIS Quarterly, 29*(1), 35-57.

Chapter XI

Changing Role
of CIO to CEO

Introduction

Both the CIO and the CEO are practicing leadership. One of the defining characteristics of leadership is the ability to develop and implement appropriate responses
to a variety of problem situations. Leaders must solve an array of problems including resource allocation, interdepartmental coordination, interpersonal conflict, and
subordinate morale to name a few. In order to effectively solve such problems,
leaders must draw on a body of knowledge gained from formal education, advice
from other leaders, and personal experience (Hedlund et al., 2003).

Sternberg (2003) presented a model of leadership in organizations. According to
this model, the three key components of leadership are wisdom, intelligence, and
creativity. The basic idea is that one needs these three components working together
(synthesized) in order to be a highly effective leader.

Sternberg (2003) argues that one is not born a leader. Rather, wisdom, intelligence,
and creativity are, to some extent, forms of developing expertise. One interacts with
the environment in ways that utilize to varying degrees one's innate potentials. The
environment strongly influences the extent to which leaders are able to utilize and
develop whatever genetic potentials they have. Many people with substantial innate
potential fail to take much advantage of it; whereas others with lesser potential do
take advantage of it.

Practical intelligence is the ability to solve everyday problems by utilizing knowledge gained from experience in order to purposefully adapt to, shape, and select environments. Thus, it involves changing oneself to suit the environment (adaptation), changing the environment to suit oneself (shaping), or finding a new environment within which to work (selection). *Creativity* refers to skill in generating ideas and products that are relatively novel, high in quality, and appropriate to the task at hand. Creativity is important in leadership because it is the component whereby one generates the ideas that others will follow. *Wisdom* consists of reasoning ability, sagacity, learning from ideas and environment, judgment, expeditious use of information, and perspicacity (Sternberg, 2003).

Demand Side CEO Requirements

From the demand side, there is a need for a new CEO. The question we raise is whether or not the CIO is a candidate for the job. Promoting the CIO to the post of CEO represents an inside succession. It can either be a relay or non-relay succession. If the CIO is selected and crowned as an heir apparent, it is a relay succession. An incumbent CEO works with the CIO as an heir apparent and passes the baton of leadership to the heir (Zhang & Rajagopalan, 2004).

To become an heir apparent, the CIO must be identified as a high-potential candidate. As the candidate enters the development pipeline, managers must constantly align education and on-the-job experience with the emerging landscape. They also must rigorously assess the candidate's performance at each development stage (Charan, 2005).

There is a need for a new CEO, is the CIO a candidate? Zhang and Rajagopalan (2004) did shed some interesting light on this question in their studies of inside or outside successions.

If a headhunting firm is involved, the chances of external recruitment might increase, thereby reducing the chances for the internal CIO to be promoted.

If the performance of the firm is poor, the chances of external recruitment increase, thereby reducing the chances for the internal CIO to be promoted.

According to Charan (2005), it is important to be identified as one of those very rare people who might one day be CEO.

The demand side for a new CEO is dependent on firm performance, in general, and initiation of strategic changes in response to poor firm performance, in particular. In the case of poor firm performance, corporate boards might have to initiate strategic changes. Part of the change will often be the departure of the current CEO. However, pluralistic ignorance on corporate boards sometimes prevents CEO succession. Pluralistic ignorance is typically defined at the group level as the extent to which group members (plural) underestimate the degree to which others share their concerns (Westphal & Bednar, 2005).

In another study, Westphal and Khanna (2003) considered the social process by which the corporate elite may have resisted pressure from stakeholders to adopt changes in corporate governance that limit managerial autonomy. Such resistance can influence both the likelihood of CEO succession and the potential selection of a CEO successor. For example, directors who are positive to CEO succession can experience social distancing and can be deterred from participating subsequently in governance changes that threaten the interests of fellow top managers.

CEO succession can be solved by duality, where one executive holds two positions. For example, if the president is promoted to CEO, he or she may still remain in the president position. In this case, there is no real vacancy, hence there is no demand for a new president. Similarly, when a CEO is promoted to chair of the board, the person might remain in the CEO position, and there will be no demand for a new CEO (Davidson, Nemic, & Worrell, 2001).

Supply Side CIO Qualifications

Taking a supply-side perspective, Zhang and Rajagopalan (2003) drew upon three theoretical perspectives: the executive human capital, agency theory, and power perspectives. First, the executive human capital argument indicates that the requirements of the CEO job are substantially different from those of other organizational positions (such as the CIO position). This is a position with considerable responsibility for overall firm performance, and hence only a small group of executives with experience at the highest levels of a firm are likely to possess the relevant managerial skills and expertise to be considered serious candidates for this position. To improve his or her chances for promotion to CEO, the CIO must develop relevant executive human capital by involvement in tasks related to overall firm performance.

Examples of tasks CIOs should perform — or attempt to perform — to develop their executive capital and potential have been presented throughout this book. Tasks such as mobilizing strategic IT resources, applying IT resources to the value configuration, and participating in corporate strategic management are important general tasks. More specific tasks include developing e-business, sourcing IT services, supporting IT governance, and linking information management and knowledge management.

Second, the power perspective suggests that in order to qualify for consideration, an internal candidate needs an established power base, especially in relation to the incumbent CEO and the board of directors. Holding a formal job title like CIO may or may not evidence such a power base. To improve his or her chances for promotion to CEO, the CIO must develop a relevant and strong power base.

The CIO can perform different tasks to build a power base. Communication and interaction with top executives are often stressed as important tasks. However, the content of communication might be more important than the frequency of communication. When knowledge transfer is defined as change in the recipient's behavior, then the content of communication of the CIO with the incumbent CEO should be such that the CEO changes behavior.

Finally, from an agency theory perspective, a candidate is more likely to be considered seriously for the CEO position if the board of his or her firm has relevant information on the candidate's skills and competencies. Interactions with the board help to reduce the "adverse selection" problem that arises from information asymmetry between a board and a potential successor. One potential arena for such interactions is the presentation and discussion of IT strategy with the board.

The CIO should use relevant approaches to provide information to the board to ensure they know about the CIO's skills and competencies. One approach is self-nomination for project work. Another approach is IS/IT to reduce the workload of board members.

If the CIO is a qualified person, will he or she become the next CEO? In this book, we have seen some of the contingent answers to this question:

- Yes, if he or she can handle the power game as discussed in the first chapter
- Yes, if he or she has important decision rights concerning strategic resource allocations
- Yes, depending on the stage of growth in terms of IT maturity
- Yes, depending on the value configuration of the organization
- Yes, depending on reporting level 2, 3, or 4
- Yes, depending on the level of involvement in governance structures

In a survey by Earl (2000), some CIOs had experience being a CEO. The traditional responsibilities of the CIO job require technological competence plus the management know-how required to lead specialists and integrate the function with the rest of the business. Most CIOs in Earl's (2000) survey acquired these capabilities by having considerable experience in the IT function. The new responsibilities also involve business acumen and leadership skills. Those CIOs who had experience being a CEO of a business or head of a business unit considered that to be an excellent training ground for developing these capabilities. In particular, they said it helped them judge where IT should lead or lag in business thinking. CEO experience from a subsidiary or another organization is likely to be considered a strength when the CIO is a candidate for the CEO position in the current organization.

If the CIO has the chance of being a follower successor or contender successor, research by Shen and Cannella (2002a) is of interest. They studied effects of alternative successions on firm performance. They predicted a positive association between contender successor and post-succession firm performance. The statistical coefficient for contender succession was positive, but not significant. Thus, the hypothesis was not supported. However, the coefficient for outsider successor and post-succession operational performance was negative and significant. Based on this research, it seems that a CIO who would like to become the next CEO might choose the contender strategy if firm performance is bad, the departing CEO's position is weak, and the departing CEO's tenure is short.

Another study by Cannella and Shen (2003) is also of interest to CIOs aspiring for the CEO position. If the CIO is an heir apparent, two contrasting outcomes emerge — promotion to CEO or firm exit. Cannella and Shen (2003) propose that the distribution of power among an incumbent CEO, outside directors, and an heir apparent influences these outcomes. Results suggest that outside director and CEO powers are important influences on heir promotion and exit and that heirs who arise from within a firm are less likely to exit.

If the CIO is an heir apparent, his or her heir apparent power should be developed. As a competent and ambitious individual, the CIO is looking forward to run his or her own show as the CEO. Promotion to CEO is top priority for the CIO. As the second-in-command, an heir apparent also has his or her own sources of power, although the heir apparent is usually weaker in comparison to incumbent CEOs and outside directors. Further, some of the factors that are associated with CEO power are not correspondingly useful in gauging heir apparent power. For example, stock ownership, long a key measure of CEO power, is far less relevant for an heir apparent. Further, position tenure, certainly an important measure of CEO power, does not have a corresponding association with heir apparent power. An heir's tenure is designed to be relatively short. When it stretches longer than five or six years, the likelihood of the final promotion diminishes.

Canella and Shen's (2003) study examined two characteristics of heirs apparent — insider status and director status — as indicators of power. For example, an heir apparent who has many years of service at a firm may have already built his or her coalition and power base. Heir apparent power may have significant implications in a relay succession because, as research on executive turnover has shown, when firm performance is low, less powerful executives are more likely to be dismissed. Insider heirs and heirs who serve on their firms' boards may not only be able to reduce their risk of dismissal, but also may even use their power to challenge incumbents and promote their own ascensions to the CEO positions.

In addition, company tenure indicates the extent to which a person has invested time and effort in a firm, developing firm-specific knowledge and skills, and therefore the perception of a better chance of promotion. This perception makes heirs apparent with longer company tenures more reluctant to leave their employing firms for outside opportunities. Finally, heir apparent director status itself signals high commitment on the part of the incumbent CEO and outside directors to the heir. When a firm is highly committed to the heir apparent, it will grant more power (such as seat on the board) to that person. Therefore, it can be expected that an heir apparent who is promoted from within a firm and an heir who serves on its board of directors is more likely to be promoted to CEO and less likely to leave the firm, regardless of its performance (Cannella & Shen, 2003).

Changing Leadership Roles

Six out of 10 leadership roles defined by Mintzberg (1994) were explored for the CIO earlier in this book. Four leadership roles were not considered relevant for the CIO by Grover, Jeong, Kettinger, and Lee (1993). The six relevant roles were personnel leader, liaison, monitor, spokesman, entrepreneur, and resource allocator. The four irrelevant roles were figurehead, disseminator, disturbance handler, and negotiator. When the CIO moves from CIO to CEO, those four neglected leadership roles become important.

The CEO as *figurehead* performs duties of ceremonial nature. In this role, the CEO is a symbolic head of the organization. The figurehead role belongs to the interpersonal roles together with liaison and personnel leader.

The CEO as *disseminator* transmits information to other organizational members and to external stakeholders. The chief executive expects to be questioned on detailed issues by various groups: union leaders, the press, customers, politicians, and members of staff. The disseminator role belongs to the informational roles together with monitor and spokesman.

The CEO as *disturbance handler* and *negotiator* both belong to the decision roles together with entrepreneur and resource allocator. However, chief executives might be constrained in their decision-making ability as discussed in the first chapter. Chief executives have to negotiate with individuals. Mintzberg (1994) used "negotiation" to refer to sessions in which chief executives met outsiders in attempts to reach agreements between their two organizations.

Then Comes CIO Succession

If a CIO becomes the next CEO, then the organization needs a new CIO. Perhaps this book suggests an acid test for selecting the new CIO. Does he or she have the potential to become CEO? If we could develop and appoint such executives, not only will we have CIOs fit for today's challenges, we may be lining up future CEOs (Earl, 2000).

Ordonez (2005, p. 9) wrote about the art of being a CIO in his own role as CIO:

> *It takes a certain kind of individual to be a good CIO. You have to love the challenge of a rollercoaster industry. You have to learn constantly, not just about technology, but also about the world you operate in. And, you must learn from your peers. Our CEO is a good example of this, his dedication and passion for the job inspires me and keeps me on my toes.*

A Final Note

In the process of moving up the corporate ladder, there is so much more to consider than what has been covered in this book. Based on research literature, this book has focused on general insights that can make a difference. In addition, there are the "how" and the "who" nuts-and-bolts details that CIOs need to perform well in a competitive environment — competing against the CEO, the sales VP, and the manufacturing VP for consideration as CEO. How to behave in the public, in private, with the media, with investors, with peers, with the board, and with staff is just as important as who to talk with, listen to, share (or not share) information with, and try to impress.

This book never lists or describes these actions or activities, simply because successful actions and activities represent contingent variables that have been presented throughout this book. Similarly, this book does not provide actual examples or case studies of successful or unsuccessful executives. We know all too well that case studies of successful executives today (e.g., Michael Dell, Bill Gates, Jack Welch, Scott McNealy, Jeff Bezos, etc.) might turn out as case studies of unsuccessful executives tomorrow, leaving the door open for successors.

At this time, there are no recognized academic degrees for CIOs, according to Dearstyne (2006). However, post-appointment training courses and institutes are growing in numbers. Three of these demonstrate varying approaches: Gartner's CIO Academy, UNC Chapel Hill School of Government's CIO Certification Program, and CIO University.

References

Cannella, A. A., & Shen, W. (2003). So close and yet so far: Promotion versus exit for CEO heirs apparent. *Academy of Management Journal, 44*(2), 252-270.

Charan, R. (2005, February). Ending the CEO succession crisis. *Harvard Business Review*, 72-81.

Davidson, W. N., Nemic, C., & Worrell, D. L. (2001). Succession planning vs. agency theory: A test of Harris and Helfat's interpretation of plurality announcement market returns. *Strategic Management Journal, 22,* 179-184.

Dearstyne, B. W. (2006, January/February). Information program leaders in transition. *The Information Management Journal*, 44-50.

Earl, M. (2000, March-April). Are CIOs obsolete? *Harvard Business Review*, 60.

Earl, M. J., & Feeny, D. F. (2000, Winter). How to be a CEO for the information age. *Sloan Management Review,* 11-23.

Grover, V., Jeong, S. R., Kettinger, W. J., & Lee, C. C. (1993). The chief information officer: A study of managerial roles. *Journal of Management Information Systems, 10*(2), 107-130.

Hedlund, J., Forsythe, G. B., Horvath, J. A., Williams, W. M., Snook, S., & Sternberg, R. J. (2003). Identifying and assessing tacit knowledge: Understanding the practical intelligence of military leaders. *The Leadership Quality, 14,* 117-140.

Mintzberg, H. (1994). Rounding out the manager's job. *Sloan Management Review, 36*(1), 11-26.

Ordonez, A. (2005). When technology is your business, your business strategy, & your point of difference. In *CIO Leadership Strategies*. Aspatore Books. Retrieved from www.aspatore.com

Shen, W., & Cannella, A. A. (2002a). Revisiting the performance consequences of CEO succession: The impacts of successor type, postsuccession senior executive turnover, and departing CEO tenure. *Academy of Management Journal, 45*(4), 717-733.

Sternberg, R. J. (2003). WICS: A model of leadership in organizations. *Academy of Management Learning and Education, 2*(4), 386-401.

Westphal, J. D., & Bednar, M. K. (2005). Pluralistic ignorance in corporate boards and firms' strategic persistence in response to low firm performance. *Administrative Science Quarterly, 50,* 262-298.

Westphal, J. D., & Khanna, P. (2003). Keeping directors in line: Social distancing as a control mechanism in the corporate elite. *Administrative Science Quarterly, 48,* 361-398.

Zhang, Y., & Rajagopalan, N. (2003). Explaining new CEO origin: Firm versus industry antecedents. *Academy of Management Journal, 46*(3), 327-338.

Zhang, Y., & Rajagopalan, N. (2004). When the known devil is better than an unknown god: An empirical study of the antecedents and consequences of relay CEO successions. *Academy of Management Journal, 47*(4), 483-500.

About the Author

Petter Gottschalk is a professor of information and knowledge management at the Norwegian School of Management in Oslo. He teaches at the Arab Academy in Alexandria, Fudan University in Shanghai, and Nanyang University in Singapore.

Dr. Gottschalk has written several books published by Idea Group: *Strategic Knowledge Management Technology; Managing Successful IT Outsourcing Relationships* with Hans Solli-Sæther; *E-Business Strategy, Sourcing, and Governance; Knowledge Management Systems in Law Enforcement: Technologies and Techniques; CIO and Corporate Strategic Management: Changing Role of CIO to CEO;* and *Knowledge Management Systems: Value Shop Creation.*

Dr. Gottschalk earned his MBA at the Technical University of Berlin, Germany, his MSc at Thayer School of Engineering, Dartmouth College, and Sloan School of Management, Massachusetts Institute of Technology, USA, and his DBA at Henley Management College, Brunel University, UK.

For more than 15 years, Dr. Gottschalk was an executive in business organizations. He was the CIO of ABB Norway, the CEO of ABB Datacables, and the CEO of the Norwegian Computing Center.

Index

H

heir apparent 18
human assets 216
human capital 89
human resources 91
hybrid manager 45

I

industry conditions 89
industry standards 193
information broker 166
information sharing 220
information systems 38, 248
information technology 38, 190, 248
infrastructure planner 192
innovation 170
inside-out resource 108
integrating 102
integration 170, 195
integrator 60
intellectual capital 241
intellectual property (IP) 217
interaction 260, 286
internal market 188
internal role 79
Internet 148, 154
Internet strategy 154
interview 52
intrapreneurship 247
investment management 63
IT governance 213, 223

K

knowledge 89, 169, 244, 248, 283
knowledge application 258
knowledge champion 242
knowledge coordination 236
knowledge creation 252
knowledge inventory 239
knowledge management 236, 251
knowledge management system 260
knowledge manager 235
knowledge partner 243
knowledge retrieval 254
knowledge reuse 237

knowledge sharing network 247
knowledge skeptic 243
knowledge sponsor 243
knowledge storage 254
knowledge transfer 237, 256

L

leadership 52, 239, 283
leadership role 72, 82
learning 89
lecturing 52
legal bond 218
liaison role 80

M

management 77
market responsiveness 109
memory 254
mentor 49
mixed sourcing 192
monitor 74
monopoly supplier 192
mutuality 219

N

negotiator 73, 288
neo-classical economic theory 201
Norway 77

O

online marketplace 167
online service provider 167
ontology 169
open information sharing 220
organizational change 193
organizational memory 254
outside-in resource 109
outsider successors 24
outside succession 4
outsourcing 78, 190, 192, 195, 225
outsourcing governance model 225

P

parental developer 125
partnership 109, 204, 223

performance 196
personality 39
personnel leader 74
physical assets 217
portal 167
portfolio manager 124
power perspective 12
practical intelligence 284
president 9
principal-agent theory 31
product developer 76
project manager 79, 193

R

rarity 106
realized strategy 128
relational exchange theory 205
relationship assets 217
relationship management 109
relay succession 3, 19
resource-based theory 88, 102, 198
resource allocator 74
restructurer 124
resurgere 102
revenue 157, 162, 165, 169

S

scenario planning 131
SECI process 261
self-organization 132
senior management 225
senior manager 190, 244
shareholder 123, 154
social exchange theory 206
socialization theory 57
solidarity 219
sourcing 170
spanning resource 109
spokesman 74, 80
stakeholder 38, 123, 206
stakeholder theory 206
stock options 30
strategic alignment 112
strategic drift 128
strategic fit 126
strategic innovation 132

strategic intent 132
strategic leader 127
strategic management 102, 125
strategic planning 120
strategic resource 104
strategic thinking 222
strategist 49
strategy 112, 118, 153, 191, 216
succession decisions 8
supplier 156
supply chain integration 170
synergy 124
synergy manager 124
systems analyst 193
systems provider 192

T

teamwork 89
technical skills 108
technology leader 49
technology provocateur 76
transaction broker 167
transaction cost theory 200
transformational outsourcing 192

U

Uniform Commercial Code (UCC) 218

V

value 105
value chain 91
value configuration 96
value network 92
value shop 92
vendor 151, 190, 204, 225
virtual community 162, 167
virtual storefront 166
visualization 256

W

Web site 156
wisdom 284

Y

Y Model 119, 134

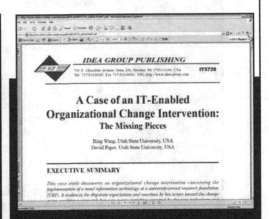